THE GREAT COVER-UP

THE TRUTH ABOUT THE DEATH OF MICHAEL COLLINS

GERARD MURPHY, from Cork, is the author of the ground-breaking *The Year of Disappearances: Political Killings in Cork 1921–22* (2010), as well as two critically acclaimed novels. He holds a PhD from University College Cork and lectures at the Institute of Technology, Carlow.

THE GREAT COVER-UP

THE TRUTH ABOUT THE DEATH OF MICHAEL COLLINS

GERARD MURPHY

The Collins Press

FIRST PUBLISHED IN 2018 BY
The Collins Press
West Link Park
Doughcloyne
Wilton
Cork
T12 N5EF
Ireland

Reprinted 2018

A CIP record for this book is available from the British Library.

Paperback ISBN: 978-1-84889-337-5

Inside cover photographs
Front: (top) Michael Collins addresses a crowd in Skibberreen
(WikiCommons); (bottom) Florrie O'Donoghue's handwritten
recollections of IRB meetings held in the 1922 (National Library
of Ireland); *Back:* The shell of the GPO on Sackville Street (later O'Connell
Street), Dublin in the aftermath of the 1916 Rising (WikiCommons).

Typesetting by Carrigboy Typesetting Services
Typeset in Sabon LT Std
Printed in Poland by Drukarnia Skleniarz

Contents

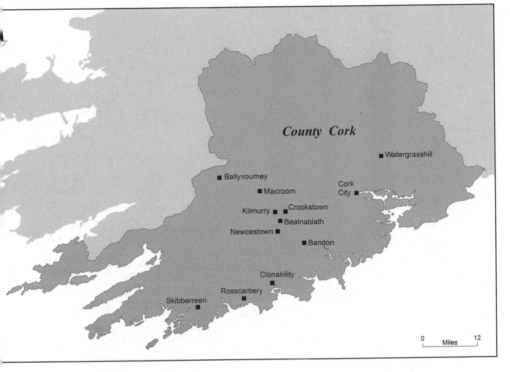

Map of County Cork (Mike Murphy, Department of Geography, University College Cork)

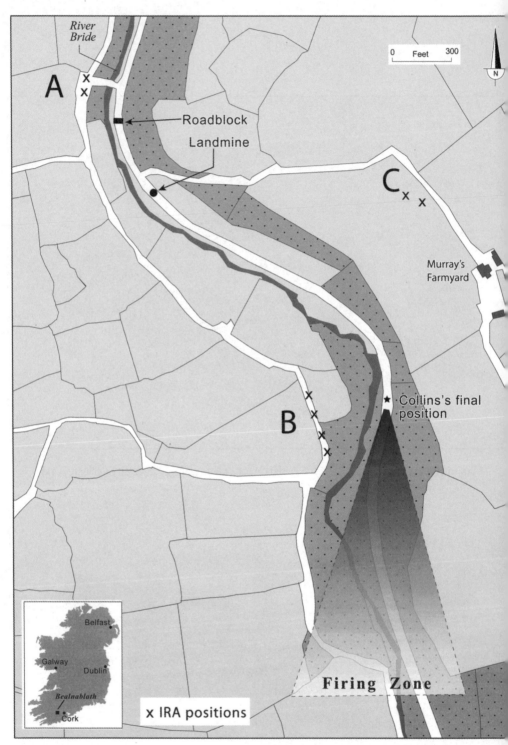

River
Bride

A

Roadblock
Landmine

C

Murray's
Farmyard

B

★ Collins's final
position

Firing Zone

Belfast

Galway

Dublin

Bealnablath

Cork

x IRA positions

Map of the ambush site at Bealnablath, County Cork. Known IRA positions indicated by X.
(Mike Murphy, Department of Geography, University College Cork)

There is no use in going to work like a horse or an ass or a beast of burden. Put your heart and soul into everything you do. That is the only way to succeed.

Michael Collins
(*Sunday Independent*, 27 August 1922)

A man of immense ability and untiring energy, and thoughtfulness for others. At the end of the day, when most people would look for a rest, I have known him to go around looking for relatives of people who had suffered a loss, to try and give them some comfort. And this was from a man who never had a free moment for himself. He was a patriot, a most courageous man, and a great, great gentleman.

Emmet Dalton
(P.J. Twohig, *The Dark Secret of Bealnablath*, Cork, 1991)

It has come to a very bad pass when Irishmen congratulate themselves on the shooting of a man like Michael Collins.

Éamon de Valera, upon hearing of Collins's death
(E. Neeson, *The Life and Death of Michael Collins*, Cork, 1968)

Such a claim is a claim to military despotism and subversive of all civil liberty. It is an immoral usurpation and confiscation of the people's rights.

(George Count Plunkett referring to the proposed trying of Michael Collins for treason, in 'Manifesto to the Irish People', De Valera Papers, UCD P150/1630)

Prologue

Last year I was fortunate enough to attend a public talk given by the well-known physicist Professor Brian Cox. He made a comment which, though it was about science, is relevant in a historical context. Scientists, he said, rarely if ever set out to answer Big Questions. Rather they set out to answer small questions. And if these offer clues to the Big Questions, then that is how the process of inquiry works. Science has many examples of this, but history has them too – or should have. I did not set out to write a book on Michael Collins, much less on his death. I had little interest in Collins's death, believing like most historians that the matter was long settled. However, even if it was settled, it must still rank among the big events in Irish history. For Collins's death surely changed Irish history in ways that, by definition, can never be established. So if there was a question about it, then – by definition again – it was a Big Question.

I stumbled into Bealnablath, much as Collins did, by accident. I was studying the papers of Florence O'Donoghue, former Adjutant of the 1st Cork Brigade of the IRA and later of the 1st Southern Division, and the IRA's chief intelligence officer in Cork during the War of Independence – and later one of the first historians of the Irish revolution. One of the striking things about O'Donoghue's papers is how often they contain material that is at odds with reality, when the motivation for their writing was clearly propagandist. O'Donoghue often felt the need – sometimes to an alarming degree – to defend his own particular version of events and to mould the historical record in ways that suited his own ends. In this, he was largely successful. The historical establishment, for the most part, have accepted his accounts to the extent that it is almost a historiographical mortal sin to try and contradict them. Only recently have serious questions been asked of this.[1]

This is not the place to deal with these broader issues. Suffice it to say that one of the subjects that seemed to exercise O'Donoghue's pen to an unexpected degree, though he never wrote about it in book form, was the death of Michael Collins. As a supposed 'Neutral' during the Civil War, one would expect he would have no direct part in, or first-hand knowledge of, the topic. Yet time and time again when articles appeared in newspapers or when biographies of Collins were published, O'Donoghue was sending off missives to newspapers or having articles published, usually in the *Sunday Press*, promoting his view on the subject: that Collins was killed – and could only have been killed – as a result of an accidental shot fired during a haphazard, hastily convened ambush.

And so, from trying to answer one of the 'small questions' – why was O'Donoghue so interested in Bealnablath? – I stumbled on one of the Big Questions: why did Michael Collins die the way he did, in that particular set of circumstances at that particular time? This will almost certainly not be the last word on the death of Collins. Nor does it answer some of the most basic questions, such as who was 'the man who shot Michael Collins'. But I believe it does ask many of the right questions. Collins's death is not a 'done deal'. Far from it. A lot of unresolved issues remain. But the book establishes, in my view, that the accepted model on the death of Collins, though perfectly plausible, is very likely to be wrong. My conclusion is that Collins was assassinated rather than was the victim of a virtual accident. That the whole thing is shrouded in mystery and that almost everybody concerned tried to lie about it – for perfectly understandable reasons in many cases – is incontrovertible.

So how does one thread through the minefield of lies and half-truths that surround Bealnablath? By giving primacy to documentation produced during the week of the ambush itself and shortly afterwards. What emerges from this is a picture quite at odds with the accepted version of events. This is what happens to Big Questions when you start digging to find answers to smaller questions: you find yourself in quite unexpected places.

Introduction

In a review on the publication of Tim Pat Coogan's biography of Michael Collins, historian and broadcaster John Bowman stated that 'Michael Collins is sexy: probably in both senses of the word, but certainly in the sense in which it has lately gained currency.' Bowman seemed to imply that there had been far too many books written about Collins, many of them poor, most of them falling somewhere between hagiography and conspiracy theory. 'Collins's fascination to so many writers is a liability,' Bowman wrote. 'Too often it is the legend of Collins which attracts: the swashbuckling man of violence, the man who turned the heads of London's society hostesses; above all, the lost leader, cut down in his prime.'

But if Collins is sexy, that is no reason to write another book about him. Perhaps there should be a moratorium on further books on Collins, at least unless significant new information is released from state and private archives – which is probably unlikely at this stage. So what do you do if you come across what you believe is new evidence on Collins's death – or at least evidence that has been overlooked for almost a hundred years? Do you ignore it, on the basis that enough has been said already? After all, do you want to be like the conspiracy theorist who goes to heaven only to be told that JFK was simply shot by Lee Harvey Oswald, a lone gunman? Or do you say your piece, on the basis that if you don't, somebody else probably will? At the risk of adding to the conspiracy theories surrounding the death of Collins, I decided, when I came across what I believed to be such evidence, to take the latter course.

However, this book is not about the swashbuckling Collins or the legend of Collins. It is rather about the sad and grim manner in which he met his death, a death which, given that political assassination was a significant part of his own modus operandi from 1919, should have come as no surprise to anyone, least of all to himself.

Of course, the conspiracy angle affects much that has been written about the death of Michael Collins, who was killed in an IRA ambush on a back road in west Cork in August 1922. In the hundred or so years that have passed since, conspiracy theories have abounded: that he was killed by British Intelligence; that he was killed by a cabal of ministers within the Provisional Government in order to secure the Treaty with Britain, which he had signed only nine months earlier; that he was killed by some other shadowy forces for the retrospective beneficiaries of his death, namely Éamon de Valera and the British government. One book on the subject suggests, with almost comical Hibernocentricity, that the British government staged the assassination of Sir Henry Wilson – whose death precipitated the Civil War – in order to force the Irish into conflict, despite the fact that two IRA men were hanged for shooting Wilson after bravely and defiantly admitting at their trial that they had done so and saying why.

What is clear, however, is that the death of Collins, who, regardless of his penchant for intrigue, was still the most capable and charismatic of the revolutionary leaders, had a significant influence on subsequent events. At the very least it was an unfortunate tragedy that he was lost at such a young age. What difference he would have made to the evolution of the Irish Free State, given the economic, political and social circumstances of the time, is entirely speculative, but it is fair to say that he would have made some difference. However, what happened, happened and history is about events, not about what might have occurred had things taken a different course. Before I stumbled into the research that led to this book, my view – insofar as I had a view – was to agree with the conventional wisdom of most historians on the subject: that Collins died as a result of being hit by a stray bullet fired by the IRA at Bealnablath, County Cork on 22 August 1922. After all, common sense alone suggested that this was by far the most plausible explanation. If any of the above groups wanted to assassinate Collins, they could have done so at any stage and would hardly need to stage an IRA ambush – let alone one as haphazard as Bealnablath – to do so.

As briefly stated in the Prologue, my interest in Collins's death came about not because of any conspiracy theories or preconceived notions or because I wanted to push a particular agenda, but because I was studying the papers of Florence (Florrie) O'Donoghue. O'Donoghue left a lot of paperwork behind him, covering all aspects of the revolutionary years, and this is a major source for historians of the period. There are curious gaps in O'Donoghue's published accounts of the revolution in Cork and equally curious gaps in his papers. And one of the subjects he treats in a rather odd manner is the death of Michael Collins. The vast majority of IRA veterans, including most of those known to have been at Bealnablath on the day of the ambush, regretted Collins's death. To quote one of them, Liam Deasy, who led the ambush party: 'I considered him [Collins] then to be the greatest leader of our generation and I have not since changed that opinion ... His death caused nothing but the deepest sorrow and regret and brought about in many of us a real desire for the end of the war.'[1] The vast majority of Republicans felt the same, and said so on many occasions. O'Donoghue, on the other hand, who by his own admission was in contact with Collins almost on a daily basis during the War of Independence, makes only one grudging reference to Bealnablath in his published work. Almost half of *No Other Law*, his biography of Liam Lynch, is given over to the events of the spring and summer of 1922, and no detail is too minor to be recalled over eleven chapters and 134 pages, yet Collins's death – surely one of the most significant events that year – gets a mere sentence. In a list of the principal figures who died in the Civil War, Collins gets tagged on: 'Michael Collins had been ambushed and killed at Bealnablath in his native county on the 22nd of the same month. There were many others.'[2] In other words, Collins, in O'Donoghue's view, was only one of many who died that year and merits no more significance than that.

However, the opposite is true in O'Donoghue's correspondence, for he spent a lot of his career as a historian putting out fires and dashing off letters scotching various rumours concerning Collins's death and trying to establish his own version of the event by writing to newspapers and to his fellow veterans. You simply get the feeling that he was trying too hard – and too often – for something he had almost ignored in *No Other Law*. Several times during the 1950s and '60s when the topic came up – usually with the publication of a book on the life and death of Collins – O'Donoghue was on the typewriter firing off missives and writing articles for newspapers defending his version of events.[3] Finally, in 1964, he got together with the surviving members of the ambush party at Bealnablath to write what they wished to put out as the definitive version of the events of 22 August 1922 from the ambushers' point of view. The occasion for this was the imminent publication of Eoin Neeson's history of the Civil War.[4] When this book, Neeson's first on the Civil War, contained nothing that did not tally with the accepted view of the time, the piece went unnoticed but remained in O'Donoghue's papers until they became publicly available in the 1990s. (Neeson's next book, *The Life and Death of Michael Collins*, was an entirely different matter, but that did not appear until after O'Donoghue's death, in 1968.)[5]

Starting with the O'Donoghue papers, it quickly became clear that all was not as it seemed in the story of Bealnablath. I was also astonished to find that a lot of early material, most of it available since the time of the event itself, had been ignored by historians – who preferred, or so it appeared, to concentrate on the reminiscences of various survivors of the ambush rather than look at the data that appeared in the days immediately afterwards. New material was also becoming available, most notably the records of the Military Pensions Board, to which former IRA and National Army men had submitted applications. Various papers and photographs of the ambush site appeared as a result of initiatives to gather material on the revolutionary years. It was also apparent that some previous writers on the topic had amassed much valuable information on the ambush and that they too were sceptical of the accepted version, or versions, of events. All these combined to shed new light on the death of Michael Collins and what has long been accepted or ignored, depending on your point of view. I think it is safe to say that the version of events surrounding the death of Collins that has been handed down to us is very wide of the mark. Is this a new conspiracy theory? No doubt some will dismiss it as such. But it is one that has the weight of most of the evidence behind it.

The death of Michael Collins has been the subject of much speculation over the years, a lot of it based on rumour. Those involved, on both sides, were pestered for years by commentators of various kinds looking for details of the ambush. While quite a few of those present gave various accounts of what happened, over the years these accounts almost all contradict one another, which is not surprising since they were often gathered up to fifty years or more after the event. Given that people in an ambush tend to keep their heads down, it is difficult to understand how they would see much other than what was visible from their own position(s) vis-à-vis the main event.

The emphasis in this book will be on the documentary evidence that emerged in the immediate aftermath of the ambush, rather than comparing the many diverse and confusing accounts that have accumulated since – what one commentator has referred to as 'the fog'.[6] This book will be an attempt to examine the death of Michael Collins at Bealnablath and the run-up to it primarily in the light of contemporary documents, rather than reminiscences. It will also look at Collins's death in the broader context of the split in the IRA and the Republican movement as a result of the Anglo-Irish Treaty with Britain. And it takes cognisance of the fact that most of those involved, on both sides, for perfectly understandable reasons, lied about the circumstances of the ambush: something that has recently been shown in detail to have been the case.[7]

A lot of information about Bealnablath has lain hidden for almost a hundred years. This is an attempt to drag it into the light and, while not every 'i' can be dotted and every 't' crossed, there is enough evidence here to show that much of what we have been told about Bealnablath is fabrication, to cover the tracks of those who had Collins killed on the one hand, and the careless military outfit that let it happen on the other – even if much of that carelessness stemmed from Collins himself. It can also be stated that had Collins not been killed at Bealnablath, it is likely that he would have been assassinated at some other point, since he was not one to remain holed up in Government Buildings for very long. Every valley and bend on the road in the south and west of Ireland was a potential Bealnablath in the summer and autumn of 1922. Bealnablath just happened to be the one at which Collins actually died.

I

In the Wrong Place at the Wrong Time

The general circumstances surrounding the Bealnablath ambush are well known. On 22 August 1922 while on a visit to Cork, Michael Collins – the Commander in Chief of the army of the Provisional Government of Ireland, and the man who had more than anyone else led the fight against the British in the earlier War of Independence and then negotiated a treaty settlement with them – was shot dead during an ambush near the small village of Bealnablath in County Cork. It is now pretty much accepted by historians that Collins was in Cork that week for a number of reasons, one of which was that he was hoping to meet some of the leadership of the opposing anti-Treaty Republicans in an attempt to bring an end to the Civil War, which by then had been going on for just under two months.

The accepted version of events is that Collins was spotted passing through Bealnablath by a scout of the anti-Treaty forces early that morning on his way to west Cork and that the Republicans in the area, consisting mostly of officers and men of the 3rd West Cork Brigade, then decided to set up an ambush in the hope that he might return later in the day by the same route. The glen to the south of Bealnablath, through which the road passed, provided an ideal ambush spot, since one side of the road consisted of a steep incline to the east, while to the west across a narrow stream ran a boreen roughly parallel, which provided perfect cover for the ambushing party. If the ambush had gone according to plan, the attackers would have been able to rain down fire on Collins's convoy, pinned in as it would have been by the high ground on the opposite side, where it would have provided perfect targets. As one young man on the Republican side put it: a bird could not have escaped from the trap if everything had gone according to plan.

However, it did not go according to plan. Collins spent the day travelling around west Cork and when around 6.00pm there appeared to be no sign of him returning, the Republicans – originally between thirty and forty in number – decided to withdraw. Some of them headed to the small hamlet of Bealnablath to the north and the rest to Newcestown to the south. But withdrawing was not easy. They had a hastily constructed mine consisting of a box of gelignite under the road and, farther along, a brewer's cart disabled and placed across the road as a barricade, and broken bottles scattered everywhere. According to local lore, they felt obliged to clear the barricade and remove the mine so as to have the road clear for farmers going to the creamery the following morning.

Some six men were detailed to clear the obstructions, remove the mine and act as lookouts. Around 7.30pm – accounts vary as to the precise time – while the clearing-up operation was in progress, Collins's convoy arrived from the south. The convoy consisted of a motorcycle outrider, Lieutenant J.J. Smith, followed by an army lorry – a Crossley tender, manned by two officers and around eight soldiers. Some distance behind, Collins was travelling in a bright yellow Leyland touring car. As the IRA report on the ambush stated at the time, making what was no doubt a salient point: 'During the journey Ml. Collins travelled in the touring car and made himself very prominent.'[1] Collins was indeed clearly visible in the car, sitting in the back seat along with General

Emmet Dalton, his commandant in Cork. The car had two drivers, Privates Michael Corry and Michael Quinn. Behind these and bringing up the rear of the convoy was a Rolls-Royce armoured car manned by two drivers, two officers and a machine-gunner, Scotsman John McPeak.

According to Republican accounts, the men on the boreen opposite fired a few shots at the convoy to warn their comrades who were down the road in the narrowest part of the valley and thus were vulnerable if the convoy were to suddenly come upon them. Dalton, on the other hand, claimed the touring car was hit by the initial volley and the windshield shattered and a clock on the dashboard broken. Members of the Free State party are adamant that while Dalton wanted his men to drive on 'like Hell', it was Collins who overruled him and opted to stand and fight. The battle, such as it was, was an entirely one-sided affair, with the convoy heavily armed with machine guns and significant manpower using rifles against half a dozen IRA men armed only with rifles.

There were in effect two battles going on: one between several IRA men and the men from the Crossley tender, who were stopped down the road near the barricade and were trying to move it out of the way; and, several hundred yards back, a second involving Collins's party. This consisted of himself, Dalton and the two drivers. They appear to have been joined at some point by Joe Dolan, Collins's personal bodyguard, who had been travelling on the armoured car. They took cover by a low ditch on the left-hand side of the road while the armoured car moved backwards and forwards spraying with lethal machine-gun fire the boreen opposite where the rest of the IRA party, no more than three or four, were hidden.

After about twenty minutes of this intermittent shooting – again the length of time varies, depending on who is telling the story – the armoured car's Vickers machine gun jammed. This allowed the IRA men on the boreen opposite to make their escape. At this point, it appears, Collins spotted them retreating and pointed them out to the other members of his party. He stood up, moved initially behind the armoured car for cover and then, inexplicably from a military point of view, appeared to walk on his own some 15 yards up the road and around the bend to the south of the armoured car in the direction of where he had seen the enemy retreat. He was, it seems, reloading his rifle to continue shooting when he was killed by a single shot that came – and most accounts agree on this – during a lull in the firing brought about by the jamming of the Vickers gun. There was then another burst of firing, presumably from both sets of forces and, according to the accounts of several of the Free State party, including Emmet Dalton himself, from Republicans on both sides of the road.

It took Dalton and Seán O'Connell, the officer in charge of the Crossley tender, some minutes to get to Collins, who by this time was dead, the back of his head blown off in what Dalton called an 'awful' 'gaping' wound. As they were trying to get his body onto the armoured car, there was a final outbreak of firing from the Republicans, in which Lieutenant Smith was hit in the neck. Though only slightly wounded, Smith was the one other casualty on the Free State side. After many stops and starts, mainly because of trenched and blocked roads, the Free State convoy, minus Smith's motorcycle and the touring car, managed to get back to Cork, where Collins's body was brought to Shanakiel Hospital, a former British army hospital on the north side of the city. Dalton and O'Connell were broken-hearted and would never live down the night when their leader was killed.[2]

In December 2012 a small item appeared in the Irish newspapers. It concerned the discovery of a photograph of the Bealnablath site taken on the day after the ambush (see page 15). The photographer was a local sixteen-year-old, Agnes Hurley, who – unusually for that time – owned a camera and had taken several hundred photos around the area over the years. It was apparently found in an attic in Dublin by her niece, who submitted it to an exhibition in Clonakilty organised by the History Department of University College Cork. All expert opinions consulted agree that the photograph is genuine. Cork City and County Archives archivist Brian McGee described the find as 'extraordinary', adding: 'The fact that it survived is remarkable.' This is especially so since it is often stated that no picture was taken of the site at the time of the ambush. (In fact, another photo taken by Agnes Hurley, showing a broader view of the ambush site, has been available since the early 1990s. See page 16.) 'Aggie went to Beal na Blath to see what had happened because they'd heard gunshots the previous day,' her niece said. 'She took hundreds of photographs over the years and dated the back of every single one.' The photo, date and all, can now be found in Cork City and County Archives.[3]

✓ The photograph shows the road at Bealnablath where the ambush took place. It is taken facing north, with the higher ground beside the road to the east of the site clearly visible. The photograph tells us a number of things. It shows a white and almost certainly dry road surface with a mottled dark area that may correspond to bloodstains, and what appears to be a piece of white cloth on the grass margin on the right-hand side of the road, which is claimed to be Collins's shirt collar. From the slope of the hill behind, it is clear that the spot is more or less where the Collins monument now stands, which means that, when it was built, those who erected it knew where their Commander in Chief had fallen. In other words, all speculation that Collins was killed either farther north or farther south of that position – and several books written on the topic claim that this was the case – are working on a false premise.

It is fair to assume that when Agnes Hurley took the photos, this is where she believed Collins had died; it is also fair to assume that she herself saw the collar and the bloodstains and identified them as such. Indeed, Father Patrick Twohig, in his book *The Dark Secret of Bealnablath*, quotes Agnes Hurley's

The spot at which Michael Collins fell as photographed by Agnes Hurley on the morning after the ambush. Note the extended dark area on the left, which is probably Collins's blood spattered along the road. Also note the white collar on the other side of the road, which was most likely Lieutenant Smith's. (Cork City and County Archives)

The position where Michael Collins was killed photographed from another angle by Agnes Hurley. Again note the apparent bloodstain on the spot where he died – marked by a cross – and the fact that the bloodstain runs parallel to the road. (Father Patrick Twohig)

sister Julianna, who accompanied Agnes along with their brother, as having seen a large congealed bloodstain, 'like a bastable cake' across the road from where the monument now stands.[4] As for the collar, of the detachable type worn by men in Ireland until the 1960s, Julianna Hurley claimed it had a bloodstained bullet hole on its left side, though it lies across the road from the big bloodstain.[5] This suggests that it belonged to Lieutenant Smith rather than Collins since, as we have seen, Smith was shot on the left side of his neck while trying to get Collins's body onto the armoured car. Another local girl, Ellen Allen (née Long), who was nineteen and who went down to the ambush site after the combatants had left, confirmed the scale of the bloodstain. ''Twas not a very nice sight. Blood all over the road, and brains.'[6] Allen suggested that an attempt was made to clean it up the next day, but clearly that had not been done by the time Agnes Hurley got there.

But the prime importance of the photograph – apart from the fact that it pinpoints the place of Collins's death – is that, when viewed in conjunction with the second surviving photo Agnes Hurley took that morning, it shows the bloodstain spread for what looks like up to two metres along the road. We can tell this because at the lower left-hand side of the bloodstain a footprint is clearly visible. This must have been made when someone stood in Collins's blood, either trying to minister to him or during attempts to move his body. And before anyone thinks this is a gratuitously gruesome detail, try imagining the effort it would take to move a man as big as Collins and doing that without standing in his blood, which was spattered widely over the road.

Another myth that the picture puts to bed is that it was raining during the ambush. Apart from the fact that the road is bone dry, the footprint is perfectly defined on the road surface from the night before. It would have been far less defined if it had been raining and would have been at least partly, if not entirely, washed away.

Yet the most important detail is not the footprint or the collar, but the scale and the direction of the bloodstain. The stain is large and diffuse and it is clear that Collins suffered a catastrophic head wound. But what is most significant about it is the direction in which it lies: it is aligned in a north–south direction, almost exactly parallel to the road.[7] This is easy to see in the photograph since there is the track of a wheel running right through the middle of it. Also, if we are to go by Julianna Hurley's description of the human material on the road as resembling a bastable cake, who would bet against the dark mass at the top of the stain being a part of Collins's skull? To judge from the size of the footprint, the stain is at least a metre and a half and probably well over two metres in length. It is also clearly visible on the second photograph since it extends down the road from the black cross that indicates where Collins had fallen.[8] What all this tells us is that Collins suffered a most appalling wound that resulted in his blood and brain matter being blown for up to two metres along the road.[9] Only a high-velocity bullet could have caused such a wound and scattered blood over such a distance. It also suggests that the shooter was not too far away, since even a high-velocity bullet when fired from a long distance would have lost much of its power and would not have caused such extensive damage. This also precludes the possibility that Collins was killed either by a ricochet or by a revolver bullet, neither of which would have had the power to inflict such damage.[10] (Again, the suggestion that the enormous stain of blood and brain matter could have been caused by the body being dragged along the road is contradicted by the fact that Smith's collar is on the right-hand side, indicating that the car was there at the time. Indeed, there is a much thinner line crossing the road in that direction in the photograph which may indicate where the body was dragged.)

What this means is that the bullet that killed Collins – almost certainly a high-velocity bullet – was travelling along the direction of the road. According to most accounts of the ambush, Collins had spotted two IRA men across the glen at the far side of the stream to his right just before he was shot and was beginning to walk in their direction. He was moving south around the bend from where the armoured car – the last vehicle in the convoy – was parked and was therefore out of sight of most of his party when he was killed. As such, he was the farthest south of the entire convoy, which indicates his reckless bravery, and was out of the cover of his own men and thus extremely vulnerable.

Most accounts have Collins reloading his rifle and preparing to fire on the departing men on the lane to the west when he was killed. If so, he could not have been killed by any of these men – despite the fact that several of them claimed they may have done so – because if that were the case, the direction of the bloodstain would have been across the road rather than parallel to it. The occasional suggestion that he was shot through the forehead is disproved by the fact that

Michael Collins's greatcoat on display in the National Museum of Ireland showing bloodstaining on the right epaulette and collar. (Author's collection)

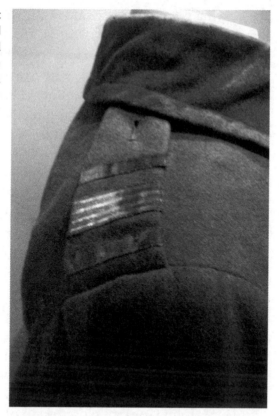

on his death mask his forehead and the hairline above it show no trace of a wound. Furthermore, the damage to Collins's cap – a jagged rip at the back towards the right-hand side of the seam – shows no hole or other mark of entry at the front. Since his cap was always well pulled down over his forehead, this more or less precludes that he could have been hit from the front.[11] What is more, the greatcoat he wore at Bealnablath is on permanent display in the National Museum of Ireland. It shows the right-hand wing of the collar and the epaulettes on the right shoulder to be bloodstained. All this shows that the bullet that killed him came from his left and exited the right side of his skull.

Since the road was curving at this point and was much narrower then than it is now, this can only mean that the fatal bullet must have come from the roadside itself, from behind the curving ditch on either side of the road or from the hillside just beyond that. In other words, the bullet can have come only from a southerly direction, something attested to by Joe Dolan, Collins's bodyguard, who was nearby when Collins was killed. Carlton Younger quotes Dolan as saying that the fatal bullet 'was fired, not from directly opposite Collins, but from much further along the valley so that it hit the back of his head at an angle'.[12]

We also know that the fatal bullet could not have come from the north because the forensics of the wound – agreed by Dr Oliver St John Gogarty, who embalmed the body and carried out an autopsy, and Dr Patrick Cagney, who studied Collins's wounds when the body was brought to Shanakiel Hospital in Cork, immediately after the ambush – indicate that Collins was hit by a bullet that entered his head just behind his left ear, exiting behind his right, effectively blowing off the back of his head in the process.[13] According to Bill McKenna, one of the Free State troops present at the ambush, who was also present when Collins's body was being laid out:

> Dr St. John Gogarty, close friend of Collins, had prepared the body for lying in state, drew attention to the minute entrance wound behind the ear, the puncture 'blueish'. Sadly the exit of the same bullet destroyed [a] massive portion [of the] other side of [the] head. This cavity the good doctor filled with wax.[14]

Gogarty told former Cork IRA man Connie Neenan many years later that the entry wound of the bullet was no bigger than a fingernail.[15] Photos of the body in Shanakiel Hospital show a heavily wrapped bandage with a wad of cotton wool covering the area immediately behind the left ear, and the angle at the back of the bandage suggests that not much of the back of Collins's head was left.

In other words, Collins was facing west when he was killed and the bullet could only have come from the south, where, according to all Republican accounts, there were no IRA men hiding. What this also means is that he was unlikely to have been killed by one of his own party, either by accident or design, because they were all to the north of him when he was hit. The shooter would have had to be either on the road itself – which curves gently to the south of where Collins was standing – or behind one of the ditches on either side of the road or on the hill slightly to the left. It should be pointed out that the ditches on both sides of the road at this point are flanked by swampy ground. There was a stream on the right and a drain on the left. However, this would not preclude someone hiding in either since, for the relatively minor inconvenience of getting one's feet wet, one would be in a very good position for getting off an accurate shot.

The damage to Collins's cap shows that there is only one hole, the rip at the back. If the bullet entered his head behind his left ear, the shooter would have had to be level with Collins when he fired or else slightly below his level. This is because the cap sloped back, covering most of the back of his head, while the area immediately behind his left ear was uncovered. This means that the bullet must have come from someone low on the roadside level with Collins's head or from the ditch to the south of the spot where he died, rather than from the hill. As mentioned above, at that time the road was considerably narrower than it is now and the stream on the west side did not quite flow to the edge of the road. There were clumps of sallies here and on the side opposite which would have given plenty of cover. (It is of course possible that the killer might have been a member of Collins's own party. However, there is no indication that there were members of his own party on his southern flank.)

But is there any other evidence gathered at the time that might support this? Tom Daly, a National Army soldier based in Macroom, was a member of a detachment of troops who went out to investigate the site shortly after the ambush:

When the report came to Macroom that Collins had been ambushed there were two lorries of us sent out. We dropped the lorries and had to take to the hills. We did not know if they were waiting for us or not ... We got no one. But I saw the cartridges and I knew that there were only a few shots fired. The cartridges weren't there [meaning they were scarce]. There were no more than two or three men there, judging from where we found the cartridges. I saw one little heap of six or seven shells. The cross[road] was coming that way down to the Bandon road and this ditch was going away in a kind of slant and there was great cover in it. When they fired, the troops could not see where the shots were coming from.[16]

This is a reasonably accurate description of the lie of the land to the south of the spot where Collins was killed: the ditch curving away 'in a sort of slant' towards Bandon. This also nails another of the myths surrounding the death of Collins: that it was almost dark when he died. There was still enough light for Daly's party to find the cartridges an hour after Collins's convoy had departed. Some writers claim this was because the British government had reintroduced Daylight Saving Time in 1922, having previously used it during the Great War, and it is fair to assume that the Free State went along with this. If this is correct, it means that the south of Ireland was operating on British Summer Time with one hour added. In other words, sundown, which would have been at 8.40 BST, would now have been at 9.40pm with at least half an hour of twilight after that.[17] The weather forecast for the day stated that 'a small disturbance will cause slight rain in places, some morning mist, day visibility moderate, rather warm, light variable winds'; in other words, a somewhat dull but largely dry summer's day.[18]

Now contrast what Tom Daly found with what Julianna Hurley found when she and her sister checked out the boreen across the stream from where Collins was killed: 'On the hundred yards stretch from Long's crossroads to the first bend they saw the impression of the gunmen on the fence. They counted nine. They collected thirty-six empty rifle-bullet cases.'[19]

Tom Foley was a seventeen-year-old local lad who helped the ambush party to prepare the position during the day. Foley was adamant all his life that many of the stories surrounding Bealnablath were false and that some were downright lies. He claimed he travelled to Newcestown with some IRA men on the day of the ambush to collect the landmine that was put in position to block the retreat of Collins's convoy. When he returned, he found Liam Deasy, O/C of the 1st Southern Division of the IRA, drawing the battle lines and organising the ambush along the boreen to the west of the site. As we have seen, Foley claimed that had the ambush gone as planned, 'a bird could not have escaped from the trap'. Foley was not present during the ambush but returned early the following morning. Along the cart track across the stream where most of the IRA party were shooting, he found 'a lot of shells were strewn about, some empty, some full'.[20] There is a big difference between these discoveries – lots of shells spread out along the lane opposite where most of the IRA men were firing from, and the handful of cartridges Tom Daly and the Free State army party found the night before, which led Daly to believe that no more than three men had fired from the position he described. Clearly they were describing two different places: Daly down on the road to the south of where Collins died and where the forensics suggest the fatal shot must have come from, and Foley and the Hurley girls the long ditch on the boreen on the opposite side of the glen which was the ambush position of the men of the 3rd Brigade, from where most of the firing came.

There is further evidence that there were men hidden on or near the roadside at the southern end of the ambush site. Father Twohig tracked down a former Kerry IRA man, Robert J. ('Bobs') Doherty. Doherty, from Glenflesk near

Killarney, had long since emigrated, like many Republicans, to the United States. On the day of Bealnablath, he was on his way back to Kerry with a colleague, having being part of a column being organised by the IRA from Ballincollig barracks before it was evacuated. Travelling westwards across the fields, they stumbled into Bealnablath just as the ambush was taking place. 'They dashed over the hill on the near (or eastern) side of the road and rather suddenly came across the scene of battle. "We dived for cover," said old Bobs, still remembering the wet of the grass where they landed.'[21] The grass was indeed wet there, and it still is, since this is the stretch of marshy ground behind the ditch near where Daly claimed he had found the handful of cartridges.[22]

> There were some men already in position near us and a little distance away. I didn't know who they were. There was an armed column on the road below us and a big man started to walk away from it. Someone near us fired just then and I saw the big man fall. I heard a man say: 'I put two into him!' That's all I know.[23]

This appears, on the face of it, to be an eyewitness account of the death of Michael Collins. It fits the forensics of the bloodstain, the wounds in the dead man's head and the direction from which the bullet must have come. It corresponds to most of the accounts left by members of the Free State party, who agree that Collins walked away south from the cover of his own troops and that of the armoured car and was some distance to the south of everyone when he was killed. It also agrees with the accounts of the Free State men who claim that there was some firing from the eastern flank as well as from the western side where the 3rd Brigade men were hidden. What it does not fit with is any of the accounts left by the members of the 3rd Brigade itself, who either were unaware that there was another party hidden to the south of the ambush position or have chosen not to divulge it. The late

Edward O'Mahony, one of the better-informed writers on Collins's death, who was from the area and grew up among many of those who took part, wrote:

> As a young man I experienced reluctance among old IRA men to talk about Michael Collins and Béal na mBláth. I would be told he was a great man and then the subject would be changed ... Men who had been interned said they feared for their lives and property if it became known that they were in any way connected with Béal na mBláth. They swore an oath of silence about the incident and, when captured, surrendered under false names and false addresses.[24]

What the above analysis tells us is that the generally accepted accounts of the death of Collins – that he was killed by one of the departing IRA men on the boreen across the glen, that he was killed by a ricochet bullet that came off the armoured car or that he was killed by one of his own party – are almost certainly wrong. It is also highly unlikely that he was hit by a revolver bullet. In other words, all the 'accepted models' are likely to be incorrect. The forensics of the wound alone – a classic head shot of the kind inflicted by military snipers the world over – suggest that this was an assassination and that there was nothing accidental about it. The statistical chances of an accidental shot hitting Collins in the back of the head are slim – especially given that all his supposed enemies were in front of him. A trained sniper, on the other hand, will always aim for the head (destroy the brain stem and there is only one outcome: instant death), so the statistical chances of this happening are high.

Further evidence that at least one such marksman was in position was the shot that hit Lieutenant Smith as he tried to get Collins's body onto the armoured car. Smith was hit on the side of the neck. The shot missed his spine and his carotid artery by an inch. The notion that it was not possible to get off an aimed shot might have been true in the case of the men on the lane opposite who were pinned down by machine gun fire from the armoured car, but clearly it was not true of everyone who was present. What this suggests is that there was someone on the IRA side who was able to get off perfectly aimed shots. Who he was is a question that may never be answered and it is probably not particularly important anyway. But the circumstances that brought Collins into the situation in which he was killed are surely important. This is what we shall look at in the next few chapters. Because Michael Collins was not in Bealnablath by accident; this was no fortuitous or accidental killing. This was a well-planned military exercise, even if its implementation was chaotic and haphazard.

2

Bealnablath: Some Essential Facts

And so we enter the historiographical nightmare that is 'the day Michael Collins was shot'. So much has been written about this that to even attempt a synopsis of the various strands of analysis of the evening of 22 August 1922 would require an entire volume in its own right. A recent book on the subject, the provocatively entitled *The Assassination of Michael Collins* by S.M. Sigerson, analyses most of the information currently available on the events of the day, and its broad conclusions are that almost everybody, on all sides, was lying about what happened at Bealnablath. In assigning blame for Collins's death, Sigerson points the finger speculatively at the two agencies that she claims ultimately had most to gain, namely the British government and Éamon de Valera. But this is surely a case of retrospective determinism, the use of consequences as predictors of events. However, Sigerson, having looked at the evidence and finding that the case against Sonny O'Neill – whom many claim fired the bullet that killed Collins – does not add up, is entitled to look elsewhere for explanations. Her book contains most of the evidence and saves a lot of footwork for the inquisitive researcher, even if it makes no attempt to avoid the 'fog', i.e. the claims and counterclaims as to what happened at Bealnablath.

According to an army report written by one of the Free State men present, the ambush itself was a desultory affair. The convoy, as we have seen, consisted of a motorcycle outrider and an open Crossley tender under Commandant Seán O'Connell with two drivers and eight soldiers, followed by the open touring car with Collins and Dalton sitting at the back. Farther back was the armoured car, armed with its Vickers machine gun. According to the report, the convoy stopped when it encountered an upturned dray on the road which was also littered with broken bottles.[1]

> Fire was opened up on the Crossley, by no means heavy but quick or rapid and lasted at most two minutes. When it ceased, [the] sound of firing from the armoured car was heard; this also ceased in a very short time. (It is at this time it is alleged, a lone shot was fired.) Comdt. O'Connell went towards [the] remainder of convoy (still out of sight) where he found General Dalton ministering to [the] already dead Collins, shot through the head. Sadly we returned to Cork which we reached after many delays and breakdowns. The dead body was brought to Shanakiel Hospital where staff bandaged up the head. The body was taken by sea from Cork to Dublin and brought to St. Vincent's where it was viewed by members of his family.[2]

I do not intend to repeat the reams of information that are available on what is claimed to have happened at Bealnablath, where no detail is so minor as to have escaped scrutiny. But there are salient points which, taken together, point away from 'the standard model'. These constitute many of the inconsistencies surrounding Bealnablath. Some of them are worth repeating.

- Collins's convoy was well stretched out along the road, with more than one account suggesting that there was up to 400 yards between the leading motorcycle rider and the armoured car which brought up the rear. This confirms that there were in effect two battles going on during the ambush: between the men on the Crossley tender at the front and the IRA; and between the men in the touring car and/or the armoured car farther back along the road and the IRA. The latter IRA men were adamant that their fire could not have reached the Crossley tender.

- As we have seen, according to Dalton, the touring car stopped when fired on – the windshield being shattered. Dalton wanted to drive through but Collins overruled him. The IRA's own report on the ambush states that all their firing was on the Collins end of the convoy.

- Most accounts have Collins standing up and reloading his rifle when he was shot, having noticed the departing IRA men on the glenside opposite.

- Collins was shot in the back of the head, the bullet entering behind his left ear and exiting behind his right. Gogarty found two bullet wounds: a small blueish entry wound in the hairline behind the victim's left ear and a larger exit wound that effectively blew out the right-hand side of the back of his skull.[3] The suggestion that Collins was shot through the forehead, even at the hairline, is probably incorrect, as his cap shows only one (exit) wound on the right hand side – the right collar and epaulettes of his greatcoat are bloodstained and his death mask shows the front of his head to be completely unmarked. So Collins could not have been shot by the main IRA party, who were to the west in front of him and at whom he was firing.

- It is highly unlikely that Collins died from a ricochet, since a ricochet would not have made a small entry wound. Besides, a ricochet by a bullet fired from in front of him would be technically impossible. At least one officer present at the scene, Joe Dolan, believed that the bullet must have come from the south or south-east of where Collins was standing; that is to say, from neither of the IRA parties known to have been present. This means that the killer must have been positioned to his left and shooting from the south.

- The ambush was a comparatively minor affair. It went on for no more than twenty or thirty minutes, and most of the fire came from the Free State party, who had a machine gun on the armoured car and another on the Crossley tender. These sprayed the ditches around the IRA men so that they had to keep their heads down and, according to their own account, were hardly able to get off an accurate shot during the entire ambush.
- Despite later claims to the contrary, the IRA men did not know that anyone had been killed in the fight until afterwards.
- Only about six IRA men from the 3rd Brigade are believed to have been in position across the glen from the convoy and these were withdrawing by the time Collins was killed. Eoin Neeson quoted one of those who was there:

> We had rifles and were under continuous fusillade from the road. It was hard enough to fire in their direction at all, let alone get off an aimed shot, at dusk and at 500 yards' range. Our purpose at this stage was merely to keep them pinned down long enough for the large party to get to safety, which we did and then retired. We did not know we had shot anybody, much less Collins.[4]

- Most Free State accounts mention that Collins had spotted two IRA men just before he was killed.
- Collins was shot during a lull in the fighting. Accounts vary, but suggest that it was either a single shot, two shots or a brief outbreak of shooting, followed by a general fusillade.
- There was then a final burst of shooting from the eastern side of the road. Various parties claimed that they could see the turret of the armoured car and let off a few rounds, after which the column moved off and left Bealnablath.

This is where several accounts find Collins's killer. He is (1) a subsequent resident of Cork city, usually either Tom Kelleher or Jim Hurley;[5] (2) a returning Kerry Volunteer;[6] or (3) Pete Kearney.[7] Each of these believed he might have fired the fatal shot.

- They are all probably wrong because the officer who was hit in this last volley was Lieutenant Smith, who was shot through the neck, the bullet exiting near his clavicle. Smith was hit by a rifle bullet which passed right through his shoulder but did not cause the kind of damage that was inflicted by the bullet that killed Collins. The convoy moved off just afterwards.

- Most accounts agree that Collins was shot when he stood up after the firing had ceased. He had wandered off some distance to the south of the armoured car – anything from 15 to 50 yards has been stated – and was towards the left-hand side of the road and loading his rifle when he was killed. While this supports the contention that his lack of combat experience contributed to his death, there has never been an adequate explanation for Collins's very strange decision to leave the cover of his vehicles. What was he doing wandering off on his own out of the cover of his men? Even if the firing had stopped, it seems a very foolish thing to have done.

- There are also serious question marks concerning the actions of the armoured car during the ambush. Initially, it was too much to the rear to be of any benefit to Collins, though it does seem it came closer to the touring car during the ambush. While the gunner, McPeak, sprayed the hedges with bullets for a while, he then stopped because the ammunition belt failed to feed properly into his machine gun. There is also a suggestion that the armoured car reversed up the lane where the main IRA party were firing from and may even have got stuck there, at least for a time. And there are claims that two men – namely Jim Conroy, who had been one of Collins's drivers during the

War of Independence, and Peter Gough – had transferred from the Crossley tender to the armoured car before they left Bandon.

These are most of the important facts as they relate to the fight itself. But other very serious question marks arise in the wake of the ambush.

- The Cumann na nGaedheal government, when it left office in 1932, had its file on Collins's death destroyed. By all accounts, the file was very substantial. The reason given at the time was that had the file fallen into the hands of the new Fianna Fáil government, it might have led to a 'loss of life'.
- No official inquiry was carried out, though a Garda John Hickey led a team of gardaí in the area investigating the death in the mid-1920s. His findings, published eventually in the *Limerick Weekly Echo* in 1972,[8] provide a fascinating account of the events surrounding the ambush. This may or may not contain similar evidence to the file destroyed in 1932.
- Any coroner's account or forensic analysis of Collins's body also mysteriously disappeared, though Gogarty's account of the embalming of the body has come to light.
- The IRB, which Collins had led from 1917 and which was his primary power base, did not carry out an inquest into Collins's death until 1966, long after it had apparently ceased to exist as a functioning organisation and so long after the event that it made no difference. It seems very strange that the organisation did not bother to investigate the death of the man who was its effective leader.
- There is no doubt that some of the most important participants on the day were economical with the truth. This is even true in the case of Emmet Dalton, whose accounts are inconsistent, to say the least, and often downright misleading. For instance, he denied that there were any

peace negotiations going on, despite the fact that his own memos to GHQ in the days before the ambush state that he was party to organising them himself. However, most writers accept Dalton's account of the relative position of the vehicles.

For all these reasons, the death of Collins has fed a host of mutually contradictory theories. Very few events in Irish history have had so many untruths written about them. All kinds of doubts have been cast on the circumstances surrounding it. This is not to denigrate the many writers who have tackled this topic, all of whom made honest, sincere attempts to get to the bottom of the story. It is just that they were often working with faulty data, at least some of which was deliberately released over the years by parties who had an interest in burying the truth. Is there any way through the maze of detail, much of it irrelevant? I believe there is, and it comes from studying what was written in the days before and immediately after the ambush before the various participants, all with reasons of their own, set about creating a fog of disinformation on the circumstances surrounding Collins's death. This is what we shall attempt to do in the next chapters.

3

Evasive Actions

On Tuesday, 15 February 1964, seven men met at the Metropole Hotel in Cork. They were Liam Deasy, Tom Kelleher, Jim Hurley, Dan Holland, Pete Kearney, Tom Crofts and Florrie O'Donoghue. All but O'Donoghue were known surviving members of the IRA party that had ambushed Michael Collins in Bealnablath on 22 August 1922. They were there to draft their version of the events of that day, a decision brought about by the imminent publication of Eoin Neeson's history of the Civil War.[1]

The article they put together was for publication and it is quite clear that their intention was to make their message public before Neeson's book came out. In the event, there seems to have been little need for them to do so, since Neeson, at least in that book, stayed away from controversial accounts of the ambush.[2] Their article is broadly similar to the now accepted version of events, except in one regard: it denies that there was any intention to kill Collins.

> Statements which have been made to the effect that the Division and Cork No.1 Brigade were aware of Collins' intention to visit posts in Cork and that a general order was issued to kill him are without foundation and completely untrue. His presence in the South was known

to the officers in the Division and of the 1st and 3rd Brigades only on the morning of the 22nd and no order had been issued by either of the commands. The ambush was decided on as part of the general policy of attacking Free State convoy [sic].[3]

The implication is that the killing of Collins was the result of circumstance and that he merely happened to be in the wrong convoy in the wrong place at the wrong time: in other words, nobody really set out to kill Collins; it just sort of happened, to borrow a contemporary phrase.

Their description of the ambush is short and to the point:

> Immediately on hearing the noise of the approaching vehicles, seven or eight of the Cork No. 3 section took up poor positions on the bohereen west of the road and opened fire on the oncoming convoy. Jim Hurley fired at the motor cyclist and missed him. Tom Kelleher fired at the following vehicle. The convoy stopped and opened fire. The Republican party were armed with rifles and revolvers only, they had no machine guns, but there were two machine guns in the convoy and fire from them raked the section of the fence from which the Cork No. 3 section were firing. The action lasted between 20 and 30 minutes and, before it ended, darkness had fallen to the extent that it was possible to see the flashes from the gunfire. Conditions were such that it was not possible to get off an aimed shot.
>
> Firing stopped at almost 8 o'clock. The Cork No. 3 section remained in position and the Free State convoy withdrew under fire. No one in the Republican party knew that Collins had been killed or that the convoy had suffered any casualty. It was only when Seán Galvin [a local Volunteer] came to Bealnablath about 11 o'clock that they got their first report of his death.[4]

This more or less corresponds to what is now the accepted version of events – in fact, it has made a substantial contribution to what most historians now believe. And there are no falsehoods in it, as such. What it states is that there was an ambush, that it was held by Cork No. 3 Brigade, that it was a minor affair in which it was not possible for the anti-Treaty men to get in an accurate shot, that the attackers left the scene without realising anybody had been shot, let alone killed, and that they heard about Collins's death only later that night.

It is simple and straightforward and, most importantly, plausible. Technically speaking, it is correct that the ambush put in place by the Cork No. 3 Brigade at Bealnablath was in effect a failed ambush in which the attackers were driven off by the superior firepower of the convoy, and it probably reflects the view of the majority of those who signed the document. However, it is not the full picture, or anything like it. Because what happened at Bealnablath was considerably more complex than the above account would have us believe. In fact this is a cover-up that neglects to impart a lot of additional information that must have been known to at least some of those who met on that day in February 1964.

What is of concern to us at this point is not so much the content of the article, which is what you might expect would have been put together by the ambushers some forty years later. The real question is: what was Florrie O'Donoghue doing among them, seeing as he apparently played no act or part in the ambush and appears, on the face of it, to have had nothing to do with it? Daniel Murray suggested that O'Donoghue was taken on merely as a scribe for the meeting. 'As a man who knew the value of information and the use of the pen, O'Donoghue was the ideal choice to record on behalf of the group their version of events.'[5] Yet they hardly had need for such a scribe. They had in Liam Deasy the author of what would turn out to be probably the best military history of the War of Independence, who was also the officer ultimately in charge of the Republicans at Bealnablath. Deasy was a cogent and clear-thinking writer and his books would prove that he had an excellent memory of the events of those years. The men did not need another scribe. Yet here was O'Donoghue acting as apparent secretary to the meeting and, seeing as the person who takes the minutes creates the record, it is fair to say that the finished article was largely the work of O'Donoghue, presumably with the agreement of the others.

So why was Florrie O'Donoghue involved? Was it just part of his general cleaning-up of historical loose ends in order to present as neat as possible a record of the events of the time – something he spent his whole life doing? Or was he hiding something?

The general background to the events of the day is by now largely beyond dispute. On 19 August 1922, some two months into the Civil War, with the Free State side rapidly gaining the upper hand, having taken all the major towns and cities in Munster, Michael Collins, having nominated himself as Commander in Chief of the Free State forces, paid a visit to his native County Cork. This was one of several tours of duty he made during August. His intention was to encourage his troops in their various outposts, to visit his family and friends in west Cork and to try to iron out as many logistical problems as he could while he was doing so. He also wanted to recover a large sum of Customs and Excise revenue that had been taken by the IRA and was lodged in several Cork banks. But what is now also beyond dispute is that one of his main reasons for coming to Cork was that he was in the process of making contact with the anti-Treaty IRA in the hope of bringing the Civil War to a speedy end.

There were major stumbling blocks on the road to peace. Liam Lynch, the head of the anti-Treaty forces, was in no mood for compromise and would, over the next nine months, lead his forces against the wishes of most of his own officers on what can be described as a near-suicidal road to destruction. Collins, at least in his own published pronouncements, wanted the anti-Treaty forces to simply surrender their weapons to the State, something they obviously were not prepared to do. However, there is much evidence that this may have been a negotiating position and that Collins genuinely desired peace.

One of the factors that brought Collins to Cork at that juncture was that over the summer of 1922 a number of prominent business people with Republican sympathies in Cork had set up a People's Rights Association (PRA) in an attempt to broker a settlement between the two sides. Liam Lynch was not interested and, when contacted by the PRA in July, he 'said he had had six months of negotiations and was fed up with them ... war or peace for him; he was tired of the situation'.[6] Nonetheless, the PRA's efforts to open negotiations were to continue.

And leading these efforts at this point were Florrie O'Donoghue and Seán O'Hegarty, respectively Adjutant of the 1st Southern Division and former commandant of the Cork No. 1 Brigade of the IRA. Both were also the leading IRB figures in Cork. As a note to Collins from Cork at the end of July put it: 'Seán O'Hegarty and Florrie O'Donoghue are not taking any interest in the war. They are out for peace.'[7] There is little doubt that O'Hegarty and O'Donoghue wanted to end the war, at least according to their own accounts; they had never wanted it to happen in the first place; this was the main reason they gave for trying to avoid taking sides in the early summer of 1922. As O'Hegarty put it when he addressed the Dáil – one of the few non-deputies ever to do so – in May: 'It does not matter what you name the Government; when a crisis occurs in a country it is not the name of the Government that counts. It is the men ... because when the opportunity comes to set up a Republic it can be set up. Let the country drift into civil war ... you do not help the Republic but you smash it utterly.'[8] O'Hegarty and O'Donoghue were to attempt to mediate again in the spring of 1923 when the situation was considerably more serious from a Republican point of view. They were to fail again, largely owing to increased intransigence on both sides and the uncompromising stance of Lynch, who still thought there was a chance of winning the war when all the evidence was to the contrary.

The immediate lead-up to Collins's death is well known. He arrived in Cork for his tour of duty on Saturday, 19 August. He stayed in the Imperial Hotel in the city and on the Sunday and Monday made several trips to various outposts in the Cork area, encouraging his troops as he went along. His notebooks for the weekend showed that he concerned himself with various logistical problems regarding his forces. He also spent much of the Monday meeting members of the banking and business community in Cork in connection with an attempt to retrieve as much as he could of the £120,000 of Customs and Excise revenue that had been taken by the IRA a few weeks earlier.[9]

On the Monday afternoon he made his way to Macroom to inspect the troops stationed there. Macroom had been taken by Free State forces under Commandant Peter Conlon only a few days earlier and was on the front line and close to Republican headquarters at Ballyvourney, some 10 miles to the west. Collins must have known that he was entering dangerous enemy territory. Nevertheless, a surviving account suggests that there were high jinks among Collins's party and plenty of drinking and carousing that afternoon in Williams's Hotel in Macroom. According to one account, Collins lifted up a pretty barmaid and carried her up the stairs, depositing her on the top step before coming down again to the applause of his men. (How willing a party the barmaid was in these shenanigans is not mentioned.)[10] The following day, Tuesday, 22 August, Collins planned to visit his homestead in Clonakilty to meet up with family and friends after spending the night back in the Imperial Hotel in Cork.

Collins, always an early riser, got up at 6.00am on the morning of 22 August. However, instead of going the direct route to west Cork – via Bandon – he opted to return to Macroom and from there to make his way to Bandon and farther west by a circuitous route. The main road to Bandon, which had been closed the previous week because anti-Treaty forces had blown up two bridges, had been reopened. Seán Hales, the Free State commandant in Bandon, had travelled it that very morning.[11] Many commentators, including survivors on the Republican side, such as Liam Deasy, have wondered what Collins was doing travelling some 20 miles west to Macroom and then going the much longer route to Bandon, rather than taking the direct route, which would have been around 25 miles shorter, particularly when he had been to Macroom the previous evening.

He may have been dropping off a Lewis gun to the garrison in Macroom, as has been claimed, but surely he could have got somebody else to do that for him. What is now pretty much accepted, however, is that he met Florrie O'Donoghue in Macroom at 8.00am, and he may also have had a meeting with him the previous day. It appears they spoke for half an hour in one of the hotels in the town before Collins left on his ill-fated journey. O'Donoghue claimed to noted IRA man Ernie O'Malley that this meeting came about entirely by accident. He said he was making his way from Cork to County Kerry to visit his mother who was sick; he had borrowed a car and received passes from Emmet Dalton, who commanded the Free State forces, and Tom Crofts, who commanded the IRA, and was passing through Macroom when he was arrested by 'a fool' of a Free State soldier and 'put in clink'. Except that most people would go to Rathmore, where O'Donoghue's mother lived, via Mallow or Lombardstown, rather than Macroom.[12] O'Donoghue also said that he saw Collins out of a window and managed to make contact with him. According to O'Donoghue: 'I had the impression that he wanted to leave politics and take charge of the army. He was really talking big, but was surprised that it had been found so easy to move around Co Cork.'[13]

Whatever may or may not have passed between Collins and O'Donoghue that morning, Collins, with his party, according to all accepted accounts, left Macroom around 8.30am and went to Bandon by the only route open, the road that would bring him through Bealnablath and within a few hundred yards of a house where an IRA meeting was scheduled for that very day. The convoy was spotted as it passed through, Collins was recognised and an ambush was put in place in case he should return by the same route. (This, as we shall see, is likely to be another fabrication.) Collins then visited Bandon, Clonakilty and points west, where he met with members of his family and former colleagues before returning via the same route. Again, he could have gone the shorter and more direct route via the main road, but it appears he had his own reasons for returning to the Macroom area. Dalton in an interview many years later claimed that 'I advised against returning by the route which we had come, but I was over-ruled.'[14] In fact, if Collins had not insisted on overruling Dalton at every hand's turn during his trip to Cork, he would probably have survived it.

Meanwhile, the ambush party, who had lain in wait all day for Collins to return, got tired of waiting and were in the process of dismantling the mine they had laid under the road; most of them were either leaving the ambush site or had already left. By the time Collins arrived, only a handful of IRA men were still in ambush position.

As O'Donoghue told Ernie O'Malley: 'I was talking to Dalton years later. He said: Mick wouldn't keep down. If he had ever been in a scrap he'd have learned to stay down for I was flat down and so Mick was killed by standing up.'[15] Many thousands of words have been spent in describing the circumstances of that day, but nobody disagrees with the simple truth of it: that Collins died because he had no combat experience, that he was suffering from hubris and was careless about his own security and he underestimated the determination of his enemies. From their point of view, by passing through their command area and so close to their headquarters, he was simply rubbing their noses in it.

On one level it was a tragedy that should never have happened, though with Collins's general carelessness and self-belief – his larger-than-life character which saw no danger anywhere – he would have been extremely lucky if it did not happen at some point anyway. He had already had several narrow escapes in Dublin and an ambush had been put in place near Watergrasshill on the main Dublin–Cork road the previous Saturday in case he was travelling from Dublin to Cork by that route.[16] He avoided another near Listowel, County Kerry, because he had to attend Arthur Griffith's funeral. As Richard Mulcahy put it many years later: 'I simply accept it that, in the dare devil kind of way that Collins did things, that when he got into an ambush position of that kind he felt he was in Parnell Square doing a job that required to be done and he never thought of looking behind him or around him or never thought of what was in front of him.'[17] There were a lot of potential Bealnablaths in Ireland at that time.

4

Some Orchestrated Manoeuvres in the Dark

Anybody who reads about the death of Michael Collins knows that just as in the case of John F. Kennedy, there is substantial literature devoted to 'Who shot Michael Collins?' The first book devoted entirely to the ambush, John M. Feehan's *The Shooting of Michael Collins*, begins from the standpoint that Collins was shot by British Intelligence but provides no credible evidence in support of this theory other than a general slur on the character of Emmet Dalton, commander of the Free State army in Cork, who was accompanying Collins on the day. The very basic forensics outlined in Chapter 1 suggest that it would have been next to impossible for Dalton to have killed him, because not only was Collins out of Dalton's line of vision, but Dalton was in the wrong place to have fired the shot and he had the wrong weapon.

Feehan claims that Dalton may have been a British agent but provides no evidence to back this up. He further implies that Dalton became an MI6 agent during the Second World War, but provides no evidence for that either. His other 'evidence' for British involvement is that news of Collins's death was carried by the *Daily Express* in London on the following day, before even the *Cork Examiner* had got hold of it. However, the *Irish Times* and the *Freeman's Journal* also had the story on the same day, suggesting that the earliest reports had come out of Dublin. This should not surprise us. Telegraph correspondence between Cork and the Free State headquarters in Dublin came through Andy Cope, the British envoy in Dublin, who was effectively given the job of nursing the Free State administration into being.[1] Cope was almost certainly going to inform London right away about such a momentous and politically significant event.

The next published book, Meda Ryan's *The Day Michael Collins was Shot*, is a better-balanced report of the events of the day. Ryan makes some unsubstantiated claims based on the recall of Jim Kearney, a Volunteer whose claim to have been at Bealnablath is disputed. Among Ryan's hypotheses is that Collins was walking north when he was hit and that his death took place some 400 yards to the south of where it did in fact take place. Nonetheless it is a very worthwhile book; it is clearly written and contains quite an amount of valuable information. Meda Ryan dismisses Feehan's claims and makes the most obvious case: that Collins was simply shot by one of the IRA party who were ambushing him. She names the most likely candidate as Sonny O'Neill, the ex-British army and RIC man who was now in the IRA, on the basis that he is said to have claimed that he 'dropped one man' towards the end of the ambush and that he was a trained marksman and may have used dumdum bullets, which some say might account for the kind of wound Collins suffered.

But by far the most interesting book that deals with the death of Collins, particularly from a Republican point of view, is Eoin Neeson's *The Life and Death of Michael Collins*, and this brings us back to the objections Florrie O'Donoghue and the ambush survivors were about to make against Neeson, as described in Chapter 3.[2] It is clear that they were trying to set the agenda before the publication of Neeson's history of the Civil War – in which, as it turned out, he said nothing controversial about the shooting of Collins.[3] However, what is clear is that they had good grounds for wanting to get their retaliation in first, so to speak, because *The Life and Death of Michael Collins*, published in 1968 – only a few months after O'Donoghue's death – shows that Neeson knew a lot more than he had included in his first book, and possibly did not publish it then because he had been scared off. It is significant that he does not thank O'Donoghue in his acknowledgements for the second (though he did in the first book), and it is immediately clear from the text why he did not do so.

Coming from a strong Republican background, Eoin Neeson had the ear and the trust of several of the survivors of Bealnablath, and what he writes is quite at variance with the O'Donoghue-penned account described in the previous chapter. Far from there being no plan to shoot Collins, what Neeson shows us is that a whole strategy had been worked out to that end well in advance – and by the senior divisional IRA leadership, not just by the No. 3 Brigade group who were there when it happened. It is worth recounting in detail what Neeson wrote because, as will become clear, much of what he says about the planning of the ambush is likely to be correct.

Neeson wrote that a meeting was held at IRA headquarters in Ballyvourney on the Saturday or Sunday before Bealnablath, at which it was decided to ambush Collins, and that de Valera may have been present at that meeting. Two things are important here: (a) the IRA knew that Collins was coming to Cork before he arrived and before the news had reached the press, and (b) the IRA planned to kill him if possible. Neeson refers to 'The controversial meeting at Ballyvourney ... controversial because the fact that it took place at all, had been denied by two officers of the Cork brigade, one who was neutral at the time [almost certainly a reference to O'Donoghue], the other being the late James Hurley of University College Cork.'[4]

But the meeting did take place ... among those present was the O/C of the Cork City Brigade, who told the

45

meeting that it was known that Collins was on his way to Cork. He also said that all units – meaning in this context, all the units of which he had control – had been alerted with instructions to ambush Collins's convoy. The road between Cobh and Cork on which he was due to travel, was mined. De Valera, who was in the area trying to make contact with Liam Deasy in an effort to secure some kind of agreement with Collins, was told that Collins might not leave Cork alive and he replied that he knew that and was very sorry for it. Lynch's instructions to Deasy were: 'Dev is in the area trying to make peace. Give him no encouragement.' Dev, for his part, stated at the meeting: 'He [Collins] is a big man and might negotiate. If things fall into the hands of lesser men, there is no telling what might happen.'[5]

This is the opposite of what O'Donoghue wrote in his 1964 article, which states that the ambush, such as it was, was convened on the spur of the moment by men of the 3rd Brigade. Neeson, however, wrote: 'When [3rd] Brigade staff Tom Hales, Brigade O/C, Tadhg Sullivan, Brigade Q/M and Jim Hurley, Brigade staff officer, arrived about one in the afternoon to attend the meeting, the ambush position was already occupied. So the decision had been taken at higher than local level.'[6] But the ironic thing was that, as Neeson put it, 'while a number of officers on the anti-Treaty side knew in advance that Collins was coming to Cork and made plans to ambush or kill him, those who in fact laid the fatal ambush did not know that he was in the south at all until he was seen on the morning of the day of the ambush by one of their members'.[7] So O'Donoghue's article is right in stating that the ambushers of the 3rd Brigade found out about Collins's arrival in the area only that morning. What he does not tell us is that by the time they got around to setting up their ambush, there were others already in ambush position. Neeson was also clear on why Collins was in the area in the first place:

'He was to meet with members of the opposing forces on the subject of peace negotiations.'[8]

Neeson even ventures to suggest how the IRA headquarters at Ballyvourney got wind of Collins's impending visit to Cork, and is in no doubt that there was also the belief on the IRA side that he was there to talk peace: 'Collins's real purpose in travelling south was to end hostilities ... Collins had an appointment with neutral officers in Cork on the night of 22 August in Desmond's Hotel, Seán O'Hegarty being one of them.'

> For some time Seán Hales [pro-Treaty army commander in Bandon and brother of anti-Treaty Commandant Tom Hales] ... had been negotiating with some of the other side on Collins's behalf for such a meeting. For obvious reasons, Collins would not want this information to be generally known, particularly, one takes for granted, by some of his cabinet colleagues in Dublin. A leak from one of the anti-Treaty officers involved, or indeed from one of the neutrals, many of whom were *unbelievably un-security conscious*, would readily account for Collins's proposed visit being known to the officers at the Ballyvourney meeting [emphasis added].[9]

Neeson goes on to state that Collins's bona fides on his peace mission are indicated by the fact that he sent ahead Frank Thornton, one of his most trusted lieutenants, to try to make contact with Deasy to bring Deasy or someone representing him to the peace meeting in Cork. Thornton, unfortunately, after meeting with Dan Breen in County Tipperary, failed in his mission when he was ambushed at Ninemilehouse near Cahir and was so severely wounded that he was lucky to survive. So Thornton never got to contact Deasy.

What is clear from all this is that O'Donoghue's article, which claims, in effect, that Collins was killed by what amounted to a stray shot by a hastily contrived ambush, is well wide of the mark. Neeson's analysis shows that there was a clear intention to ambush Collins, that the decision to do so was taken by senior divisional IRA officers and not simply by the members of the 3rd Brigade, who we know manned the ambush and who came to know of Collins's presence in the area only that morning. It is also clear that Collins was in Cork to talk peace and that his presence had been leaked, probably by those who were acting as intermediaries in the negotiations: as Neeson diplomatically put it, 'one of the anti-Treaty officers involved or indeed one of the neutrals'. Neeson's claim that 'many of the neutrals were unbelievably un-security conscious' is surely a dig at O'Donoghue and/or O'Hegarty. It is hard to avoid the conclusion that Neeson was not too subtly pointing the finger at 'the neutrals', that is to say O'Donoghue and O'Hegarty, as the source of the leak that led the IRA command to plan to kill Collins.

The claim that 'many of the neutrals were unbelievably un-security conscious' might sound strange as a reference to O'Donoghue and O'Hegarty, who would be regarded by historians as among the most discreet of all the Munster IRA men. Yet it looks from this almost as if they wanted the knowledge of Collins's impending arrival to be generally known. (And an intriguing minor point here: how did they know that Collins was planning to visit Cobh – which he did – where the mine placed to 'welcome' him did not go off? Clearly someone very close to what Collins was planning must have told them. As we shall see, there is a strong suggestion of collusion between individuals in Collins's command and the anti-Treaty forces.)

So clearly there is much more to this than meets the eye, and O'Donoghue's venture into the Bealnablath debate suggests that he may have had a larger role than he claimed. Was he simply embarrassed in case it might be pointed out that he was one of those responsible for leaking Collins's visit to the anti-Treaty leadership? Or is there more to the story? What is astonishing is that Neeson's book, the closest thing we have to an insider's view, given his contacts in the Cork IRA, has largely been ignored in the various debates around Bealnablath.

There are some hints as to why this might be the case in the next book dedicated to the subject of Michael Collins's death. This is *The Dark Secret of BealnaBlath* by Father Patrick Twohig, a somewhat speculative but well-informed analysis which provides much information that is not available elsewhere.

As in his other books, Father Twohig in *The Dark Secret of BealnaBlath* does not provide any references. However, such was his obsession and enthusiasm that he left no stone unturned in his search for information. He was also a Macroom man and knew some of those involved in the events of the day. Indeed, it appears that he spent much of his life digging up material on Bealnablath. His approach was to gather every piece of evidence available from his various sources and throw them all into a melange that is sometimes confusing but also very detailed and informative. His overall conclusion was that Collins could have been shot by any of several IRA men who happened to be in the area that day, including Sonny O'Neill. He names several other potential shooters, all on the IRA side, particularly focusing on the group of Kerry Volunteers on their way home from the fall of Cork. Like Meda Ryan, he dismisses the suggestion that Collins was killed by one of his own party.

But Twohig's book has a strange subtext. He seems to imply, without saying it straight out, that Florrie O'Donoghue had some connection with the death of Michael Collins. His evidence for this is interviews he carried out with O'Donoghue himself and with members of the O'Donoghue family. What Twohig seems to imply is that Collins was in Macroom on the morning of the ambush mainly because he was meeting with O'Donoghue and that he was returning to the area in the evening to meet with him again. In other words, Collins travelled the circuitous route to Bandon via Macroom and back because he was to meet O'Donoghue at both ends of the day, presumably to pursue the peace negotiations that O'Donoghue and O'Hegarty were trying to set up. This means that the peace meeting, which Neeson claimed was scheduled for Desmond's Hotel in Cork city, may actually have been planned to take place in or near Macroom.

Twohig's account of the meeting between Collins and O'Donoghue on the morning of the ambush appears to be a re-enactment of a conversation he may have had with O'Donoghue (Twohig knew O'Donoghue in the 1950s). This is a very odd piece of writing since it is the only part of the book to be written in dialogue. In it, he has Collins meeting O'Donoghue in the Victoria Hotel in Macroom. There is no mention of a sick mother or of O'Donoghue's claim to Ernie O'Malley that he was thrown 'into the clink', which is almost certainly a fabrication, if only because all the 'clinks' in town – namely Macroom Castle, the local courthouse and the former RIC barracks – had all been burned down by the departing IRA forces a few days earlier so that they would not fall into the hands of government forces. Nor is there any mention of O'Donoghue getting arrested by 'a fool of' a soldier.

Instead, Twohig has O'Donoghue waiting for Collins to arrive from the larger Williams's Hotel,[10] and even has Dalton suggesting they should still go to Bandon via Cork since the bridges had been repaired. And he has Collins stating that he would be back that evening. The evidence for this is a statement – 'a long-standing family secret' – he got from Nancy McCarthy, whose brother was married to O'Donoghue's sister, that Collins was to meet O'Donoghue again that evening in Macroom.[11]

There are reasons to believe that the peace meeting arranged that evening was not scheduled for Macroom, where it would have been difficult for Republicans to attend because it was being held by National Army forces, or for Cork, which would have been difficult for the same reason, but for nearby Crookstown, which was neutral ground. Crookstown was just down the road from Bealnablath and not far from Macroom. Garda John Hickey, one of three officers sent in by the Free State government in 1924 to put together a report into Collins's death, was stationed at Crookstown for some years. Hickey's account, which was serialised over several weeks in the *Limerick Weekly Echo* in 1972, is so detailed and full of useful information that it is included here as an appendix (see Appendix VI).

Hickey claimed on local evidence that Collins was heading back to Crookstown that evening to meet with intermediaries, probably O'Hegarty, O'Donoghue and presumably at least some anti-Treaty officers. The meeting was to be held in the house of Canon Tracy, the parish priest of Crookstown. According to Hickey, the local IRA unit became aware of the meeting and had another trap waiting for Collins at Farran, between Crookstown and Cork, with a view not to killing Collins, in this instance, but to kidnapping him. The meeting originally was to have been held the previous night. Trees were felled, the ambush was in place and when Collins did not turn up, the Crookstown IRA had enquiries made in the Imperial Hotel in Cork where Collins was staying. Collins's route the next day was telephoned back to Crookstown; the Farran ambush was reactivated and remained in place all day. So it appears from this that had Collins passed through Bealnablath unscathed, he would have been in trouble when he reached Farran. As it was, the touring party carrying the body of its dead commander had enormous difficulty in getting from Crookstown back to Cork after the ambush with trenched roads and felled trees, suggesting that a plan had indeed been in place that evening to send him down a particular route.[12] In his biographical notes on Seán O'Hegarty, O'Donoghue states that O'Hegarty was due to meet Collins that evening and that he (O'Donoghue)had a letter from O'Hegarty to that effect.[13]

The 'dark secret' of BealnaBlath is essentially that Collins was in Macroom that morning only because he was meeting

O'Donoghue and that he was to return to meet him again that evening, that this was in connection with possible peace negotiations, and that he met his death because of these meetings. Like Neeson, Twohig hints that O'Donoghue may have informed the anti-Treaty forces of Collins's movements by heading out to Ballyvourney, where the Cork city IRA commandant, Dan 'Sandow' O'Donovan, now had his headquarters, but he gives no evidence of this.

Whatever way you look at it, the balance of evidence now points to the fact that O'Donoghue was part of the story of Bealnablath and that he may have had good reason for being the author of the anodyne statement put out in 1964.

Twohig also states that O'Donoghue's daughter Breda wrote to him to tell him that Collins had called to the family home on the Blackrock Road upon his arrival in Cork, with the present of a Kerry Blue terrier for O'Donoghue's wife, Josephine, who had acted during the War of Independence as an IRA spy in British army headquarters at Victoria Barracks, Cork, where she worked as a typist. 'I only remember one slight incident, of very little importance, which was spoken of when we were very young children. I believe Michael Collins did give my mother a present of a Kerry-Blue dog when he visited them (Dad and Mother) the day before he was killed.'[14] This has a ring of authenticity since Collins was an avid breeder of Kerry Blues and had the habit of giving pups to those he considered his friends. He was on the point of giving one to Lord Birkenhead, and may even have done so.[15]

It also appears that O'Donoghue tried to expunge any evidence of visits by Collins to members of his family during the post-Truce and Treaty periods. His sister Agnes McCarthy, in her IRA pension application statement, lists Michael Collins among those who visited the shop in Castle Street which she ran as an office for O'Donoghue after he went on the run at the end of March 1920. Only four words are redacted in her entire Military Service Pension statement – though it is still possible to read them since they are poorly crossed out. These are 'Mrs. Brown' in the sentence: 'I also spent a considerable time on intelligence work and I believe with good results and was associated with "Mrs. Brown", my sister-in-law'. The other crossed-out words are 'Michael Collins' in a list of IRA officers who visited the premises.[16] It is highly unlikely she would have made the claim that Michael Collins had made a visit at some stage if he had not. And considering that there is no evidence that Collins was in Cork city during the War of Independence, this can refer only to the Truce or early Civil War periods.

5

The Lead-Up to Bealnablath

So the balance of evidence suggests that there was a plan to kill Collins and that he was effectively drawn into the trap that Bealnablath turned out to be. However, the evidence also suggests that if not Bealnablath, it probably would have happened somewhere else. Liam Lynch at the time certainly seemed to welcome the death of Collins because he felt it gave his side a tactical advantage. The reality, of course, was the opposite: the killing of Collins unleashed unprecedented savagery from the Provisional Government forces, resulting in a bitterness that was to last for generations.

The Farran kidnap plan claimed by Garda John Hickey may have actually existed, as there is evidence of other plans to kidnap senior Pro-Treaty political figures. Lynch wrote to Ernie O'Malley on 2 August 1922 about a plan to capture 'big bugs', as he called them, and the need for secure places of captivity, and he bemoaned the fact that this was less likely to happen now in the south since Free State forces had moved into garrisoned areas of Munster – they were about to land in Cork a few days later.[1]

Furthermore, Lynch had what he believed was information – whether it was reliable or not – that Collins may have had a plan to assassinate members of the anti-Treaty leadership. Given his record of arranging the assassination of his enemies, from the Secret Service agents killed on Bloody Sunday to

Sir Henry Wilson, this was entirely plausible. A letter from Con Moloney, Adjutant General of the anti-Treaty forces, to Ernie O'Malley, written a few days before Collins arrived in Cork, asks if O'Malley can find out in Dublin 'definitely if [a] policy of assassination has been decided by the enemy'.[2] The reason for this was that a Free State communication had been intercepted which suggested that such a policy had been put in place. Considering that in the previous few months Collins may have arranged for Wilson to be assassinated in London and had sent his men to kill the official British hangman and his assistant, political assassination was still very much part of his way of doing business even though he was de facto leader of a new sovereign state. The intercepted letter is worth quoting:

Dear Dick,

The men arrived via Enniskillen and well drunk. Two of them have hellish English accents and I doubt if the men here will fraternize with them. Besides the people around will soon get to know they are English. One of them told me he belonged to 'N' Coy of the Auxiliaries stationed at Longford during the terror. Are we so far gone that we must employ these men to assassinate our erstwhile comrades? If the assassination of the Republican leaders starts, Collins might rue it. Is there no moderation in the Cabinet, or has he got leave of his head completely? It is all very well to say we will not be asked to commit murder, but who will accompany the new arrivals in their deeds of blood. I am fed up with the whole thing. [How] are you keeping in Portobello? Let me know what I asked in my last.[3]

What is clear is that if these visitors from Enniskillen were who the Republicans thought they were, then this was an early taste of some of the tactics employed by the Free State which were to cause so much rancour later. There is little evidence to suggest that Collins was about to introduce a campaign to assassinate his former colleagues. However, regardless of its accuracy, the fact is that this note with all that it implies was on Liam Lynch's desk during the week that Collins visited Cork. It would be hard to see how Lynch could ignore it. It has been stated on numerous occasions by various commentators writing about Collins's death that, had the shoe been on the other foot, Collins would not have had de Valera assassinated. But the historical record suggests otherwise. Tom Flood, one of Collins's deputies and a member of the famed Dublin Guard, waited all night with two of his most trusted men at an abandoned railway station at Twopothouse, a few miles north of Mallow, in the summer of 1922, expecting de Valera to emerge from a train. Their plan was not to kidnap him but to shoot him on the spot.[4] Dick Barrett, one of the four senior IRA men executed by the Free State at the end of 1922, claimed that Collins had 'stated his plans in detail; he would operate a *dark hand* and, according as undesirables pushed their way forward, the *dark hand* would assassinate them [emphasis in original]'.[5]

So, considering that there is evidence the anti-Treaty IRA had plans to kidnap senior government figures and that they had information that Collins might be about to assassinate their own leadership, it is hard to see how they would pass up the opportunity to either kidnap or shoot the most senior figure of all, especially since he seemed willing to present them with the opportunity. Was Collins lured into a trap at Bealnablath by using the bait of the potential opportunity of negotiation with his opponents? If so, those behind it used the good offices of the self-appointed People's Rights Association, which was trying to get the two sides together. And this is not to question the bona fides of some members of that group, such as Canon Tom Duggan and Alfred O'Rahilly, who were genuinely seeking peace.

It is instructive to compare Florrie O'Donoghue's public utterances on the PRA with his private notes on these attempts at negotiation. In *No Other Law*, his biography of Liam Lynch, O'Donoghue states that the PRA was first constituted on 17 July 1922 at a specially convened meeting at the offices of the Cork Harbour Commissioners.[6] However, the attempts at negotiations seem to have predated this by a week or two and are claimed by O'Donoghue to have been instigated by Frank Daly, the chairman of the Cork Harbour Commissioners. Daly had also been part of a group of Cork businessmen who in the spring of 1921 had tried to negotiate between the British government and Sinn Féin with a view to accepting Dominion Home Rule as a compromise option that both sides might accept.[7]

Now he was back, leading a similar group that was hoping to make peace between the factions of the Civil War. This time, his right-hand man was the 'enigmatic' T.P. Dowdall, as Liam Deasy called him, a Cork butter merchant and a long-time Republican supporter. O'Donoghue claimed that Daly and Dowdall were the instigators of the PRA and that he, rather reluctantly, had decided to help them in their search for peace. However, from his own notes taken at the time, it is clear that backroom attempts to contact both sides were going on well before 17 July and that he himself was intimately involved in, and busy with, the initiative. 'On 5 July,' for instance, he states, 'Daly went to see Lynch but did not succeed. Deasy would not commit to this or any other subject. I would have been surprised if he did.' The following day: 'there was a meeting today of O'Rahilly, Daly, Dowdall, [Barry] Egan, [Micheál] Ó Cuill and myself. Rahilly's proposals were discussed. Dowdall, O'Rahilly and Egan left for Dublin to contact Govt people.' The next day, 7 July, 'another attempt to contact Lynch, this time by Fr Duggan.' According to O'Donoghue's notes on 9 July: 'Duggan is back' with news that Lynch was tired of negotiations.[8] All these toings and froings took place under the auspices of the Cork Harbour Commissioners but before the PRA was launched, and it is clear that O'Donoghue was at the heart of them, rather than being on the periphery as he claimed. As to the claim that Lynch was 'tired of negotiations', that may not be true either. On 14 July he sent a note to Daly instructing him to travel from Cork to Lynch's base in Clonmel: 'wish to see yourself and friend at my office here immediately'.[9] This is not suggestive of a man who is 'tired of negotiations'. There is no doubt that O'Rahilly and Canon Duggan were seeking peace, and probably Daly and Dowdall as well – they decried the 'drifting towards the greatest calamity in Irish history' – but was an ulterior motive lurking in the background?

The peace negotiations proceeded in this one-step-forward, one-step-back fashion over several weeks. Ó Cuill wrote to Collins on 1 August outlining the Republicans' position. Essentially, Lynch was requesting that 'if Prov Gov cease their attack on us, defensive action on our part will cease'.[10] They also wanted the Second Dáil to be reconvened, something that was never going to be acceptable to a government that had just been elected to serve on the as yet unconvened Third Dáil. The tone of Ó Cuill's message was dictatorial: 'Mr Collins' was requested to convey 'his final answer' in time for a public meeting to be held in Cork on Saturday, 5 August. Officials in Dublin noted the tone of the 'ultimatum' and 'insolent communication', where 'General Liam Lynch, Chief of Staff' is contrasted with 'Ml Collins'. Nonetheless, a lenient approach was taken in view of the possibility that Ó Cuill might have been under duress from the IRA when he wrote it.[11]

W.T. Cosgrave, on behalf of the government, replied on 4 July stating that they would be prepared to negotiate only on the basis of the anti-Treaty forces declaring obedience to Parliament, surrendering their arms and seized property and giving particulars of mined bridges, roads and railways. Collins was more obdurate: 'the choice is definitely between the return of the British and the Irregulars sending in their arms to the people's Government, to be held in trust for the people'. Negotiations appear to have broken down at this point.

However, in the two weeks before Bealnablath, the 'neutrals' in Cork moved into the gap vacated by the PRA. From the government point of view, 'another Peace offensive has been launched from alleged "neutral sources" in Cork. The terms proposed are a distinct advance on those of a previous occasion and on the face of it look innocent enough.' These proposed a week's truce during which time a peace could be negotiated on the basis that men of the anti-Treaty forces would be accepted into the army with their rank and service recognised, that a general amnesty would be given for all political prisoners and that Republicans were to limit themselves to constitutional actions against the government.[12] Noting the tone of the Republicans – 'dictatorial – careless of anything but their own, defiance of the facts, ignoring the will of the people' while at the same time seeming 'ready and anxious for a peaceful settlement' – the government also noted the position of the so-called 'Neutrals': 'Between the two are the peace makers, busy protesting neutrality, but betraying in every line their manifest bias', with the inconsistencies of their statements, their 'shirking of the facts', clouding of essential features and vague phrases. 'When all these implications are understood, the impossibility of acceptance of such terms becomes manifest.'[13] Nonetheless, it was this proposal – sensible enough on the face of it, and issued through the 'Neutrals' – that Collins was acting on when he went to Cork on 19 August.

Notwithstanding the genuine desire for peace on the part of many of those involved, was there also an element of a trap in all this? One William Murphy wrote from Cobh to Mulcahy in early August to warn of the PRA offering 'an armistice'.

> I regret to say that Frank Daly is, perhaps unconsciously, causing mischief by linking the weight of his name and influence to the Plotters who are engaged in an attempt at forming the so-called People's Rights Association.

> Rightly or wrongly the impression is slowly crystallizing in the minds of the people here in Cobh and in Cork that Mr Daly is playing a double game.[14]

This was written ten days before Collins was killed. It is clear that William Murphy was of the view that the aims of the PRA were not as altruistic as they appeared and that they were 'Plotters', and he took the time and trouble to warn the government about it. O'Donoghue told Ernie O'Malley that Daly, even though he was part of the Cork business community, had 'been of great use to us in Cork', which seems a rather odd thing to say given that the peace negotiations came to nothing. But if being 'of great use to us in Cork' refers to helping to pull Collins into the trap that ultimately found its expression in Bealnablath, then it makes sense. Interestingly, Frank Daly's house was searched by government forces a few days after Collins was killed, which did not go down well with Mr Daly.[15] However, it is clear that it was the proposals of the 'Neutrals' rather than those of the PRA that Collins was attempting to follow up on when he went to Cork, and that the PRA, with O'Donoghue in the background, was merely an initial attempt to get the two sides together. Bearing in mind that O'Donoghue also told O'Malley that 'I was in touch with him [Liam Lynch] and with Tom Crofts and with Liam Deasy all the time during the Civil War',[16] it is obvious where all this is leading: the anti-Treaty IRA wanted either to kidnap Collins or to have him shot – and its different factions might have wanted different things at various times – just as Collins might have had them shot. As in all wars, it was an eye for an eye. Bealnablath was simply the opportunity that presented itself.

6

Words, Too Many Words

The death of Michael Collins appears, in the words of one eminently sensible historian, to be based on evidence 'which seems straightforward enough'.[1] The published material on it points mostly in one direction: that Collins was shot by an IRA man in an ambush in west Cork, and that it is as simple as that. After all, several IRA men who were in the ambushing party that day claimed to have shot him, and one of the Kerry Volunteers who came on the scene as he was returning home after the evacuation of Cork claimed that he was standing beside the man who fired the fatal shot. Indeed, the day after the shooting, when Collins's older brother Johnny was on his way to Dublin for the funeral and was captured and held overnight by an IRA party outside Bandon, one of them 'boasted that it was he "who plugged Mickeen" and was joyous about it'.[2]

It was not my intention to add to the mountain of theory that has been erected around the death of Collins, nor did I wish to engage in an analysis of many of the finer points of the debate. Any evidence will be contested anyway, especially since this is a subject on which many people have strong views. However, seeing that close analysis of the circumstances surrounding Bealnablath points to the likelihood that

Collins was assassinated, rather than just dying in unfortunate circumstances, is there any other evidence from contemporary records to suggest that this was the case?

John Feehan was the first to put forward a detailed assassination theory. His argument was that Collins was assassinated by a cabal of his own colleagues in the Provisional Government, which Feehan termed 'the Junta', and that Major General Emmet Dalton was the man who pulled the trigger.[3] The logic of the argument, if it could be called that, was that W.T. Cosgrave, Richard Mulcahy, Kevin O'Higgins and others in the Free State government wanted to get rid of Collins because he was becoming a liability – and that they had 'demoted' him to commander of the army. Leaving aside the fact that Collins put himself at the head of the army and that the 'demotion' was part of his own efforts to take full control of events on the military front, Feehan produced no evidence to support this claim.

As for his other claim, that British Intelligence was involved and that Dalton may have been a British plant: as we have seen, Feehan provided no evidence of this either, other than speculation – that Dalton resigned from the army shortly afterwards and that he may have been recruited by MI6 during the Second World War, which is probably a lie. (It appears that Dalton was approached to join the Special Operations Executive but declined.)[4] All Feehan did was cast aspersions on Dalton's good name with nothing to back them up. Almost all serious writers who have looked at this since have disagreed with Feehan and stated the obvious: that there is little or no evidence to suggest Emmet Dalton was responsible.[5] Shrewd journalists who interviewed Dalton for TV documentaries in his later years concur with this. The only conclusion one can come to is that either Dalton was an extraordinarily convincing actor, to the extent of weeping openly as he cradled Collins's head on the tortuous journey back to Cork after the ambush, or he had nothing to do with the death of Michael Collins. For his part, Seán Boyne,

Dalton's biographer, has no truck with the argument and dismisses it out of hand.[6]

It is reasonable on the other hand to suppose that the fatal shot was fired by an IRA man – the dubious honour usually being given to Denis 'Sonny' O'Neill, an ex-RIC man and ex-army marksman, who was in Bealnablath most of the day but who had probably gone by the time the ambush took place.[7] Indeed, some have claimed that O'Neill himself believed it was his bullet that killed Collins. A supposedly signed statement made by O'Neill to that effect is claimed to exist but has never been made public. Meda Ryan claimed that no fewer than seven IRA survivors of the ambush believed that O'Neill had fired the fatal shot. His family, however, dispute this, and I have been told by a reliable source close to the family that when asked on his deathbed if he had shot Collins, he said he had not.

Another figure who is sometimes named as 'the man who shot Michael Collins' is Jim Hurley. Hurley was a very well-known figure in Cork. He was a native of Clonakilty and went on to win several All-Ireland hurling medals with Cork in the 1920s. He ended his career as Bursar of University College Cork in the 1960s. Hurley was at Bealnablath; he claimed he fired some shots and believed that it was he who had shot Collins. Kerry Volunteer Greg Ashe, brother of Thomas Ashe who died on hunger strike in 1917, was a prisoner in Tintown internment camp in the Curragh in late 1922 when, he claimed, he heard a Free State officer called Doherty point to Hurley and say 'That's [the] so and so who shot Michael Collins.' 'Jim Hurley asked me what Doherty had said about him and I replied "You look like Mick Collins".'[8]

Tim Pat Coogan reported that Hurley turned up at the home of Johnny Collins, Michael Collins's brother in Dublin, on more than one occasion, greatly upset and in tears. 'How could we do it?', he asked. 'We were too young, I was only nineteen.'[9] This suggests that Hurley may have believed that he was personally responsible and clearly regretted it. He was to request many years later that he be buried beside Johnny Collins, a request that was granted.

However, this may simply have been Hurley's conscience playing on him. According to Neilus Connolly, Skibbereen IRA commandant and later pro-Treaty officer in west Cork, Seán Hales had Hurley arrested and was about to court-martial him for the shooting of Collins.[10] Connolly and Gearóid O'Sullivan, Adjutant General of the National Army, travelled to Bandon to see Hales. They told him that in their opinion Hurley was innocent and that he did not know what he was firing at; they threatened to join the Republican side if Hurley was executed.[11] It is clear from internal IRA correspondence that they were concerned for him.[12] Hales backed down and Hurley was spared. He was moved to Cork Female Prison and thence to Tintown, where the incident described by Ashe took place. Hurley is unlikely to have fired the bullet that killed Collins, however, since he was down the road at the barricade along with Tom Kelleher – who could not have fired it either – some 400 yards to the north of the spot where Collins was killed. He was in the wrong place and in the wrong direction. If the maps and the accepted positioning of the IRA men at Bealnablath are correct, then neither Hurley nor Kelleher could have fired the fatal shot.

Another man who believed he might have shot Collins was Pete Kearney. According to Meda Ryan, Kearney and Liam Deasy were at Bealnablath Cross when they heard the firing coming from the ambush site. They made their way via a back road to the east of the ambush until they could see the convoy in the valley below. According to this account, while they could see very little, they let off some shots to distract the convoy and draw attention away from their own men in the lane opposite. They could not have killed Collins from where they claimed they were standing since they were on the wrong side and too far away in any case.

However, Father Twohig gives a completely different account of Kearney's position during the fight. According to Twohig, Kearney had gone south towards Newcestown rather than north towards Bealnablath. If that was the case, he would have been at the right side of the convoy to have shot Collins:

> Until his death he [Kearney] was tormented with the conviction that he himself had killed Michael Collins. He had left Bealnablath in charge of six men and headed across country towards Newcestown. At the sound of gunfire they returned. Pete was impeded by the fact that he had broken his arm in the process of cranking a Model-T (a common occurrence at the time for the unwary), or so he told his family, but he managed to fire a single shot at a man facing him obliquely on the road far below. The man fell. He believed the bullet bounded off a rock or stone wall to the rear and returned hitting Collins in the back of the head. This he confided before his death to Fr. Jerome Hurley of the Dublin Diocese, parish priest of Avoca and a native of Enniskeane, Co. Cork.[13]

This at least might put Kearney in the right place to have fired the fatal shot. If he had gone towards Newcestown and returned upon hearing the shooting, he would have been coming from the south. And if he was coming along the road or anywhere near the road then he and whoever was with him would have ended up more or less where the shot must have come from. His 'confession' ties in closely with the IRA account of the ambush written two days later, which states that six men remained in ambush position after the rest had withdrawn but that three others managed to get back during the fight itself.[14] However, the very fact that he believed the bullet must have ricocheted from a rock or a stone wall in order to hit Collins in the back of the head suggests that the place he had returned to was the lane across the valley to the west, where his men were firing from – where most accounts place the returning men. Nonetheless, this account of Kearney's movements, if correct, is the only one of the many confessions of people who thought they might have shot Michael Collins that places the shooter in a position where he may have actually done so.

What is more, Kearney's Military Pension application is evasive when it comes to Bealnablath. In contrast to others named in connection with it, such as Sonny O'Neill, Denis Long and 'Bobs' Doherty, Kearney never mentions Bealnablath at all.[15] However, the application does contain useful information. He claims that he was in his own district at the time, that he was in engagements 'north of Bandon, Ballineen and Dunmanway' and that he had attended a meeting of the 1st Southern Division around this time. He states that he was O/C of the 3rd Battalion of the No. 3 Brigade and that he was also O/C of the Brigade's flying column. This adds credence to his account above since, as O/C of the column on the day, it was he who would have been technically in charge. So when he said he 'left Bealnablath in charge of six men', this has the ring of truth to it.

What his evasiveness, and the fact that Liam Deasy left a completely contradictory account of his and Kearney's movements, tells us is that Kearney probably genuinely believed he shot Collins, and that he at least fired some shots during the ambush. However, he could have killed Collins only if he and whoever was with him returned from the south via the road that Collins had travelled on. No account places them on the road to the south of Collins – though it should be noted that Liam Deasy was extraordinarily reticent and uncomfortable in his interviews with Father John Chisholm when it came to Bealnablath, claiming that he had what amounted to a 'mental blank' regarding some aspects of Collins's death.[16] Meda Ryan and others have the returning men – who do not include either Deasy or Kearney – on the southern end of the lane across the glen to the west where the rest of the ambush party were firing from. If that was the case, they were in the wrong position to have killed Collins.

However, regardless of who was responsible, the entire episode throws very strange shadows. You would expect that one side would blame the other for Collins's death. This does not seem to be the case. We have the anomalous situation that the IRA men believed they had killed Collins, though it would have suited their interests to claim that the Free State side had shot him, while rumours coming from the National Army – or so one supposes, because Feehan does not tell us – seem to suggest that he may have been shot by one of themselves. Again it would suit their interests to suggest what is now regarded as the accepted version of events: that Collins died as a result of a Republican bullet fired by one of the ambushers. Several other anomalies have been gone into over the years – that there was no official inquiry into the killing, that the autopsy report went missing, that all the material dealing with it was destroyed by the government of the Free State in 1932, that Dalton's behaviour was very erratic subsequently – and there was plenty of debate over the exact nature of the wound from which Collins died. In other words, there is no shortage of fuel to run the industry of conspiracy.

In the previous chapters we saw that Collins would almost certainly not have passed through Bealnablath except that he was hoping to meet with some of his former comrades that evening for talks designed to bring about an end to the Civil War. There is a reasonable case to be made that Collins was due to meet with neutral IRA men and probably active anti-Treatyites that evening at the parochial house in Crookstown, a few miles away. Even the IRA men waiting in ambush were only half-hearted in their efforts, if not in their intentions: 'All during the day it was freely rumoured that the war would soon be over. We had no great mind to shoot anyone.'[17] Indeed, one of the biggest tragedies arising from Collins's death is the bitterness it led to and the prolonging of the Civil War beyond its logical end. Had Collins not died that day, the Civil War would have fizzled out much more quickly than it did.

So, the most important question we need to ask is: was Collins led into a trap and was this trap disguised as peace negotiations? Seán O'Mahony, a lifelong writer on Republican matters, gathered a large amount of material on various aspects of the Irish revolution, and appears to have been particularly interested in the death of Michael Collins. He managed to track down many of the sources used by Feehan, as well as finding new material himself.[18] It should also be pointed out that accounts given by some prominent witnesses, especially on the Free State side and which have been widely quoted in books and documentaries, are erroneous and indeed some are deliberate lies. Indeed, much of the accepted narrative is, as we shall see, based on falsehoods. As one student of the episode put it, 'somebody is telling lies'.[19]

On the matter of why Collins found himself in Macroom and went to west Cork by a circuitous route, O'Mahony unearthed an army report, written by one of the Free State men present and quoted by Feehan, which leaves no doubt that Collins was very much on a mission to establish negotiations with the anti-Treaty side and that the People's Rights Association was at the heart of it:

> On the 18th August 1922, General E. Dalton was handed terms by prominent Cork citizens and after consultation with his staff, agreed to communicate them to General Michael Collins. The terms were that a week's truce was to be immediately arranged on the basis of the existing military position to allow the Republican leadership to hold a meeting to discuss the making of peace. The report went on to list the conditions for peace, conditions which, it has to be said, would not be not too onerous on the Free State side. Republicans were to be allowed to return to civilian life 'without molestation or penalization' or else should be free to join the National Army 'with

due recognition of rank and service' and there would be a general amnesty for all political prisoners. Finally Republican arms and munitions were to be handed in 'to a committee to be mutually agreed upon'.

The above was wirelessed to General Collins C.I.C. Portobello Barracks Dublin, who replied early morning of the 19th August to General Dalton requesting names of prominent citizens making the offer, and if the Republican leaders, military and political, agreed to the offer and if it were on their behalf.

General Dalton replied in the affirmative and gave the following names: M. Aylward, Frank Barrett, Frank Aiken.

General Collins agreed to a meeting and the Republican forces supplied ([as] far as possible) General Dalton with details of laid mines, mined bridges, etc., generally assuring a safe conduit for the C.I.C. As the time would not allow the contacting of every outlying post and, for this reason only, an armoured car escort was included to serve as a deterrent to possible attack and/or identification. [20]

This confirms what we generally know about the proposed peace talks but gives more details of the conditions. One new piece of information is that Frank Aiken, Frank Barrett and Michael Aylward were named among those trying to set up the peace negotiations. The names of Frank Daly and O'Donoghue's 'prominent Cork citizens' are not given, though it is clear that these were also trying to get the two sides together.

It appears that Collins was somewhat sceptical of the overtures of these three Republicans. On the margin of the original document he wrote what presumably are quotations from public utterances made by two of the three.

'Alyward [*sic*] – Shoot them down.'
'Frank Barrett – Spare no Free State.'
'Aiken – Something else.'[21]

The report is quite clear on why Collins took the route he did. Dalton had been given details of where the anti-Treaty forces had laid mines and blown up bridges. Collins went the only route to west Cork that the Republican details allowed him to. Other routes might have been cleared later, but the Bealnablath route was known to be clear. The very fact that Collins would have been able to travel this way in both directions suggests that this was the case – in contrast with what the convoy later had to encounter when it was trying to make its way to Cork after the ambush. This is confirmed by Bill McKenna, one of the last surviving members of Collins's party on that evening. 'They had maps provided by the IRA, to show the blocked and mined roads. Dalton knew Collins was on the way to Cork and was expecting him.' McKenna claimed to have seen 'messages between Collins in Portobello and Dalton in Cork concerning the programme for his visit and matter referring to a ceasefire'. If indeed McKenna did see such messages, it is not difficult to understand how they might have fallen into the hands of the anti-Treatyites.[22]

The late Michael Hopkinson, in his history of the Civil War, gives what is probably the most succinct and balanced account of the death of Michael Collins. While accepting the generally held view that Collins was killed owing to unfortunate circumstances, he admits that there are some serious question marks around it. Like most historians, he is highly sceptical that Dalton may have been responsible for Collins's death. 'Any implications that Emmet Dalton was involved in a conspiracy appear patently absurd, given Dalton's closeness to Collins and how devastated he was by his death.' Hopkinson, however, had little doubt of why Collins risked 'a journey to one of the strongest areas of Republican resistance' and cites three other attempts he made to arrange for meetings with the Republican leadership during his journey to Cork. He quotes Liam Deasy telling Ernie O'Malley that Collins 'saw Seán Hegarty and Florrie the night before he was killed and was to have met Deasy himself the following evening', and also repeats the fact that Collins had met with O'Donoghue on the morning of his death. And yet Liam Lynch was vague about the peace negotiations, while confirming that they were going on. 'There have been peace negotiations started again in Cork recently, I understand, and probably arose out of Collins's visit to Cork. However, there can be no negotiations except on the basis of the recognition of the Republic. Recent events may change [the] situation.'[23] According to Hopkinson: 'At the same time as Collins was travelling through West Cork, de Valera was meeting with Deasy near Beal na Blath and urging peace negotiations. There is no evidence that there was any prospect of a meeting between de Valera and Collins.'[24]

However, some sources suggest that de Valera might well have been due to meet Collins that evening and this may have been the focus of the meeting in Crookstown that was to have taken place in the house of Canon Tracy, as Garda Hickey suggested in his report. According to Jimmy Flynn, de Valera's aide-de-camp, who arrived along with de Valera and stayed a few miles to the south-west at Muinegave on the night of 21 August:

> On the night of the 21/22 August 1922 de Valera was the guest of a family only a short distance from Crookstown village.
>
> The driver of de Valera's car was in the village of Crookstown when he, like other members of the local Irregulars, saw a convoy of Free State troops pass through around 9.00am in the direction of Bandon. The driver recognized Gen. Collins as one of the party and went immediately to de Valera about what he had seen.
>
> Shortly afterwards de Valera joined the Irregular officers who were having a conference. It was there and then that de Valera heard that they planned to ambush Collins's party when that convoy must return to Cork city using the same route. When de Valera heard this he addressed those present and asked them not to ambush

Collins as he himself was in the area with the expressed purpose of meeting Collins. Arrangements had already been set in motion to bring them together. The officers were not impressed and de Valera virtually pleaded with them but to no avail – he went so far as to imply that they would soon have to surrender and when that happened they would negotiate better terms from Collins here in his home county rather than in Dublin, where he might by influenced by his friends there.

The upshot of all this was that de Valera was told that, while he was in the area, his status was that of a Staff Officer under the Area Commander Liam Lynch – they were the active service under command of the same Liam Lynch *and they would carry through his wishes to plan the ambush*. On hearing this de Valera stormed out from the meeting in a rage, collected his belongings and accompanied by his ADC [Flynn], left the area – apparently having abandoned any hope of meeting Collins in Cork [emphasis added].[25]

This account has often been quoted by historians studying the death of Collins and many of its details are well known. Yet the detail that de Valera was about to meet with Collins seems to have been passed over, as has the statement that the ambush was arranged on Lynch's orders.[26] Flynn went on to state that he and de Valera proceeded to Kilworth, County Cork and went from there to Fethard, County Tipperary, where Flynn's parents had a drapery shop. These facts can be broadly confirmed from several sources. Moreover, the outline of the fractious meeting that de Valera had with the IRA officers on the morning of the ambush and the fact that de Valera tried to prevent the ambush from taking place are often overlooked. De Valera at the time was talking peace and Lynch was having none of it. So we have an anomalous situation whereby O'Donoghue and O'Hegarty were ostensibly organising peace meetings while the Republican leader Liam Lynch wanted no truck with peace and was planning ambushes.

While de Valera's biographers do not mention that a meeting with Collins was being planned, this could be put down to understandable reticence on de Valera's part. It is consistent with the known facts. Dinny Long, the IRA scout who spotted Collins passing through the area on the morning of the ambush, stated in his IRA pension application that he was guarding the house in which de Valera was staying 'previous to the ambush at Beal na Blath'.[27] Joe O'Connor told Ernie O'Malley that Frank Daly and Alfred O'Rahilly of the Cork PRA had earlier gone up to Clonmel to see de Valera (and Lynch) about peace negotiations.[28] The priest's housekeeper went to buy in extra groceries and drink on the Sunday night for 'some important visitors'.[29] This would explain the extraordinary, almost freakish, coincidence that de Valera and Collins were within a stone's throw of each other on the day of Collins's death, a coincidence that has often been commented on. Given how things worked out, it is easy to see why de Valera would not want too much made of it subsequently. Of course, the irony of all this is that de Valera was blamed for Collins's death when in fact he was trying to prevent it. But then, politics is often as much about lies as it is about the truth.

7

The IRB and the Shooting of Collins

There is little doubt that Florrie O'Donoghue and the anti-Treaty survivors of Bealnablath were effecting some kind of cover-up when they released their statement in 1964. However, one would hardly imagine they could have been doing so for the benefit of either British Intelligence or the Free State. Even O'Donoghue's powers of persuasion and tenacity are unlikely to have convinced the IRA survivors of Bealnablath to issue a statement for the benefit of the pro-Treaty forces, let alone some shadowy forces operating on behalf of Britain. Common sense, which may not always be correct, suggests that some protagonist on the Republican side must have been the beneficiary of all this cover-up and attempted cover-up. Ironically, the clue to the identity of this protagonist comes from British Intelligence itself in one of the last reports it produced before the British military left the south of Ireland for good.

It is a well-known fact and is widely reported by those who were around Collins during his trip to Cork that he appeared depressed in the weeks leading up to his death. This is put down to a bout of flu or a similar illness he was suffering, and also the pressures he was under and the death of Arthur Griffith – all of which were no doubt important factors in limiting his legendary *joie de vivre* that weekend. However, on 19 August, the day before he left for Cork and two days after his touring car was 'riddled with bullets' near Stillorgan, County Dublin, British military intelligence in Dublin relayed an earlier intelligence report in their file on Collins:

> A report received from the USA dated July 29th 1922 states that on reliable authority it is known that Michael Collins was tried by a Court of the Inner Circle of the Irish Republican Brotherhood in Ireland and was found guilty of treason to the IRB and condemned to death. Twelve trusted men were given orders to carry out the sentence on Michael Collins and have joined the F.S. Army. (Ix/1417, 19 August 1922.)[1]

On the face of it, this might easily be dismissed on the basis that the Supreme Council of the Irish Republican Brotherhood, of which Collins was effective leader, were pro-Treaty, so they hardly would have condemned Collins to death for treason for signing the Treaty. But the Supreme Council – mostly hand-picked nominees of Collins after 1917 – were not reflective of the mood of much of the IRB membership. As one of Collins's biographers, Peter Hart, put it: 'Most of the anti-Treaty officers were IRB men, and didn't care what the Supreme Council told them.'[2] Moreover, British Intelligence's understanding of the workings of the inner sanctums of Republicanism was often confused – particularly in day-to-day intelligence briefings. If we were to broaden the term 'inner circle' to mean those at the core of the Republican movement from before 1916 – most of whom were IRB members – then the above statement might make a lot of sense.

For, in a 'Manifesto to the Irish People', adopted at a 'conference of the available deputies of the Republican Party' issued on 15 July 1922, a few weeks after the start of the Civil War, Count George Plunkett – father of Joseph Mary Plunkett, one of the 1916 leaders – issued a savage denouncement of Collins and his colleagues for their performance from September 1921 to July 1922:

> A brazen usurpation masquerades as Constitutional Government in Ireland today with the approval of a corrupt press and the benediction of all the traditional enemies of our national liberty. Trusted men of our race, sent to London a year ago to explore possible avenues to a lasting peace, have prostituted the authority conferred upon them and arrogated to themselves an authority never conferred upon them.

The manifesto goes on in this vein, and while it does not call on Collins and his fellow Treaty supporters to be tried for treason, this is implied in every sentence and is its logical conclusion.[3] From the words used – 'a self-seeking clique have sought to circumvent the manifesto by the most outrageous acts of political usurpation known to history' – one would never think that the anti-Treaty party had lost the June 1922 general election by a margin of almost five to one. However, in a foretaste of the future of Irish politics, Plunkett calls upon Rome for spiritual guidance: 'While they [Collins *et al.*] were in London the President of the Republic took the occasion of a letter to His Holiness the Pope to proclaim to the world that the Irish people acknowledged no allegiance to the King of England.' Notwithstanding the fact that the vast majority of the Irish Catholic hierarchy also were in favour of the Treaty, Plunkett – who was, after all, a Papal Count – managed to find a 'recent ecclesiastical pronouncement' to support the Republican position:

> Such a claim [the authority claimed by the Treaty] is a claim to military despotism and subversive of all civil liberties. It is a moral usurpation and confiscation of the people's rights.

This quotation is important not because it betrays the sanctimonious tendencies of the leadership – this would have been true of any strand of Catholic Ireland at the time and for many years afterwards – but because of its reference to 'the confiscation of the people's rights'.[4] As we have seen, the 'People's Rights Association' was the name given on 17 July, two days later, to the group in Cork aspiring to draw Collins into talks in the summer of 1922. It is clear that the term arose directly out of Plunkett's manifesto since Frank Daly's Cork Harbour Commissioners group became the PRA on that date. O'Donoghue's correspondence of the time suggests that the Harbour Commissioners group was effectively hijacked by O'Donoghue's Republicans in the weeks after he had resigned from the IRA.

The PRA's own pronouncements mirror those of the more extreme 'Inner Circle' civilians. 'The Army is simply fulfilling the oath [to Dáil Éireann] and in the present instance are defending themselves against a treacherous, unjust, unconstitutional and illegal attack ordered by a group of individuals who are usurping government and acting as a Military Dictatorship.'[5]

Plunkett's statement is reprinted here (Appendix IV) in full, largely because it illustrates the heightened political passions of the day. It leaves one in no doubt about the sense of betrayal felt by Republicans at Collins's acceptance of the Treaty and his behaviour up to and including the shelling of the Four Courts and the start of the Civil War. There was a history here. Collins had been Count Plunkett's economic adviser in the run-up to 1916 and had been Joseph Mary Plunkett's adjutant during the Rising itself. IRB membership does not come much more 'Inner Circle' than the Plunketts. From the point of view of someone like Count Plunkett – and Seán T. O'Kelly, since the document was countersigned by him – there can have been no greater act of treason than for Collins to repudiate 'the Republic' – in the terms understood by Republicans themselves – in favour of what was politically feasible. (It is not beyond the bounds of possibility that British Intelligence had a source in this corner of the Republican movement even at this stage. In 1916, the police had an agent called 'Granite' placed in the Plunkett circle at Larkfield in Kimmage, County Dublin.[6] Contrary to the mythology that the British knew nothing of the Rising in advance, 'Granite' and another agent, 'Chalk' who had attached himself/herself to Tomás MacDonagh at University College Dublin (UCD), had provided the authorities with some warnings. But Dublin Castle choose to ignore them. Perhaps 'Granite' was still providing information to the remnants of the military authorities as late as the summer of 1922.)[7]

Laurence Ginnell, a lawyer and maverick TD, put Plunkett's document into legal language and issued a detailed statement calling for the Supreme Court of the Dáil to be reconvened 'to compel the production of witnesses and evidence, to try Arthur Griffith, Michael Collins and Eamonn Duggan, members of Dáil Eireann, on the charge of HIGH TREASON to be substantiated under the following headings ...'.

Ginnell goes on to list, in very substantial detail, the crimes the three were guilty of, recommending that they be immediately arrested, placed in safe custody and put on trial (see Appendix V).[8] These statements are so passionate and overwhelming in their detail that it is hard to see from a Republican point of view how Collins could *not* have been tried and almost certainly found guilty of treason. Republican courts were still functioning throughout the country, though they would soon have no legal standing in Provisional Government terms.[9] On 11 August Kathleen Clarke, widow of Tom Clarke, another 1916 signatory and one of the most 'Inner Circle' Republicans of her generation – who also excoriated Collins and carried a long list of his alleged treachery – conveyed an order of the 'Supreme Court' on Eoin McNeill to reconvene the Dáil, getting a girl to deliver it personally to McNeill's home.[10] This suggests that a 'Supreme Court' of some shape or form was meeting at that time and was making decisions. One way or another, if civilian Republicans were doing their best to try Collins for treason, then the military wing was hardly going to be any more lenient. (De Valera himself was far more moderate. It is clear from his notes on these developments that, while he may have agreed that what the pro-Treaty men had done was illegal in Republican terms, he was also of the view that 'a resolution of censure against all those deputies' would be sufficient punishment.[11] De Valera knew only too well the political realities Collins had to deal with in his negotiations with the British – after all, he had instigated them himself.)

Although the IRB's Supreme Council had voted for the Treaty, by the summer of 1922 the vast majority of Republicans and IRB members were firmly against it. Its officers in Munster in particular were vehemently anti-Treaty, including O'Donoghue and O'Hegarty. So the British Intelligence report that effectively predicted Collins's death makes sense. There were a great many 'Inner Circle' IRB men who concurred with Plunkett's view and would have seen the assassination of Collins as simply carrying out the orders of the Second Dáil. Yet this almost self-evident fact has not been referred to by the many writers on the topic of Collins's death. The report states, unambiguously, that a Republican court of some kind had been convened to try Collins for treason; this implies that his death was an assassination rather than a random killing in an ambush, and that this was well planned and that the British also knew about it in advance. This would also explain the protracted efforts at a cover-up that came from different sources, invariably IRB men such as O'Donoghue, when any suggestion came up over the years that Collins had been deliberately killed. The fact that the killing was carried out in an IRA ambush, rather than by IRB members who had joined the National Army, merely means that one group rather than another got him. Besides, as we shall see, there is evidence that individuals within the army in Cork were colluding with the anti-Treaty forces at the time and at the very least probably aided and abetted the killing.

But how likely is it that the British Intelligence report on the threat to Collins – written three days before his death (though based on older information) and therefore perspicacious, to say the least – is accurate? According to the intelligence file, the message apparently originated in the United States at the end of July. This alone, and the fact that its details are specific, suggests that the report is likely to be authentic, since British Intelligence had long since cracked Clan na Gael, the American branch of the IRB, going back to Roger Casement and the landing at Banna Strand in 1916. In 1922 Clan na Gael, under veteran Fenian John Devoy, had officially come out in favour of the Treaty, while a small offshoot under Joe McGarrity eventually (perhaps influenced by Harry Boland) came out against it. In 1922/23 the British Consul in New York, Sir Harry Gloster Armstrong, had a reliable source in Clan na Gael and had access to secret circulars sent out to Clan members. It is even possible that the spy in the Clan was in Ireland at the time. Dr William J. Maloney, a Scotsman and former British officer and well-known neurologist based in New York, was long believed by Devoy and his group to have been a British agent. He was now on the anti-Treaty wing and was in Ireland during the summer of 1922, monitoring developments for McGarrity. He is known to have attended at least some anti-Treaty meetings and to have been in contact with IRB men on both sides.[12]

But are there any contemporary documents to suggest that an anti-Treaty faction within the IRB may in fact have condemned Collins to death for signing the Treaty and that the many attempted or near-attempted ambushes – two in Kerry, three in Cork and a narrow escape in Dublin – were all intended to assassinate Collins? In other words, was Collins singled out for special treatment over and above that reserved for a mere enemy, such as his other generals in the field? Considering that Emmet Dalton, Tom Ennis, Charlie Russell, Liam Tobin and even Richard Mulcahy met with anti-Treaty leaders at various stages over the next few months in efforts to bring about peace, the specific targeting of Collins appears to have been pursued with unusual diligence, suggesting that it was indeed a well thought-out plan. In order to get to the bottom of this, we must look briefly at the conflicting positions and internal divisions within the IRB in the nine months between the signing of the Treaty in December 1921 and the shooting of Collins in August 1922.

As we have seen, the fifteen-man Supreme Council of the IRB took the pro-Treaty side, voting to accept the setlement with eleven for and four against. Collins's IRB men took up many key positions in the new army. The alleged presence of a 'cabal' of IRB men, members of a secret society, in key positions in both the Provisional Government and the National Army has often been used to question the legitimacy of the Free State itself, an argument that rather ignores the fact that the Treaty received a majority in the Dáil – admittedly a narrow one – and also got overwhelming support in the general election of June 1922.

So, the argument that the army of the Free State was officered by former IRB men does have validity. What is also true, however, is that the anti-Treaty IRA was also officered, particularly in Munster, by former IRB men. It is implicit in the correspondence of Florrie O'Donoghue, Liam Lynch, Liam Deasy and others on the anti-Treaty side during the Civil War that there was no shortage of senior IRB officers opposing the Treaty.[13] At the end of the Civil War, Tom Barry called for a 'fusion of the IRB elements which are now warring on both sides', with a view to ending the 'vindictive pursuit' of members of the IRA.[14] We have the bizarre situation where the officers of the two opposing forces in the Civil War, like a divorcing couple, had until recently been members of the same exclusive and secret club. In fact, from the spring of 1922, there were far more IRB men in the south of the country opposed to the Treaty than were for it. In other words, the IRB was divided on the subject, just as the IRA and the Dáil itself were split. From April 1922, when the dust of debate on the matter was beginning to settle, it was clear from the series of 'Army Conferences' held in Dublin that, even though the largely Dublin-based Supreme Council had recommended the Treaty, the majority of the IRB membership in the provinces were against it. So, in effect, while there was a pro-Treaty IRB in the National Army, there was an anti-Treaty IRB on the other side, even if it was rarely referred to as such.

One man who was in no doubt of the importance of the IRB on the anti-Treaty side was Florrie O'Donoghue. He devotes four chapters of *No Other Law* to the behind-the-scenes machinations of the IRB that led to the breach on the Treaty and his attempts to 'reunite' the sundered Republican army: attempts that were to continue right until the end of the Civil War.[15] O'Donoghue's papers contain several files on the topic. Because the IRB was a secret society, detailed information on its operations is limited. The members of one 'Circle' did not necessarily know the membership of other 'Circles', and at the time of the Treaty the rank-and-file IRB members did not know the composition of the Supreme Council. As late as 1958 O'Donoghue was still trying to find out which members of the Supreme Council had voted for the Treaty.[16] O'Donoghue's own papers are the principal source and, as we know from other topics covered in the present book, he is not to be trusted to have left an unbiased account of events. The consensus, though, is that the IRB had effectively ceased to exist by around 1924.[17]

Historians are confused as to the reasons for its apparent demise. Its first historian, Leon Ó Broin, came to the conclusion that it had simply fizzled out by the end of the Civil War. He quoted Seán MacEoin, a member of the last Supreme Council, as saying that the IRB dissolved itself in 1924. 'Neither do we know whether any formal decision was ever taken to wind "the Organization" up.' He goes on to suggest that 'the Supreme Council may have just stopped meeting'.[18] Yet a few thousand pounds remained in the IRB coffers, which was used almost fifty years later to help fund a memorial to Wolfe Tone by Edward Delaney on the north-east corner of St Stephen's Green in Dublin, which was formally unveiled by President de Valera on 18 November 1967 (and which became known to Dublin wits as 'Tonehenge' because it resembled a circle of standing stones).

In 1966, the fifty-year anniversary of 1916, the men of the IRB who led the Rising were lionised throughout the land. There was no questioning then of their importance to the mythology of the founding of the State. Yet just sixteen years earlier, in 1950, when Diarmuid Lynch, the last surviving member of the IRB leadership who had planned the Rising, died, he was an almost forgotten figure. As his biographer, Eileen McGough, has pointed out: 'It is difficult to understand how a man at the centre of the Rising, the last person out of the GPO, who went on to play a critical part in America for the Irish Republican cause, has been forgotten so completely.'[19]

When looked at logically, this is surely very strange. Here was the organisation that ran the 1916 rebellion, that had been in existence since the 1860s in one form or another, that had funded and run a series of rebellions in Ireland which, in the words of Ó Broin, had 'brought about the Rising of 1916, the establishment of Dáil Eireann, and the Treaty of 1921'.[20] Had it, as Ó Broin suggests, simply outlived its usefulness and gone into what would now be called voluntary liquidation? One would expect that an organisation of such significance would remain in existence in some form or other, if only as an old boys' network, with yearly meetings of its ageing veterans. It had some funds and many of its members were still alive. Yet that does not appear to have happened. Nor did either side try to claim it. There was no equivalent of variants of Óglaigh na hÉireann, or competing Dáils, when it came to the Irish Republican Brotherhood. Everybody seemed to want to wash their hands of it. The question is, why did this happen? Why had 'the Organization' (as its members liked to call it), which rallied Republicanism over several generations, and took itself so seriously that it saw itself as the only legitimate government of Ireland, suddenly become a toxic brand?

8

The Great Divide (the IRB and the Treaty)

From its inception, the Irish Republican Brotherhood, though it was a secret society about which very few people in the country knew anything, saw itself as the supreme authority, the true government of Ireland – with, by extension, the power of life or death. As Ó Broin put it: 'consistent, too, with its idiosyncratic view of itself as a government, "the Organization" empowered the Supreme Council to inflict a sentence of death for treason, though one does not need to be a moralist to question the right to take the life of even the most miserable informer.'[1] But if the British Intelligence report of 29 July 1922 is to be believed, not only could a self-appointed subsection of 'the Organization' inflict a sentence of death for treason on 'the most miserable informer', but it could, and would, inflict the same on its most important member and the man who did more than anyone to fulfil its ultimate goal, independence from Britain. However, while the British Intelligence report stated that it was a 'court of the Inner Circle' of the IRB that had tried Collins and sentenced him to death for treason, this was clearly not the same as the Supreme Council – whose existence British Intelligence was also aware of, since Collins was stated to have been a member only a few months earlier.[2]

Before coming to a conclusion about this, we must look in some detail at the debate that took place within the IRB itself at the time of the Treaty and over the following six months. Luckily we have a source, which, along with the more evasive writings of Florrie O'Donoghue on the subject, allows us to paint a picture of the divisive and poisoned arguments that took place. The most senior member of the Supreme Council of the IRB at the time, apart from Michael Collins, was Seán Ó Muirthile, a Falstaffian, moustachioed figure and one of Collins's most trusted aides. Ó Muirthile left a memoir that points the finger of blame in no uncertain terms at those who he believed were primarily responsible for initiating the divisions that were to split the IRB, and by extension the Republican movement as a whole. Though he does not say it in so many words, it is clear that Ó Muirthile believed Florrie O'Donoghue and Seán O'Hegarty were largely to blame for setting in motion the wheels of division – to the extent that he could barely bring himself to mention their names.[3]

According to Ó Muirthile, it was O'Donoghue who first started throwing the word 'treason' at Collins with reference to the Treaty.[4] In fact, he had begun sowing dissension in the camp even before the Treaty negotiations had started. In the autumn of 1921 at an IRB meeting held in Cork just before the start of the London talks over which Collins presided,[5] O'Donoghue voiced his suspicions of Collins's intentions.

> Collins presided at this meeting and when some of the Officers present showed signs of 'suspicion' regarding the straightforwardness of the Treaty negotiations, Collins became somewhat annoyed and in assuring the meeting that nothing out of accordance with the desire of the IRB would be agreed to by him, he said: 'I expected to find a different spirit in Cork', meaning of course that he was surprised that his friends in Cork should suspect him. Seán Hegarty who was a delegate at this meeting, turned to the suspecting 'Centre' and said with inimitable

sarcasm: 'If you're going to be sold, you're going to be sold.'[6]

That this took place much as Ó Muirthile reported it is confirmed by some of those who attended and would go on to take the anti-Treaty side. 'Seán Hegarty was all out for ruthless warfare. If they weren't going to fight that way, he wasn't going to fight any other way. That was his attitude and he was right. Either be prepared to cut all their throats, or leave them alone and go home.'[7] And Ó Muirthile – 'a decent man and a humane prison governor', according to Tom Barry, who found himself as a prisoner in Kilmainham Gaol in the summer of 1922 when Ó Muirthile was governor – is likely to be a reliable witness.[8]

It is clear that O'Donoghue – almost certainly the 'Centre' in question since he was IRB Centre in Cork at the time – was not favourably disposed to a negotiated political peace, even before the negotiations began. This is of a piece with much of his correspondence in later years, in which he also spent a considerable amount of time trying to deny the fact that Liam Lynch had written to GHQ just before the Truce to the effect that the IRA in the south was on the ropes, something that is now accepted. In Ó Muirthile's words: 'We had not, when these terms [the Truce] were offered, an average of one round of ammunition for each weapon we had ... The fighting area in Cork which was the main area was becoming daily more circumscribed and they could not have carried on much longer.'[9] There is a file of correspondence in Piaras Béaslaí's papers on O'Donoghue's subsequent efforts to deny that this was the case, and he goes on to repeat it and to use his powers of persuasion to convince others of it well after the event in *No Other Law*.[10]

Immediately after the Treaty was signed – Collins had been very careful to keep the Supreme Council onside during the negotiations – the Cork City Board of the IRB led the charge that ratification of the Treaty would be 'utterly at variance with the principles of the IRB and treason to the Republic set up in 1916'.[11] When the Supreme Council voted in favour of the Treaty, O'Donoghue replied that the Treaty was 'utterly opposed to the spirit of the Constitution of the IRB' and that those who voted for it 'are unfit to remain as members of the SC and that we call on them to resign office'.[12] When the Supreme Council went on to recommend that the Treaty should be ratified – which, incidentally, according to the rules of 'the Organization', the membership were obliged to obey – O'Donoghue, as Centre for Cork, refused to forward the memo to members 'since it was a contradiction of the Constitution and the ideals for which the IRB was maintained and that no useful purpose would be served by having it issued to members ... A statement to the men in the Organization is urgently necessary, but not this statement.'[13]

As a result, O'Donoghue and a handful of others, including Humphrey Murphy of Kerry and Pax Whelan of west Waterford, were suspended from the IRB. According to O'Donoghue: 'Before the vote the IRB sent instructions to every TD who was IRB to support the Treaty. This was an order.'[14] But this was not an order. The Supreme Council's instructions were that IRB members who were TDs could vote in any way they wished. O'Donoghue continued: 'We refused to circulate the order to TDs in the area and were suspended. Notwithstanding this, we were subsequently invited to the later general meeting'[15] – which surely indicates Collins's naive trust in some of the men formerly under his command. In fact, it was the southern brigades of the IRA that forced their members who were TDs to vote *against* the Treaty, not the other way around. Not only that, but O'Hegarty had the Irish correspondent of the London *Times* kidnapped when he wrote that there was considerable acceptance of the Treaty among Munster IRA officers, and he was forced to recant.

O'Donoghue's accusation that Collins had 'flouted and defied the authority, not only of Dáil Eireann, but also the [Supreme Council] of which he was President' flies in the face of the fact that the Dáil and the Supreme Council had both ratified the Treaty.[16] So it is clear that it was O'Donoghue who was flouting and defying the authority of the Dáil and the Supreme Council, though it is noteworthy and perhaps significant that he did not think it worth flouting to the extent of actually fighting himself for the Republic during the Civil War. Nor did O'Hegarty, after kicking up all the fuss in the first place. Collins's reaction was: 'They call me a traitor. We will see if I am a traitor.'[17]

With regard to the actual debate on the Treaty within the Supreme Council, it is clear that some people who were originally just about in favour of the Treaty were ultimately to reject it. Liam Lynch, who felt that the oath of allegiance to the King would not be acceptable to 'the Volunteer mind', spent some considerable time, with the help of pro-Treaty officers Eoin O'Duffy and Gearóid O'Sullivan, drafting an alternative oath – where the primary pledge was to the Free State, with the monarch getting only a subsidiary mention. This was accepted and included in the final draft. However, as Ó Muirthile ruefully put it: 'in view of the subsequent action on the part of some members of the Supreme Council … I want to show that some of those present that day, afterwards gave their lives in an effort to disestablish an oath which was practically word for word their own composition.' When Ó Muirthile saw the final text of the Treaty he felt at the time that 'all would be well'[18] and that Lynch was in agreement. Subsequent events would prove that Lynch was not.

Harry Boland initially also expressed himself in favour of the Treaty, but then changed his mind when de Valera opposed it. In the United States the 'official' Clan na Gael of John Devoy, Judge Daniel Cohalan and Diarmuid Lynch were initially sceptical, feeling that the settlement fell short of the Republican ideal, but then they rowed in behind Collins's stepping-stone argument and the evidence he provided that the IRA was on the ropes in Ireland.[19] Joe McGarrity, of the rival Philadelphia Clan, who came to Ireland in January, was initially supportive of the Treaty, but changed his mind over the following months: whether under the influence of de Valera or Harry Boland or the far more insidious influence of William Maloney is hard to tell. As we have seen, Maloney himself travelled to England on 1 July 1922 on board the Cunard Line's *Scythia*, and we know from his earlier record in the US that anywhere Maloney turned up there was likely to be division and trouble.[20]

The reason for the volte-face on the part of some of the principals had much to do with herd mentality. Anyone with any level of political nous would have realised that politically the Treaty was the only settlement that the British government could swing in the face of conservative opinion both in Westminster and in the country at large – especially with the Northern Ireland state already a year in existence. However, common sense flew out of the window when passions were raging in the wider Republican community, especially when de Valera, Cathal Brugha and Republicans like Mary MacSwiney had their say. The level of outrage and betrayal is palpable in the Plunkett and Ginnell diktats.[21] As Owen McGee, the most recent historian of the IRB, states – perhaps a little too sympathetically – with reference to people like Liam Lynch and O'Donoghue: 'some bewildered young Volunteer recruits (virtually all of whom, like de Valera, had no connection with Irish politics prior to 1917) began propagating conspiracy theories regarding the meaning of the other "Irish Republic" referred to in the IRB constitution and accused the IRB of being traitors and seeing itself as the only authority in the country.'[22] They were also serving their own ends by perpetuating the myth that the IRB was completely pro-Treaty. They were 'bewildered' first and foremost because they were primarily militarists who had little interest in, or understanding of, politics and the limits of power. In fact, they wore their disdain for politics as a badge of honour. But if they were 'bewildered young Volunteer recruits', they had more than enough elders encouraging them.

Some of their reasons lay in the past and need not detain us here, while others were down to simple and perhaps overly simplistic idealism. De Valera's ego and envy of Collins may have been factors on the political front, but the main opposition came from the executive of the IRA, particularly its Munster brigades and its Munster IRB men. Indeed, as Michael Hopkinson put it: 'The 1st Southern Division's speedy publication, on 10 December, of their opposition to the settlement was probably explained by their earlier knowledge of developments through IRB sources. There had been no time for them to be influenced by any political opposition.'[23] This suggests that it was people like O'Donoghue who got the ball rolling. In Cork, the urgings of those whom Ó Muirthile termed the 'refusals' fell on fertile ground. The Cork No. 5 District of the IRB wrote to O'Donoghue in early February to 'express our approval of the action of the County and Divisional Boards in withdrawing their allegiance from the Supreme Council',[24] with the result that opposition to the Treaty was gathering momentum in Cork almost from the moment it was signed.

> From the issue of this document [Supreme Council Order of 12 January recommending acceptance of the Treaty] it became evident that some highly placed Officers were no longer prepared to obey the orders of the Supreme Council. This lack of loyalty was not confined to those outside the SC itself, because a number of members of the SC who had approved of the Document also refused to allow it to reach the rank and file of their subordinates.[25]

Ó Muirthile goes on to name Liam Lynch as one of the principal 'refusals'. It is clear from the correspondence between Lynch and O'Donoghue that Lynch was, to say the least, encouraged by O'Donoghue to throw his considerable weight against the Treaty. In this, O'Donoghue was aided and abetted by the 'Centres' for Kerry and Waterford, respectively Humphrey Murphy and Pax Whelan.[26]

But how does this fit with the perception of O'Donoghue as a 'neutral', a man who would not fight a civil war on ethical grounds? He, O'Hegarty and Tom Hales offered their resignation at the IRA convention of 26 March because they did not want the upcoming general election to be stopped by force – O'Hegarty even expressing the view that the Free State was inevitable.[27] (Their resignations were not accepted since they were 'officers of ability with influence in the 1st Division [and] there was little use in preventing elections in some places if it were to be allowed in others'.)[28]

At this stage O'Donoghue was named as Adjutant General of the IRA and would soon be proposed at a similar rank in a 'unified' army. 'In April, shortly after the 14th which was the date upon which the Irregulars took possession of public buildings, Florry [*sic*] O'Donoghue, *whose name I have to repeat in these pages*, intimated to Collins that he saw possibilities of unity if informal discussions were initiated from an IRB point of view'[29] [emphasis added]. What is interesting about this is that the Republicans saw it the other way round. In their words, it was the

> Beggar's Bush people [pro-Treaty military headquarters, who] by underground and devious channels were trying to disrupt the Republican forces by negotiation. The IRB offered the best opportunities for this but their efforts for the time being came to nought. Messrs O'Hegarty and F O'Donoghue continued, without the knowledge of the [IRA] Executive, to be in touch with Beggar's Bush. Their efforts at secret diplomacy resulted in the publication on April 21st of a statement signed by Collins, Mulcahy and other Free State officers and Sean O'Hegarty, F O'Donoghue, Tom Hales and Humphrey Murphy containing an appeal for unity in the army – based on acceptance of the position created by the Treaty.[30]

These conferences broke down but were renewed at the time of the election pact between Collins and de Valera in June. 'Mulcahy pressed for the inclusion of O'Donoghue [in a compromise Army Council] but met with objections from Republicans.' Despite this, a 'Pact' Army Council was proposed with O'Donoghue and Gearóid O'Sullivan rotating the posts of Director of Intelligence and Adjutant General between them. Collins was due to meet the new Army Council but failed to turn up – a failure for which he gave no explanation.[31]

Were the seeds of Bealnablath sown during these abortive efforts at secret diplomacy? As we shall see, many of the dramatis personae who can be connected to Bealnablath were involved in these efforts on 'army unity', just as they were involved in the 'peace negotiations' that brought Collins to Bealnablath in mid-August. There would seem to be some grounds for seeing a sense of personal animus against Collins emerging out of these talks. However, concrete evidence of this, other than disgust at Collins's behaviour, which is evident in much Republican correspondence at this time, is hard to find.

In any event, all these attempts at unity failed, which is hardly surprising. Humpty Dumpty had long since fallen off that particular wall, and positions had become so entrenched that the 'possibilities' of putting him back together again were slim, to say the least. By then the anti-Treatyites in the IRB were probably in the majority anyway.[32] However, after reading *No Other Law*, you would be forgiven for thinking that O'Donoghue did nothing from the Treaty onwards other than to try to heal the wounds between the two sides. He gives no hint that he was one of the main instigators of division in the first place.

As for the British Intelligence claim of late July that a 'court of the Inner Circle' of the IRB had court-martialled Collins in his absence and condemned him to death, there is evidence that this was the case. As early as January, Jim O'Donovan, the IRA Director of Chemicals, at a meeting at Marlborough Street in Dublin turned to Collins and said: 'You are a traitor and you should have been court-martialled long since for treason.' When asked to withdraw the remark, O'Donovan refused to do so. Also in January, Tipperary Commandant Seamus Robinson charged Collins and Griffith with 'being guilty of high treason.[33]

But there are reasons to believe that such a decision was taken and that there was a plan to assassinate Collins, just as the British Intelligence report stated. In his biography of Collins Rex Taylor published a page from Collins's notebook in which one of the suggestions made at a meeting of the County Centres of the IRB held at Parnell Square on 19 April 1922 was 'Míceál – do away with him.' Forty years later, O'Donoghue was so concerned with this getting out that he transcribed the page word for word, presumably with the intention of doing something about it. This would go some way to explaining the way he went about attacking Taylor in the press – though, of course, he conveniently neglected to mention this particular detail. It would appear, moreover, that something like this did actually take place. O'Donoghue himself acted as intermediary between the pro- and anti-Treaty factions at these conferences. Each time he came back into the room from his side-meetings with Liam Lynch he noted that Lynch 'asserted that he should take action' – 'action' presumably meaning some kind of military action – and that he was tired of talk and tired of delaying.[34]

That there were moves at these meetings to find Collins guilty of treason are confirmed by Roibeard Langford, another senior Cork IRB man, who also attended: 'I was associated with a resolution passed unanimously at a Circle meeting held at 42 Parnell Square Dublin whereat he [Collins] was severely and unanimously castigated by the members and accused of conduct unbecoming of an officer and a gentleman and the

Transcript by Florrie O'Donoghue of Collins's notes of an IRB County Centres meeting held in Dublin on 19 April 1922 at which Collins noted that there were suggestions that he be 'done away with'. (National Library of Ireland)

Army Council was asked to courtmartial him for same . . . I have no regrets. I did what I had to do.'[35]

The very fact that this was stated so baldly and even noted by Collins himself suggests that 'doing away' with Collins was being openly discussed as early as April 1922 – according to Sean MacEoin, even as early as March..[36] This was to get far worse with the shelling of the Four Courts and the repudiation – at least in anti-Treaty eyes – of the Pact with de Valera in June. It was only a matter of time before they got to Collins. It took a month for British Intelligence to get wind of it but clearly they did – Collins even getting a warning that Irish American IRB men were on their way to Ireland to have him and Mulcahy assassinated.[37]

Around this time too, a 'very prominent opponent of Collins', a senior IRB man closely connected to the American IRB/Clan na Gael – probably Harry Boland – told a visiting American journalist that 'a meeting was held here last night and three ways of dealing with Collins were discussed: (1) Force him to bend to our will and if he did not (2) discredit him and (3) shoot him'.[38] As a note from London by Art O'Brien to Rory O'Connor put it a month earlier: 'I do not think the manager of the firm is acting quite straightforwardly in this matter. I am certainly strongly of the opinion that the sooner you act or take definite action to put matters straight, the better for all concerned.'[39]

If this were the case and shooting Collins was clearly one of the options, then the entire enterprise to pull Collins into talks was designed to assassinate him once those options had been exhausted – which they clearly were, especially when, after the results of the June general election became known and with a sweeping victory for the pro-Treaty side, Collins was no longer prepared to take bullying from anyone. Once the Civil War started and people like Plunkett began calling for Collins's head, this effectively became a fait accompli. As Seán MacEoin put it, admittedly with no small amount of pro-

Treaty sentiment: 'What a pity they conspired to extinguish "that life and breath of Ireland".'[40]

It is also clear from the subsequent inquest into the Army Mutiny of 1924 – in which a number of army officers, led by former Collins men Liam Tobin and Charlie Dalton, attempted a pro-Republican *coup d'état* which quickly fizzled out when the government learned of it – that the army, the mutineers and the anti-Treaty forces were plagued by the activities of secret societies, and that these secret societies – factions derived from the IRB – often overlapped. Of the mutineers, the report concluded: 'That the organization which brought about, and many members of which joined in the late mutiny, was in existence, at least in embryo, before the outbreak of the Civil War and that many of the officers who mutinied and those who encouraged and abetted them had become a problem to General Collins before his death in August 1922.'[41] This is an indication that anti-Treaty men had joined the Free State army, just as the British Intelligence report claimed they had. It is perhaps ironic then that Liam Tobin – expelled from the army in 1924 for leading the mutiny – was given the job by the government, when it left office in 1932, of destroying the file on Collins's death.

Several other events had possible old IRB connections. The reaction of the Free State government to the killing of Seán Hales by the IRA in December 1922 (was he killed because of his knowledge of the negotiations that led to Collins's death and because he was carrying out his own investigations into Bealnablath?)[42] was to execute four Republicans – Dick Barrett, Joe McKelvey, Liam Mellows and Rory O'Connor – as a reprisal. Why these four were selected for summary execution has long been a point of historical debate. This was an immediate and terrible revenge and did much to damage the reputation of the new state, especially since none of the four had taken any part in the Civil War, having been captured in the Four Courts at the end of June 1922. It is often claimed that they were killed because they represented the four provinces of Ireland and the government was putting out a signal to that effect. This may indeed have been the case. But another reason may have been that they were all members of the IRB on the anti-Treaty side. It is also significant that their death warrant was signed by Richard Mulcahy, himself a senior IRB man, who around this time tried to reorganise the IRB in the Free State army 'in order to stop the Irregulars from getting control of it if it were left derelict and using its name to stir up difficulties for the State'.[43]

After Collins's death, the Free State hunted down opposing IRB men with particular ferocity, especially in County Kerry. As John Joe Rice of the Kerry Brigade put it: '"Free" [Humphrey Murphy] was a big man in the IRB in South Kerry. I had an idea that any important IRB who didn't go Free State were wiped out. The F/S never used any propaganda against me but they high-spotted "Free" so that if they laid their hands on him, they would have done him in.'[44] Humphrey Murphy was the senior IRB leader in Kerry and a key figure, along with O'Donoghue, in opposing Collins in the early stages of the Treaty debates within the IRB. As such, Murphy was regarded with particular odium by the Free State authorities, who saw him as a traitor to the IRB as well as a senior anti-Treaty IRA man.[45] 'They used instead to blacken Murphy so that they could kill him more easily when they caught him.'[46] In the event, the Free State authorities never got their hands on Murphy and he remained at large until after the end of the Civil War, though he was extremely ill and was to die prematurely some fifteen years later as a result of his exertions during the conflicts.

On the subject of newspapers, the IRB's main man in Britain, Art O'Brien, who had been in almost daily contact with Collins during the Anglo-Irish war but subsequently turned vehemently anti-Treaty, took day-by-day clippings of everything dealing with Ireland from British newspapers over a three-year period. His accumulated files are an invaluable source for researchers based in Ireland, since they give the

British angle on many events.[47] But there is one week missing from his hoard of clippings, and this is the week after Collins was killed. This may suggest embarrassment or even shame on O'Brien's part at the killing of Collins which, to judge by his correspondence earlier in the summer, he was encouraging. But it may also mean that British newspapers contained details of Collins's death that O'Brien did not want recorded or finding their way back to Ireland in his correspondence.

To summarise: the picture that emerges from this truncated version of the debates of late 1921 and the first half of 1922 is as follows.

- In the autumn of 1921, Florrie O'Donoghue began suggesting at IRB meetings that Collins was about to sell out on his Republican principles. Considering that the Treaty negotiations had not even begun, either this was very perceptive of him or he was a fanatic. (All the evidence is that O'Donoghue, who was very calm and measured about everything, was anything but a fanatic.)
- Even as the Treaty was being ratified by the IRB Supreme Council, O'Donoghue was manipulating behind the scenes to make sure the Munster IRB moved against it. In this he was pushing an open door, but his closest confidant, Liam Lynch, appeared, at least initially, not to have been as opposed to the Treaty as he would subsequently become.
- When the circular from the Supreme Council recommending acceptance of the Treaty arrived in January 1922, O'Donoghue refused to forward it to the various units and, as a result, he was suspended from the IRB.
- In April, reinstated in the IRB and back at the talks, O'Donoghue was trying to pull Collins into negotiations with his opponents – a ploy that initially failed because only a working party of three members from each side was set up to talk. O'Donoghue himself was nominated to the position of Adjutant General in the proposed unified army.

- In early July O'Donoghue followed his friend and mentor Seán O'Hegarty out of the IRA. So much for his much-vaunted fidelity to the Republic: he was not prepared to fight for it. 'I cannot wish for your success', he wrote in his letter of resignation to Liam Lynch, while at the same time pledging his assistance, if needed.[48]

- Republican deputies issued their calls for Collins and his associates to be tried for treason. At around the same time the anti-Treaty IRB in Cork and/or Dublin was planning to have Collins assassinated.

- Now, outside of the IRA, O'Donoghue and other Republicans hijacked the peace initiative emanating from the Cork Harbour Commissioners and adopted a title and terminology from Plunkett's denunciation of Collins to set up possible peace meetings between Collins and his enemies. It is noteworthy that these meetings were to be with Collins himself, rather than with his officers in Cork or elsewhere – which would surely be the more logical place to start, especially when Emmet Dalton and Tom Ennis, who commanded the army in the South and South-East respectively, were open to talks.

- It appears that in the summer of 1922 O'Donoghue may also have been trying to play both sides. In June he had been nominated as a senior officer in a unified army consisting of pro- and anti-Treaty personnel. (The talks were to break down when agreement could not be reached over who should be Chief of Staff.) O'Donoghue may still have been trying to gain access to the Free State army as late as mid-August. According to Connie Neenan: 'A certain Commandant of the Irregulars had offered his services to the FS and also to join them but not presently as he would do more work by playing both sides. At a dinner in [the] Imperial Hotel FS officers refused to sit with this man, so to prove his sincerity he got 8 prominent IRA officers arrested.'[49]

- O'Donoghue's efforts eventually bore fruit when, primarily with his help, Collins was pulled into the trap of Bealnablath while on his way to one of these peace meetings.

This is all fine so far as it goes, but it remains just a conspiracy theory at this point. It might look plausible, but could it be true? It seems clear that the anti-Treaty wing of the IRB was planning to assassinate Collins. But did they actually do so? Is there any further evidence to support the suggestion that O'Donoghue (and O'Hegarty, who hated Collins)[50] deliberately drew Collins into the trap that was Bealnablath? In order to examine this, we have to look in more detail at the events of the day at Bealnablath, because they are not what we have been given to believe and are far from the 'virtual accident' account put out by O'Donoghue and his colleagues in 1964.

9

Army Matters

When the Provisional Government began to set up a National Army in the spring of 1922, it faced many difficulties. The new army consisted mostly of units from outside Munster, new recruits, many of them Irishmen who had served in the British forces during the Great War. The majority of the IRA went anti-Treaty and refrained from joining up; only those who agreed to support the Treaty were admitted. On the other hand, any Volunteer officer who declared himself to be supportive of the Treaty and was willing to join the army was likely to be appointed an officer.[1] This led to the curious situation where many of the senior officers in the army were appointed because they were close to Collins and had been Collins's men during the War of Independence, while most of those in the ranks had no background in the previous conflict. Many of the former had also been members of the IRB.

But the new army faced another major problem. During the early months of 1922 up to the Army Convention of 26 March and probably for much longer, the anti-Treaty IRA followed a policy of infiltrating the National Army. As one officer put it at the time: 'At that time we were in Beggar's Bush I did not know but the man in the next office would blow me up ... The idea was to build up a line of forts by fellows who might blow up the forts themselves ... On one occasion the late Chief of Staff and myself had to hold the Bank of Ireland for a few hours, because everybody had left it.'[2] As Richard Mulcahy put it: 'We were dealing with a difficult situation where you did not know where loyalty lay and you had to handle the threat of what was a secret society.'[3] What all this suggests is that if elements within the IRA placed trusted men in the army, they would be well camouflaged by the many anti-Treaty men who were already there. It was just one other element in the chaotic melee that was the attempt to create a standing army out of nothing. There were many Trojan horses in the force, an issue that was not tackled until after the mutiny in 1924.

As regards the Cork Command itself, Dalton in his last letter to Mulcahy before he resigned his commission gives the impression of insubordination on a grand scale among his men in Cork. In contrast to his early successes, his advance on anti-Treaty positions appears to have ground to a halt entirely in the month after Collins's death. He put this down to a lack of resources and also to the 'ignorant jealousy of Cork men of Dublin men and of old fighting men of all others'. He complained of extravagance, of 'junketing, larking, dancing and flirting'. 'I am beginning to lose hope,' he wrote to Mulcahy. 'As a whole – excluding some honourable exceptions – there is no zeal, no dash, no organization or determination, only lack of discipline.' As for the real affiliation of many of his men, he stated:

> Many of our officers are painfully indiscreet – talking loudly of taking Camden or Carlisle[4] and of burning all the old ascendency out of the country and dividing up their estates amongst their despoiled relatives now alive. In Cork we are going to be beaten unless we wake up, and soon. The state of things is bad – it is my plain duty to say so.

He advocated, among other things, 'sterner conduct towards our insolent enemies'.[5]

Mulcahy was to summarise the problems in Cork after Collins's death and Dalton's resignation:

> The Original Difficulties
> Special Report: The difficulties with Dalton in Cork – his marriage[6] – his undesire to return there. The demands for executions there. *The overtures going on underhand with Irregulars.* No executions when powers were given [emphasis in original].[7]

It emerged at the inquiry into the mutiny in 1924 that at least part of the garrison in Cork had to be broken up after Bealnablath, that some of Dalton's men had deserted their posts in Cork upon Collins's death and that others 'had to be taken out of Cork because of their inability to deal with the situation there, and of their colloguing [collaborating] with the irregulars'. It is quite clear that many of the men at the time were being accused of engaging in 'irregular activity'.[8] Within a month of Collins's death, government forces had planned a widespread sweep of west Cork into east Kerry. However, the sweep had to be aborted when someone within the Cork command leaked the plans to the anti-Treatyites.[9] As Gearóid O'Sullivan put it: 'High-placed officers collogued with Irregular leaders when the remains of the late Commander-in-Chief were not yet cold in the grave.'[10] 'The existence of secret societies, factions and political organizations undoubtedly did affect discipline among officers.'[11]

In summary, what all this tells us is that Dalton had enormous problems in Cork after Collins's death – after showing plenty of 'dash' and 'pluck' before Bealnablath. But two crucial details stand out from all the ill-discipline and shenanigans: some men deserted their posts immediately after Collins's death and others had to be taken out of Cork because of fraternising with the enemy. The evidence suggests that the desertions and the 'special break-up' may have occurred as a direct result of Bealnablath. If Collins had been shot as per 'the standard model', i.e. shot by an IRA bullet in a scrap, there would be no reason why this would have happened, or why it happened at this precise time. On the other hand, if the British Intelligence report is correct and men had been put in place with the job of assisting in Collins's assassination, then the inescapable logic of this is that they would have immediately deserted when the job was done – and gone back to the anti-Treaty IRA – and those who may have been in on the plot or at least sympathetic to it would have been moved out. All this points very strongly in the direction of involvement at some level by men within Collins's own ranks. This is not the same as saying that twelve trusted men joined the army with the intention of assassinating Collins if and when the opportunity arose, but it comes close. It suggests at the very least that if such an assassination attempt were to be carried out, there would be no shortage of men on the inside who would provide assistance.

10

Not a Shred of Evidence

One of the biggest disparities between accounts of Bealnablath left by members of Collins's convoy and those of the ambush party concern the direction from which the fire was coming (see point B on the map on page viii). Members of the ambush party, mostly Volunteers of the West Cork No. 3 Brigade, claim that the IRA fire came almost exclusively from the western flank where the ambush was set up and where its control point was situated. This was the boreen that ran parallel to the main road and which offered perfect cover. It was where the IRA men had been lined up all day and where they could have rained as much lethal fire as they wanted on the convoy below, had it not been for the fact that most of them had left by the time the convoy arrived.

Most of the 3rd Brigade men did not mention fire coming from anywhere else. The sole exception was Liam Deasy, who claimed that he and one or two others, including Pete Kearney, who he said had been at Long's pub in Bealnablath, had scrambled up the high road to the east of the ambush, crossed a few fields to the hill overlooking the site to the north-east and fired some shots into the bushes, allegedly to draw the fire of the convoy below them on the road (see point C on the map on page viii). If they were where Deasy said they were, they could not have seen Collins in the valley. Besides, they were too far away and in the wrong direction anyway to have fired the fatal shot. Of course, they may have been economical with the truth. Their real position could well have been much closer to the spot where Collins was killed. However, if they were there, they never admitted it.

Many of the Free State accounts, on the other hand, claim that there was firing from both sides of the road. This disparity is very striking. Lieutenant Smith stated that the advance group from the Crossley tender 'opened fire on the attackers on both sides of the road with a Lewis gun and rifles ... The attackers were spread out along the slopes on both sides of the road for fully a quarter of a mile.' This is almost certainly an exaggeration, but it is clear that the impression Smith had was that there was gunfire coming from both sides at various stages. He also states that where Collins and Dalton and their drivers took cover behind the low fence on the western side of the road (facing the boreen opposite) left them exposed to the party on the other (eastern) side of the road.[1] Emmet Dalton, in his original account, stated that 'it seemed that the greatest volume of fire was coming from the concealed roadway on our left-hand side'. However, he was also sure that some fire had come from the eastern side. As he told the RTÉ documentary: 'at the time I felt that there was a little fire coming from up there, from the hill up there ... Nobody seemed to have agreed with me but I felt at the time that there was ... well, very little from there but certainly, definitely, some.'[2] John O'Connell, who had joined the Free State group in Mallow as a guide and was still with them and travelling in the Crossley tender, stated that during a lull in the firing he and Smith began a survey of the site. After they found an oilskin bag with black powder in it (possibly part of the IRA's mine), 'there was more firing at this point coming from the direction of the farmhouse on the hill'. (This of course may refer to the farms on the far side of the valley but these are quite a distance away and are not clearly visible from the valley. The most visible farmhouse is Murray's on the hill to the east of the site.) The primary newspaper reports of the days following, from Lieutenant Smith and Commandant O'Connell, both state that there was firing from both sides of the road.[3]

When the first government of the Irish Free State sent Garda John Hickey and his two colleagues to Crookstown in 1924 to investigate the circumstances of Michael Collins's death, they did so for two reasons. They wanted to establish if Éamon de Valera had any part in Collins's death, but also to see if there was evidence that Collins might have been assassinated by someone from his own side: 'The purpose of the investigation was to clarify who actually shot Collins as there were strong rumours at the time that some of his own escort were responsible for the shooting. This, I am convinced, was believed in Government circles at the time.'[4] Hickey was satisfied that de Valera was not implicated. Nor did he find any evidence that Collins was killed by one of his own party, though he did claim that there was collusion from within the National Army and that Collins's route had been leaked to the Republicans by someone within its ranks.

> After the ambush rumours were rife. Four main theories were advanced as to how Collins was shot. The first, it was alleged that de Valera had shot him; second, the armoured car gunner McPeake [*sic*] had shot Collins; third, that Collins had been shot by one of his own officers; and fourth that he had been accidentally shot. Our six months' investigation eliminated all these rumours and discounted the theories put forward.[5]

What this means is that by 1925 Garda Hickey and his colleagues had already established what reams of books and articles written since have ignored: that none of the above were the cause of Collins's death. However, it is still possible to find books that make the case that Collins was shot by Emmet Dalton, who was supposedly working at the time for British Intelligence.[6] This rumour started in the Free State government of 1922–32 and was believed by some ministers at that time. Desmond FitzGerald, for instance, is said to have told a senior civil servant that Dalton had shot Collins, notwithstanding Garda Hickey's report which exonerated Dalton[7] – and it was FitzGerald who ordered the destruction of the files of the investigation in 1932. The rumour then seems to have died off, only to be reignited by John Feehan in the 1980s, who seems to have been in regular earlier contact with Florrie O'Donoghue. But the story of the spreading of disinformation is interesting because of what it tells us about what might have been going on, and about the people who were spreading those rumours and their motivation.

The framing of Emmet Dalton for the killing of Collins seems to have been grown new legs in 1968 with the publication of a letter in the *Evening Herald*. The letter, which was quite long and detailed, was written by William J. Brennan-Whitmore. Among other things it stated that:

> First, there was no ambush at Beal na mBlath; second he [Collins] was not murdered by one of his own followers; third he was in fact and deed murdered by a member of the British Intelligence Staff, who had infiltrated into the Irish army, and rose to high rank in that service: fourth, favoured by circumstances, this agent carried out his orders with well-trained efficiency ... This [the fire fight] was the intelligence agent's opportunity and he acted with well-trained efficiency. Shortly afterwards this agent resigned from the national army, tangled temporarily in the political arena; but soon returned to the foreign service section of British Intelligence, and was posted to North Africa, extending from Gibraltar to Suez.[8]

There is not a shred of evidence in support of any of this. Brennan-Whitmore, a journalist and writer, was a senior member of the IRB in 1916 and was imprisoned in Frongoch in Wales; indeed, he is regarded as the historian of Frongoch, the so-called 'university of revolution'.[9] It was assumed by everybody concerned with these matters that he was referring to Emmet Dalton in the above context. His letter is full of other inaccuracies and strange interpretations of events, which have been largely ignored. For instance, he states that the 'Headquarters Camp' at Bealnablath was commanded by Seamus Robinson, that they were expecting Collins and that there was no ambush in place; Collins merely misinterpreted the shots fired by scouts to alert the camp of his approach – he was expected for peace talks – and jumped out and started firing back. The apologists for the Dalton theory quote the above piece but neglect to mention the other inaccuracies in the letter.[10]

What is interesting, however, is *why* the letter was written: it was prompted by an article in the *Sunday Times* on T.E. Lawrence (Lawrence of Arabia) which claimed that Lawrence, who had Irish roots, became friendly with Collins during or after the Treaty negotiations in London in late 1921. Indeed, it appears that Collins may even have offered Lawrence a role in the National Army, which Lawrence turned down. However, one sentence in the article, which was in brackets and out of context, drew Brennan-Whitmore's attention: 'Collins had been ambushed by his own followers near Cork on 22 August 1922. According to papers in the Lawrence Archive, he had been betrayed by his driver.'

This would have been ignored as merely an inaccurate account of events had Brennan-Whitmore not drawn attention to it. After all, while some conspiracy theorists believed Collins had been ambushed by his own followers, most did not. The *Sunday Times* had a very limited circulation in Ireland at that time, so few in the country would have noticed the offending sentence. But the scale of Brennan-Whitmore's response and the thorough 'detail' he used to show that British Intelligence had placed its agent in position – Dalton, supposedly, with the implied intention of pointing the finger away from the driver – suggests that something was being covered up. The fact that Dalton did not sue Brennan-Whitmore and the *Evening Herald* for publishing the letter was in turn taken as proof that he was the man in question – and this was still being quoted as recently as 2013 in support of the theory that Dalton was the assassin. In fact, it appears that what Brennan-Whitmore was really doing was covering up for elements within the IRB.[11]

The rumours that Collins had been shot by someone on his own side had circulated for decades before that, however. In 1964 Florrie O'Donoghue received a letter from an Irish American, one Richard G. Lucid, thanking him for his efforts in clarifying aspects of the Irish revolution. Lucid went on to state that 'there are certain specific matters, however, such as the shooting of Michael Collins – killed by one of the members of his own party, the driver of the Armoured Car and not by the rear guard of the attacking force – that should be defined for posterity.'[12] In fact, as we shall see, it was 'the rear guard of the attacking force' – or some variation of that term – that was precisely responsible for Collins's death.

Lucid goes on to state:

> whether Collins' death was arranged by the British Secret Service or some other force has not been definitely established to my knowledge. There is no doubt in my mind that the real facts are known to a select few and also that somewhere in the archives of the Irish Government the papers relative to the attempted extradition of the suspect from England might help throw some light on the matter. There are some people here in the United States who could provide some worthwhile information on this area also. Perhaps you as former Intelligence Officer of the First Southern Division may have access to some very vital information on this matter.

But if Lucid thought O'Donoghue was the person who could 'define' the death of Collins 'for posterity', he could hardly have been looking to a less suitable chronicler. As O'Donoghue put it in a long and detailed rejection of aspects of Rex Taylor's book on Collins's life and death a few years earlier:

> General MacEoin [who reviewed the book] has done a service by dissipating the air of mystery which Taylor and other writers have built up of uncritical, confused and contradictory accounts of the conditions in which Collins was killed. For years, in this as in many other matters of the period, a mystery had been created where there is no mystery. The publication of Liam Lynch's letter establishes the simple if tragic fact: that Michael Collins fell in an exchange of fire with the forces opposed to his government in a regrettable civil war.[13]

In fact, the letter of Liam Lynch's he referred to says nothing of the sort. What Lynch actually wrote on 28 August 1922, six days after Collins's death, was:

> Nothing could bring home more forcefully the awful unfortunate national situation at present than the fact that it had become necessary for Irishmen and former comrades to shoot such men as M. Collins who rendered such splendid service to the Republic in the late war against England. It is to be hoped our present enemies will realize the folly of trying to crush the Republic before it is too late.[14]

This does not say, much less prove, that Collins died simply in an exchange of fire. Moreover, he says 'it had *become necessary* for Irishmen and former comrades to shoot such men as M. Collins [emphasis added]'.[15] 'Considering the small number of men engaged, this was a most successful operation, and they are to be complimented on the fight.'[16] This probably says it all. Not only that, but MacEoin is adamant in his review that the reason Collins was in Cork was to use his contacts in the IRB to try to heal the divisions in the movement.

But O'Donoghue was busy trying to provide a smokescreen for this very simple fact. As he put it to Captain John Feehan, who was publishing Eoin Neeson's book in 1964: 'In regard to the death of Collins, I feel that tinkering with this is undesirable from any point of view. What is the point of adding another half-baked account to Taylor's and others already known to be unreliable?' According to O'Donoghue, Collins's death was a 'virtual accident'.[17]

But rumours referring to a role played by one of Collins's drivers have persisted and they go right back to the time he was killed. Michael MacDonagh, in his biography of William O'Brien published in 1928, stated that Collins was killed by a bullet 'aimed, probably, by an old comrade-in-arms', who could have been anybody.[18] After Piaras Béaslaí published the first biography of Collins in 1926, he received a letter from an ex-National Army soldier called John Doherty who claimed to have been very close to the events in Cork on the day Collins was killed. It is clear from the letter that Doherty was known to Béaslaí from the barracks at Beggar's Bush, that they had served together, and that it was Béaslaí who had contacted him on the matter in the first place.

> You will notice from my letter where I referred to the driver of the armoured car, well Sir, that was the opinion of all my Batt[alion] and is my personal opinion today that he shot Collins. Just after when he took the car and deserted, we were ordered out to search for that car [and] had we found him, he would never have come in alive, and it is my determination should I ever come in contact with him, he will – well, lest said, easiest minded [sic].[19]

It is clear that Doherty had confused the driver of the armoured car with McPeak, the gunner on the armoured car, who did indeed abscond with the car some months later. McPeak was not the driver on the day and, despite his being tarred with the reputation of being the man who shot Michael Collins, most experts now believe he did not do so – mostly because he deserted to the anti-Treaty forces and he would hardly have done that had he been a British agent, as is claimed. Moreover, he was extradited to Ireland some years later and, while he was jailed for taking the armoured car, he was never charged with killing Collins nor was it even discussed at his trial.[20] The consensus is that McPeak did not shoot Collins, if only because it was impossible for a Vickers machine gun to get off a single shot or a small number of shots. Since Collins was moving away from the armoured car when he was killed, the wound, an entry behind the left ear and an exit that took out much of the right side of the back of his head, could not have been caused by a bullet coming from his right. Besides, all accounts of the ambush agree that the Vickers machine gun was jammed by the time Collins was killed. But all these diverse accusations, most of which are lies or bluff of one kind or another, end up doing one thing: implying that one of Collins's drivers played some significant role in the events at Bealnablath, or was in some way implicated in the tragic event. The next chapter looks at that very issue.

11

'Mick turned and fell'

The suggestion that Collins might have been shot up close, and not by a bullet fired from the departing IRA men on the boreen opposite, was first hinted at in the days immediately after the ambush. In his 1981 book, *The Shooting of Michael Collins*, John Feehan quotes an interview given by one of the soldiers who was present at Bealnablath to a reporter for the *Daily Express* when the convoy arrived back in Dublin. In Feehan's words, the soldier claimed to have 'noticed a sniper creeping up on hands and knees down the road behind him. Mick [Collins] went a dozen yards in that direction. There was a sudden burst of firing. Mick turned and fell.'[1] This is dismissed by all writers on Bealnablath, and one has to wonder why, given that if such a sniper did exist, he was in the right place to have shot Collins.

Moreover, it is a rather restrictive interpretation of what the soldier had to say. In fact, it is downright misleading and you would have to question why Feehan gave so distorted an account of something that surely was of some significance. The soldier, according to the actual text published in the newspaper, 'a boyish figure wearing a ragged civilian coat' with a Lewis gun across his shoulders, had just emerged from the ship that had brought Collins's remains to Dublin.[2] From the brevity of the account – this is not a detailed interview – it seems he was just stopped and briefly questioned by a reporter. However, he referred to Collins as by the familiar 'Mick', suggesting that he was one of Collins's original officers and not a former British army soldier or a new recruit. This would point to the speaker being either Joe Dolan or Jim Conroy, both of whom seem to have been travelling on the armoured car and may have been the only members of Collins's party to be in a position to see him fall.[3] This is what the 'boyish figure' had to say:

> Mick, during a lull in the attacking fire, noticed a sniper creeping on his hands and knees down the road behind him. Mick immediately went about a dozen yards in his direction in order to stop any movement in the part of the party. At that moment heavy firing swept across the road *from both sides*. The gun in the armoured car was jammed. The sudden burst of fire caused Mick to turn around for a few seconds; the next moment I saw him fall to the ground [emphasis added].[4]

This seems at face value to be an eyewitness account of Collins's death, yet for some reason it has been dismissed by historians who study Bealnablath, perhaps on the basis that nobody else has confirmed the presence of this 'sniper'.[5] It has also been missed by historians who trust that Feehan's version is correct. But surely it is a mistake simply to dismiss such an account out of hand. After all, why should it not be taken at face value? The *Daily Express* report of the previous day, for instance, states that Collins was hit behind the ear, which confirms Oliver St John Gogarty's finding at the subsequent embalming.[6] What is written in the immediate aftermath of an event by one of the participants is surely of more value than something written forty or fifty years later with all the vicissitudes of memory and recall and 101 reasons for giving a faulty account.

But the most important thing to emerge from it is that it seems to offer an explanation for one of the most puzzling questions about the ambush: why Collins left the cover of his vehicles and wandered off on his own, away from the protection of his men. The distance, 'about a dozen yards', is close enough to the 15 yards mentioned by several other survivors. The above would explain why Collins was standing on his own, in no-man's land, so to speak, where he was effectively a sitting duck.

A shot fired by such a sniper would precisely explain the trajectory of the bullet that killed Collins. Coming from the south, along the direction of the road and fired at a relatively close range of maybe 20 to 30 yards, a bullet from a high-velocity sniper's rifle would explain the entry and exit wounds and the elongated bloodstain along the road. A sniper firing from a position low on the road at a standing Collins would account for the fact that the bullet was either travelling horizontally – the road is beginning to slope slightly here – or rising slightly when it hit Collins, entering behind his left ear but managing to catch his cap on the way out. (This alone would preclude the bullet coming from the high ground across the valley.) Maybe, after all, Art O'Brien did have good reason for not retaining cuttings of English newspapers that may have carried something close to the truth of what happened at Bealnablath.

There was at least one person on the Free State side who was of the view that the shot that killed Collins was fired by a sniper. This was John O'Connell – not to be confused with Commandant Seán O'Connell, who was in command of the Crossley tender on the day.

John O'Connell was a young lad from Mallow who was recruited by Collins's party a few days earlier to guide them through the mined and blown-up roads between Mallow and Cork. O'Connell managed to remain with the convoy for its trip to west Cork and he gave several accounts of the ambush over the years. Rex Taylor, for one, was convinced of O'Connell's authenticity and used his version of events in his biography of Collins. Most writers on Collins's death have dismissed O'Connell on the basis that he stated that the Collins convoy visited Bandon 'via Skibbereen', which according to one writer 'shows a shocking ignorance of the location of these towns'. Yet this is precisely what the convoy did.[7] If you travel from Clonakilty to Bandon, as Collins did, and visit Skibbereen in between, you should surely be forgiven for saying that you visited Bandon via Skibbereen.[8] It seems ironic that writers can quote O'Connell when it suits them to lend colour to their accounts – for instance, Collins's insistence on attacking felled trees with an axe outside Clonakilty and the fact that young O'Connell had never seen women dressed in west Cork shawls before that day – and then dismiss his account of the actual ambush.

What can be stated of O'Connell's account of the ambush conditions is that it is probably honest in the sense that it is valid mainly in terms of what he heard, given that he was lying low along with the rest of the troops on the Crossley tender, which was quite some distance away from Collins when he was killed, and he said he saw very little. But it was what he claimed he *heard* that is significant.

According to O'Connell, as the convoy entered the valley of Bealnablath, the Leyland touring car carrying Collins was around 50 yards behind the Crossley tender on which he was a passenger. He states the armoured car was too far in the rear to be of any use during the fight, claiming that it was a slow, heavy and ponderous vehicle. His mention of the motorcycle outrider and the Crossley tender coming across the disabled brewery cart that was blocking the road is similar to most other accounts. O'Connell said there was little cover, so the men in the Crossley tender stayed where they were for a half an hour while some firing from the opposing forces went on. While he claimed some of the Dublin city soldiers on his side shouted 'Look at the fella, look at the fella', he was sceptical that anyone in the tender at that point got a clear look at the ambushers. The first outbreak of shooting went on for up to half an hour by O'Connell's reckoning – it was likely to be a lot less than that, since men under fire, and particularly someone like O'Connell who had never been in an ambush before, tend to exaggerate time because of the stress.

At some point after the initial firing stopped, O'Connell stated:

> We heard these three shots, these three peals of shots, way in the direction of Cork, and General Collins stood up. He was loading his rifle in the meantime and while he was loading his rifle, one lone shot, apparently like from a sniper, rang out and hit him on the side of the head the right-hand side ... there. He fell down and he never spoke again. The firing suddenly opened up then, just as Collins fell, so that practically nobody was able to go to his aid at that time and the firing held for about a quarter of an hour after Collins falling on the road. I'd say he was dead instantly, yes, he did fall but anyway, General Dalton and the officer who happened to be in the armoured car came over to him and rendered to him any assistance they could. All they could do was bandage his head.[9]

While there are inaccuracies in this – Collins was shot on the left side of his head, though the main wound was on the right, and Dalton was assisted by Seán O'Connell, rather than an officer from the armoured car – this account does explain some of the anomalies surrounding the ambush. The early shooting, while severe enough to prevent the men in the Crossley tender for a while from removing the brewery cart and clearing up the broken bottles that littered the road, was not severe enough to be lethal. This supports the Republicans' assertion that the Crossley tender was too far away to be accurately fired upon. This gunfire stopped, probably a lot sooner than the half an hour suggested by O'Connell, presumably when the Vickers gun stopped firing and the Republicans on the lane opposite made good their getaway. Then 'three shots, these three peals of shots [rang out] way in the direction of Cork'. This firing, coming from the eastern side of the road, most likely relates to the handful of shots fired off by Liam Deasy's group to distract the convoy.

The most important point is that John O'Connell was of the view that Collins was killed by a single shot 'apparently like from a sniper' during a lull in the shooting. There was more firing immediately afterwards because if a sniper had been responsible, there would have been inevitable gunfire from his cover party. Also, the troops in the convoy would have opened up with everything they had when they realised their Commander in Chief had gone down. It was during this firing that Lieutenant Smith was hit in the neck.

Given that Collins was killed by a classic head shot of the kind snipers are trained to carry out, this was the most obvious explanation of his death all along, and it is hard to see why it has not been the accepted explanation for his death. But given the volume of obfuscation and distortion generated over the years by various parties with an interest in burying the facts, it has been difficult to separate truth from lies. Certainly people like Florrie O'Donoghue and Liam Deasy, and others involved in the ambush, had their own reasons for a cover-up. But given the type of wound and the reports in the newspapers quoted in the previous chapters, it is hard to believe that the bluffing has been swallowed for decades. Yet the likelihood of a sniper having operated at Bealnablath has been strangely avoided by most of those writing on the topic, which suggests that some kind of cover-up was going on.

So did any other information leak out in the days following the assassination to suggest that the 'sniper' may have been real or to indicate that one of Collins's drivers may have been in some way involved, as was alleged right through the 1920s and occasionally afterwards? Is there anything to support the *Daily Express* interviewee's claim that a sniper had been crawling on his hands and knees towards Collins just before he was killed or that there were other persons in Collins's vicinity around the time he was killed?

12

Snipers and Drivers

The day after Collins's death, the *Cork Examiner* managed to get a reporter on board the SS *Classic*, the ship that brought Collins's remains from Cork to Dublin. During the trip the reporter interviewed one of the National Army officers who had been present at Bealnablath. While the source is not named, it appears likely from the context to have been Seán O'Connell, who was in charge of the Crossley tender. His account, which is much more detailed than the *Daily Express* one, confirms that there were effectively two battles going on, one centred on the Crossley tender at the head of the convoy, some of whose men were detailed to remove the brewery cart that was blocking the way, and the other centred on the touring car and the armoured car farther back along the road. This concurs with the IRA's report of the ambush, which states that the Crossley tender was out of range of the IRA's fire.[1]

> Commandant O'Connell, having noticed that the fire of the attackers had ceased, went back to the touring car in which General Collins had been travelling. When he reached within 40 yards of the vehicle, one of Commandant O'Connell's men shouted to him to take cover, as one of the Irregulars had appeared on their right, revolver in hand. That man was shot by the driver.[2]

O'Connell then reports an exchange of shots that lasted for four or five minutes, 'after which it was observed that General Collins's rifle was silent'. He eventually got to Collins's side, along with Dalton, only to find that his commander was dying, if not already dead. What follows is an overblown account of Collins's last moments that has O'Connell and Dalton whispering an Act of Contrition into his ear and is almost certainly exaggerated, since it has Collins saying 'Emmet, I am hit.' It is very doubtful if someone with the back half of his head shot off would have been able to say anything.

'The Irregular who appeared on their right, revolver in hand' is hardly the same man as the 'sniper' spotted by the *Daily Express* interviewee. While he may have been on the boreen across the valley, the account seems to imply that he was much closer, on the right-hand side of the road. Depending on who is telling it, this could mean he was north or south of the ambush position. Given that the men of the 3rd Brigade had departed by then, it is unlikely to have been one of them. Since Seán O'Connell seems to have been getting close to Collins, it is just about possible the man with the revolver was accompanying the sniper. He may even have been acting as his cover. Either way, if the *Daily Express* man is correct, Collins was heading towards the 'sniper' and spun around on the sudden burst of fire before going down. He may have turned away from the sniper for a moment before being hit. Seeing that the bullet which killed him came from his left, entering behind his left ear and blowing away half of the right side of his skull, the 'creeping sniper' was at least in the right place to have been the shooter. It is generally accepted that Collins had spotted two ambushers, not one, just before he was shot, suggesting that the 'sniper' and the revolver man were two different people.

The IRA report, produced in the immediate wake of the ambush, contains a number of unexplained details. For instance, it states that there were thirty-two members of the ambush party – 'a picked column, 32 in number'. This specific number was put together the day after the ambush when Tom Crofts, the officer who wrote it, would have been in a position to account for all his men. Yet no subsequent account has ever come up with more than twenty to twenty-five names, almost all of whom were members of Cork No. 3 Brigade.[3] The report is adamant that most of the ambush party had left before the convoy arrived. 'Fortunately, six of the men had not left their position.' These were the men on the boreen across the glen who did most of the firing on the convoy, but the report also notes that 'three more managed to get back' into position. Who these three men were is likely to be the key to the entire argument.

They may have been three members of a group of twelve ambushers, mostly members of Cork No. 1 Brigade, who formed the cavalry unit commanded by Seán Hyde and who were there all day and departed south for Newcestown before the convoy arrived. These would include Sonny O'Neill. However, there is no convincing evidence that any of these men got back. A second possibility is that they were the group under Liam Deasy who had retreated to Long's pub at Bealnablath about half a mile to the north. When they heard the firing at the barricade, they claimed they made their way quickly up the high road to the east of the site and crossed three fields to a position where they could see the convoy in the valley below them. Such a scramble by active young men would have taken no more than ten to fifteen minutes, ample time to be in a shooting position when Collins was killed. This group, which included Liam Deasy, claimed that they got to the brow of the hill somewhat north-east of the ambush site and north of Murray's farmyard, where they fired a few shots into the bushes to distract the Free State party. They could not have killed Collins from there since they were too far away – at least 300 yards – and were on the wrong side anyway. And despite what they claimed, they could not have seen most of the convoy from where they were since it would have been hidden in the valley. If, however, they were being economical with the truth in their accounts of where they had ended up and, instead, had crossed the fields a little farther to the south of Murray's farmhouse, they would have come down over the hill just at the point where Collins was killed. This would indeed qualify as a 'rearguard' action. In that case, they would have been in a perfect position to have killed Collins, even if they would have been somewhat exposed on the side of the hill to the south-east where the entire episode was witnessed by Bobs Doherty.[4] Having said that, Lieutenant Smith's account would seem to confirm that there was somebody in the position they describe – that is to say, to the north of Murray's farmhouse.

However, Father Twohig's account of Pete Kearney's movements claims that Kearney had withdrawn to the south towards Newcestown before the arrival of the convoy, rather than north to Bealnablath as Meda Ryan suggests. If that were indeed the case, then there is a possibility that he and two others were the three men who, according to the IRA report, got back in position during the fight – and might have been in the right place to have fired the shot. Kearney also appeared to have picked up a broken arm at this point which he stated to his family was caused by the starting handle of a Model T Ford.[5] Was the 'broken arm' a wound picked up at Bealnablath? If Kearney's group were down on the road, then they may have been the group that included 'the sniper' and 'the man with the revolver'. Or did Kearney and the others stealthily make their way back to the ambush along the road from the south, only to be faced with Collins strolling round the bend in their direction? While all accounts have the men returning across the glen to the laneway to the west, this is a scenario that cannot be ruled out.

But what if it was an entirely different group, one that is never mentioned in the accounts of the No. 3 Brigade men? Garda Hickey claimed that there were three separate 'columns', as he called them, in operation at Bealnablath – who were often at odds with one another.[6] We know two of them, namely the men of the 3rd Brigade and Hyde's cavalry. But who were the third? According to Eoin Neeson, the men who originally planned to shoot Collins were in position all day, even before the 3rd Brigade men set up their own operation. It is very likely that this was the group seen by Bobs Doherty. If so, there is also a strong possibility that the killers had been there all along and were responsible for the first volley of shots that hit Collins's car as it rounded the bend to begin the ambush, after which they stayed where they were, waiting for a second opportunity which presented itself when Collins walked around the corner in their direction.

So the evidence supports Eoin Neeson's claim that the ambush had been organised at the Ballyvourney meeting some two nights previously and that a plan to assassinate Collins had been put together by officers of the 1st Division, rather than by No. 3 Brigade, and that at least three of these men – who had been in position during the day – had either stayed there all day or returned quickly when the convoy came along, and one of them shot Collins. Only these circumstances could account for where the bullet came from and for Bobs Doherty at that position witnessing the shooting of the 'big man' by the sniper who 'put two into him'.[7]

Another rather odd detail of the above account is that it was written by Tom Crofts, the Adjutant General of the 1st Southern Division, and not by Deasy himself, who as commandant would have been expected to have written on such a serious matter to his own Commander in Chief. Indeed, I have been able to find no correspondence at all from Deasy in IRA documentation during that two-week period.[8] Instead, Crofts writes again to Lynch on 11 September that 'the O/C is now practically recovered', suggesting that Deasy may well have been wounded at Bealnablath.[9] Pete Kearney, as we have seen, may also have been injured since he told his family that week that he had broken his arm using a starting handle.[10]

And there is still another anomalous detail in the report. It states that 'the enemy used explosive bullets in whatever little rifle fire they indulged in'.[11] We already know that most of the gunfire coming from Collins's party was machine-gun fire but that there was some rifle fire. Free State accounts confirm this, there having been two Lewis gunners on the Crossley tender and McPeak firing his Vickers machine gun from the armoured car. Yet the IRA apparently believed that in 'whatever little rifle fire they indulged in' the Free State forces used explosive bullets.

Considering that the National Army was not in the habit of using explosive bullets, why would the IRA men present believe that the rifle fire emanating from the Free State forces was of the explosive kind? Considering the nature of Collins's wound, a small blueish entry wound behind his left ear and the entire back of his skull and its contents blown out – precisely what would happen with some types of explosive bullet – is it possible that what the IRA men heard was the report of the shot or shots that were fired at him? If this is the case, then Collins was shot by a bullet that does not fit any of those claimed to have been used by the Free State forces or the IRA on the day.

One person who studied the Free State government file on Collins's death before it was destroyed was General Michael J. Costello, who was Director of Army Intelligence in the mid-1920s. In 1981 Costello wrote to *The Irish Times* to reject the many allegations in John Feehan's book. He confirmed that the army believed that Collins had sighted two men: 'The shot could not have come from anywhere but the direction in which Collins sighted two of the ambushers.'

Costello's comments on the nature of Collins's wound also point in the direction of a 'sniper'. According to Costello, 'Collins was killed by a single shot fired by one of an ambush party who went into action for the specific purpose of attacking him.' As for Collins's wound, Costello's version concurs with that of Gogarty.

The entrance and exit [of the wound] is consistent with those caused by Mauser sporting rifles using soft-nosed bullets designed to kill elephants ... Although Dalton saw many wounds, he had no previous experience of such being used. He correctly called the exit wound – the only one he saw in the semi-darkness – 'awful' ... The man who organized and ordered the ambush told me that one of the ambush party was so armed.[12]

Costello is likely to be correct in this, since the 1st Southern Division had landed a consignment of these sporting rifles from Germany in April 1922 and had them in their armoury. They were a particularly deadly weapon and could do appalling damage; they were useful to the IRA because they were believed to be armour-piercing.[13] 'A fearful gaping wound at the base of the skull behind the right ear ... I tried to bandage his wound but, owing to the awful size of it, this proved difficult' was how Dalton put it.[14]

Costello also stated that many years later, when he was O/C Southern Command during the Emergency, 'I was approached by Liam Deasy with the advice that it would be dangerous to have an officer who had been one of Collins's "Squad" stationed in the locality because he had sworn to "get" the killer of Collins.'[15] This suggests two things: that Deasy knew who the killer was, and that he was still living in 'the locality', by which presumably he meant Cork. This would also rule out Sonny O'Neill, who had lived for many years in Nenagh, County Tipperary, where he died in 1950.

Before even attempting to come to any conclusions, or dealing with the issue of the rifle, one other key piece of evidence should be examined: the *Cork Examiner* article quoted above states that the Irregular with 'revolver in hand' was shot by one of the drivers. The report also states that the Irregulars 'had sustained at least two casualties'. The *Daily Express* report of the previous day has one of the attackers being wounded just after Collins was killed.[16] 'We picked off a couple of them and could see a couple of them fall. Another was seen crossing a gap and was hit when fired upon.'[17] Almost all newspaper accounts published on the following day report that there were several – in some cases 'many' – casualties on the anti-Treaty side. This of course is dismissed as hyperbole of the kind that often emanates from military reports, but if the mysterious wounding of Deasy and Kearney is correct, there may be some truth in it. (Two other Volunteers were shot in the backside as they fled the scene; one of these shootings was confirmed by Lieutenant Smith in his account published in several newspapers the following day.)[18]

Yet on the basis of what IRA veterans stated over the years, no other member of their party was shot and nobody fits the bill of the Irregular with the revolver or the sniper, nor was anybody 'shot by one of the drivers'. If you believe the versions given by anti-Treaty survivors, this man – or men – did not exist. The only person of significance shot at that stage of the battle on either side was Collins (Smith of course was to be shot in the neck afterwards as he helped get Collins's body into the armoured car). What is most significant about the *Examiner* report is that it has 'one of the drivers' shooting someone, which implies that that driver might have been able to recognise that someone afterwards.

According to Garda Hickey, whose sources were local Republicans in the years immediately after the ambush, there were three casualties on the Republican side. What is more, he claimed they were fatalities, referring to 'the heretofore undisclosed fact that three of the attacking party on the Michael Collins convoy were shot dead'.[19] There is no independent evidence for this and there is no concrete record of fatalities on the Republican side. However, if the casualties were wounded, instead of being killed, this might fit with the above evidence. If Collins's driver was responsible for one of these and might even have recognised the man, then the drivers – and there were at least six in the convoy – have a major significance in the death of Collins.[20] This would support the long line of subsequent rumour that a driver had some involvement in the affair.

So is there any other evidence of casualties on the Republican side that might substantiate the above account? Was a driver involved? Events reported in the *Cork Examiner* over the weeks following Collins's death confirm that this was indeed the case and that there were at least some casualties on the Republican side, and that a driver (or drivers) had a role in the affair. That the significance of this has been overlooked by writers for nearly 100 years seems extraordinary considering all the books and articles that have been written about Bealnablath. Nonetheless, that is exactly what has happened.

13

Doctors, Drivers and Wounded Plotters

If the significance of drivers has been lost on historians, it was not lost on the Cork anti-Treaty IRA in the immediate aftermath of the ambush. A week later, in the small hours of the morning of 29 August, a National Army driver called Edgar Isherwood, who lived in Blackpool on the north side of Cork city, had a knock on his door.[1] Thinking the callers might be army personnel, he opened the door to find a group of six masked and armed men who said they wanted him to drive a car for them. At the point of a revolver, they forced Isherwood to accompany them. They took him past the Fair Field, a well-known Cork north-side landmark, and into another field, and told him that he had been convicted of being a spy and that he was to be shot. But before they shot him, they had some very interesting questions to ask.

> They asked him if it were a fact that he had been driving the late Commander-in-Chief when the fatal attack had been made at Bealnablath and he truthfully replied 'No'. They also wanted to know if he had driven a doctor and nurses to Youghal the previous day for the National troops, and other questions relating to his work as motor driver were also put.[2]

They then told him the names of others they intended to shoot, remarking that these would 'soon be in Heaven with him [Collins]!'. 'They mentioned six names in all, and it was learned that these were all motor drivers, and all residing in the city.'

After asking him would he rather be shot sitting or standing up, to which he replied 'sitting', they tied his hands behind his back, blindfolded him and told him to say an Act of Contrition, and tied a card to his chest with the words 'Convicted spy. IRA. Beware.' Then they retired 'some distance away' and fired a volley of shots at him. He fell, with a bullet through his left ankle. A second volley was fired and he was hit in the left arm. Isherwood feigned death and when the men struck a match near his face they saw that he was 'lying motionless, with his mouth open, with apparently no sign of life'. One of them said it would be 'safer to put a bullet through his head', to which another replied that 'it was all right, the man would be dead in an hour or two, if he was not dead already'.[3] But Isherwood was not dead. He was too terrified to move and remained motionless in the field until 4.00am, when he managed to crawl away to safety. His ankle was smashed. Medical opinion was that it had been caused by a dum-dum bullet. His arm was slightly injured.

This is a crucial piece of evidence, because Isherwood was employed at Army Transport HQ at Johnson & Perrotts Ltd on Emmet Place, from which the transport section of the army operated. 'He was through two ambushes over the previous ten days or so, one at Macroom and another at Rathcormac. During the latter encounter he had a very narrow escape, the man sitting next to him being wounded.' The report is significant for three reasons: (1) the men wanted to know if Isherwood had been Collins's driver at Bealnablath, (2) they claimed they were going to shoot six other drivers, and (3) they wanted to know if Isherwood had driven a doctor and nurses to Youghal the previous day, presumably 27 or 28 August.

What this means is that the Cork IRA was prepared to abduct a National Army driver and shoot him as a 'spy' in order to find out the answers to these questions, which were obviously significant to them. What is more, they intended to kill another six drivers.

So the first and obvious question is: were other National Army drivers specifically targeted in Cork during this period? The short answer appears to be 'yes'. The most immediate instance arose out of another ambush Isherwood had mentioned as having taken place at Rathcormac, because the day after Isherwood's narrow escape, Richard Kearns – a native of Cork city who had been in the British army during the Great War and had joined the Free State forces as a driver – was sent to retrieve a Crossley tender that had been abandoned after this ambush. Kearns was also the driver who was sent to bring Collins's Leyland touring car back to Cork after it was abandoned near Crookstown on the night of Bealnablath, so he had a link to Collins's death. Collins's car was towed into Cork on 23 August: 'the whole structure was so riddled with bullets it resembled a pepper canister', as the *Cork Examiner* colourfully put it.[4] On the way back to Cork from Rathcormac, Kearns's party noticed a bump on the road near Watergrasshill. When they went to investigate, a mine blew up. A brief firefight ensued in which Kearns and his co-driver were both shot dead through the head. Nobody else died in the affair. Kearns had also been based at the transport depot at Johnson & Perrotts.[5]

The driver of another Crossley tender, Private Albert Cottle of the National Army, was blown up at Tubberenmire, near Carrignavar, on 30 August,[6] and on 4 September James Murray, a National Army driver, was shot dead 'accidentally' by an army sentry for 'refusing to halt' on the Bandon Road in the city. Murray's father was the caretaker of the Mechanics Hall in Cork.[7] Driver Jack Castles, a native of Kells, County Meath, was shot in the legs on his way to Carrigaline while driving a Dodge for the army. Though there were five men in the car, only the driver was hit. On 21 September, a civilian driver, Thomas Lyons, in the employ of McColls of Pope's Quay, was shot dead while driving two ladies to Tralee.[8] Lieutenant Hugh Thornton, a brother of Frank Thornton, one of Collins's Squad, was shot dead while travelling in a Lancia in Clonakilty on 29 August. This would pass as an unremarkable ambush-style attack were it not for the fact that a few days later the *Cork Examiner* denied that it had even been an ambush, reporting instead that Thornton 'was killed by the accidental discharge of a rifle'.[9] What is perhaps noteworthy about this incident is that a number of ex-British army soldiers in Collins's party had been placed under arrest in Rosscarbery on the way to Bealnablath because it was alleged that a plot had been uncovered that they were planning to assassinate Collins.[10] This meant that at least some of his guard who might have been expected to protect him in the event of an ambush were now out of the picture. Did the real plotters plant a fake plot in order to remove some of the guard and make it easier to kill Collins, and did Hugh Thornton perhaps get wind of it?

There is no doubt that some of these shootings were just normal warfare atrocities in which drivers, by definition, are in the front line, but some of the heavy focus on drivers is surely related to the threats made to Isherwood. Another warfare atrocity, though this time on a much larger scale, was the blowing up by a mine of a party of National Army troops near Macroom on 14 September. Seven men were blown to pieces when they arrived to defuse a mine under a culvert at Carrigaphooka. The mine was trip-wired. The officer in charge of the party was Colonel Commander Tom Kehoe, a former member of Collins's Squad. Kehoe died soon afterwards from horrific wounds. This was one of the worst atrocities of the early phase of the Civil War, almost on a par with the Ballyseedy massacre in County Kerry.[11] Kehoe had been the officer in command of the Transport Section at Johnson & Perrotts in the week Collins was killed.

The upshot of all this was that the transport section of the army in Cork was paralysed. What had been an effective mobile force before Bealnablath could now do very little for want of drivers. It is clear from Dalton's last memos to Mulcahy that one of the principal causes of the malaise of the men under his command was 'lack of transport'. He cites 'a horrible lack of transport, competent drivers, lack of machine guns and equipment generally'.[12] Dalton had requested more transport in early October but received nothing. 'No action was taken.' This was one of the reasons he cited for leaving the army – the last of these memos in late 1922 was in effect his note of resignation.

There are other odd questions arising out of the interrogation of Isherwood. As we have seen, he was asked if he was the driver who had brought a doctor and nurses to Youghal after Collins's death. There appears to have been no military action in the Youghal area that might have resulted in casualties during that week. Youghal had been taken by Free State forces on 8 August when the gunship *Helga*, which had famously fired on Sackville Street in Dublin during the 1916 Rising, landed with 200 troops and was met with no opposition. By the last week of August, Republican forces had retreated west of Cork city and there was nobody left to carry out actions in Youghal. Yet Isherwood's interrogators were clearly of the view that a National Army driver had brought a doctor and nurses from Cork to Youghal on 27 August. If they were going to the length of shooting an entirely innocent man, it was clearly important for his would-be killers to find out who the driver of the car to Youghal was. Was he to be liquidated as well?

Youghal had no obvious connection with Bealnablath or with the death of Collins. But Youghal had many connections to Florrie O'Donoghue. His wife Josephine – the famed 'spy in the barrack' – had a sister, Cecily, married in Youghal. It was to her home that young Reggie Brown, Josephine's son from her first marriage, was taken after O'Donoghue kidnapped him from his grandparents' home in Wales in late 1920 and where he stayed for most of the next year. It is clear from their correspondence that Florrie and Josephine were in constant contact with their cousins in Youghal and that they spent much of their time there.[13]

Indeed, Josephine's first contact with the IRA was through Michael Walsh in Youghal, who seems to have remained in contact subsequently with both O'Donoghue and his wife.[14] During the War of Independence, Youghal saw an outbreak of the same kind of 'Anti-Sinn Féin League' killing of alleged spies, including at least one Methodist.[15] This was very similar to what had occurred along the Blackrock Road in Cork where the O'Donoghues lived and may have been linked to the kidnapping of Reggie Brown.[16] It is clear from his writings that if O'Donoghue needed somewhere to lie low, or was giving assistance to someone who needed to hide out, it is very likely that he would have gone to Youghal, probably to the home of his sister-in-law.[17]

And the connections do not end there. On 25 September a Dr Richard B. Dalton, a 52-year-old physician, died at a small private hospital in Cork from acute pneumonia 'of five days' duration'.[18] Nothing unusual about that, apart from the fact that the funeral – of a very prominent citizen of Cork – was to be 'strictly private', to the extent that no details of the funeral arrangements were given in the press release.[19] But five days before he died, a Ford car had pulled up on Union Quay, across the river from Dalton's house on Morrison's Island in the centre of Cork city, and a machine-gunner with a Lewis gun riddled the house with bullets. An elderly woman who had been living with the family since the previous July, Mrs Frances Haynes, was shot dead through an upstairs window. Initial reports seemed to suggest that this was an attack on Moore's Hotel next door, which was used by the National Army as a prison for captured Republican fighters. However, it is clear from the account given at the inquest by the sergeant who was on duty outside the hotel that the fire was directed on the area 'between the AOH [Ancient Order of Hibernians] Hall and Moore's Hotel'; in other words, at the Dalton residence. Nobody else was wounded, while Mrs Haynes was hit by no fewer than eight bullets.[20] Was Dr Dalton's five days' sudden and acute pneumonia triggered by the shooting? Was Dalton also shot only to die later from complications arising from wounds? Either way, there is likely to be a connection between the two. And there is a connection between Dr Dalton and the O'Donoghues, because Dr Dalton was Josephine O'Donoghue's physician and was well known to the family.[21]

The building had also been riddled with gunfire on 9 September, and during the same week Mrs Haynes's son-in-law's brother, Edward Hawkesworth, also a doctor, died under mysterious circumstances on Grand Parade in Cork city.[22] Hawkesworth collapsed apparently of a heart attack after hearing firing in the street.[23] He had returned to Cork after eighteen years working in England and was now living on the Blackrock Road, not far from the O'Donoghues – and was connected to Dr Dalton through Mrs Haynes. This all adds up to a determined level of intimidation. Surely it is no coincidence that a doctor and nurses were ferried to Youghal in the week after Collins's death and that a week or two later a doctor known to the O'Donoghues and another doctor probably also known to them both died under mysterious circumstances? And there is a direct link between Bealnablath and the east Cork area. Garda Hickey claimed that the third of the three columns engaged in the ambush – that mysterious 'column' that nobody else seems to have written about – left for Killumney immediately after the ambush and moved later that night to east Cork and Waterford, thus bypassing the city.[24]

What this suggests is that, *inter alia*, Florrie O'Donoghue had one or more people who were wounded at Bealnablath moved to Youghal where they got medical treatment, and then went to great lengths to cover it all up. And because these lengths were so extreme – shooting drivers and having the Daltons intimidated or even shot – it suggests that the individual or individuals – most likely including the 'Irregular with the revolver' who was shot by one of the drivers – were important. We may never know for sure who the mysterious patient or patients wounded at Bealnablath were, for whom a doctor and nurses were brought from Cork to Youghal: what we can suggest is that they are likely to have been in some way connected to the O'Donoghues.

While it might be argued that it was the injuries incurred by Liam Deasy and Pete Kearney which required such medical attention, the fact that both had recovered and were back in action in a week or two suggests that these were not the men the Youghal group were trying to protect. To employ a driver to bring a doctor and nurses to Youghal and then go to the trouble of attempting to kill both the driver and the doctor suggests that a far more serious and life-threatening injury was suffered by somebody – somebody known to both the driver and the doctor.

In early October, a full month after Deasy was back in command of the 1st Southern Division, the headquarters of Cumann na mBan contacted Liam Lynch looking for funds for the support of 'some Republican prisoners' dependants' in Youghal – an area known for its traditional loyalty to Britain, and where there were never more than a handful of Republicans in the first place. 'Although the case is a very deserving one, we cannot comply with the request. Could you possibly give them any temporary assistance or even loan them some money to tide them over their present difficulties?'[25] There are no further details and no record of whether or not Lynch acceded to the request. However, on 26 October Seán O'Hegarty wrote to Ernie O'Malley looking for some financial assistance for 'maintenance'. O'Malley replied by instructing his Director of Finance to send O'Hegarty some money, with the caveat that 'on the matter of your maintenance … I can do nothing to support families of men who are on active service or who are in jail'.[26] What is interesting about this is that Republican dependants in Youghal, a town that capitulated to National Army forces in early August, should now be in need of urgent financial assistance. And why was O'Hegarty, who was supposedly 'neutral' and not on active service and presumably back at his job at the Cork Workhouse, now looking for financial help? At least he had a job to return to, which is more than could be said for many who were sent out to defend 'the Republic'.

The question of why an army driver might be employed to bring a doctor to Youghal can be easily explained by the fact that at least some officers in the Free State army in Cork were really anti-Treaty. O'Donoghue, on paper at least, was as well in with the Free State forces as he was with the Republicans. He may well have been the 'Irregular Commandant' who was 'colloguing' with the Free State forces in the Imperial Hotel during the weeks before Collins's death.[27] He could have easily got the use of an army driver in an emergency. Given that Hickey learned that an officer of the army was responsible for leaking Collins's movements to the Republicans,[28] it is entirely possible that army resources might have been used to bring medical help. A pro-Republican officer in the army could surely have approved the use of such a driver. The only leak then might come from the driver himself, especially if he was a former British army driver, and of course from the unfortunate doctor.

This brings us back to the identity of the mysterious Irregular with the revolver and the equally mysterious sniper who, according to the newspaper interviewees, was crawling towards Collins just before the latter was killed. These accounts suggest the presence of two enemies with intent to kill being within shooting distance of Collins when he died. The official IRA report of the ambush says that there were thirty-two in the ambush party. As we have seen, only between twenty and twenty-five of these can be accounted for – and these were almost all members of the 3rd Brigade. Who were the other seven? Where were the members of the 1st Brigade when all this was going on? Where, for instance, was Tom Crofts, who wrote the report? Where did O'Donoghue go after he met Collins that morning in Macroom? Was he, along with O'Hegarty, as several people have claimed, waiting to meet with Collins – and possibly de Valera – at Canon Tracy's in Crookstown? Given that Canon Tracy heard the firing from the ambush site, did they hear it too and venture the few miles up the road to see what was going on? Why were most of the IRB men on the anti-Treaty side who were in the vicinity either completely silent or very evasive on the events of that day? Why were old IRB hands like Brennan-Whitmore, a Free Stater and later a proto-fascist, trying to stitch up Emmet Dalton for the death of Collins decades later? Why did the IRB not instigate an investigation until 1966?

One clue to these questions may be found in O'Donoghue's correspondence in the months after Collins's death. In O'Donoghue's papers there is nothing at all written by O'Donoghue himself, or by O'Hegarty for that matter, from the week of Collins's death on 22 August to December of the same year. Considering that both men were involved in 'peace efforts' over the summer of 1922 and would be again in the spring of 1923, this gap is interesting, to say the least. So what were O'Donoghue and O'Hegarty doing during the three months from the end of August to early December and why were they so silent? Well, one answer may be got from their return to correspondence, again on the matter of the IRB, in December 1922.

On 29 December O'Donoghue replied to Liam Deasy, who had written to him some weeks earlier on reorganising the IRB. 'When I replied to your letter re Organization I was in very bad form and did not answer at such length as I should have done. Indeed I wasn't fit to deal with anything at the time. However, I am feeling better in health again and I wish to write more fully on the reorganization of the Organization.'[29] The date when O'Donoghue was not fit enough to reply was

7 November, when Deasy wrote to him for his views on how to restructure the IRB, given that the original Supreme Council had been in favour of the Treaty. What this note implies is that O'Donoghue was too ill to function during the autumn of 1922. But it also places the anti-Treaty elements within the IRB right at the centre of things. However, O'Donoghue was well enough again in the spring of 1923 to attend a three-day IRA Southern Division army council meeting held at Coolea, County Cork, from 19 to 23 February 1923. So much for his self-styled reputation as a 'neutral'.[30]

But O'Donoghue was not the only one who was too ill to work, for around the same time O'Hegarty wrote to him: 'I am not well enough in health to work, so you can't expect any help from me. I am telling you this for your own information only so you will not let it go further.'[31] It may also be significant that, even though he had resigned from the IRA in June, O'Hegarty, at least on the basis of one account, had been reconfirmed as O/C of the Cork No. 1 Brigade at the meeting chaired by Liam Lynch at Ballyvourney two days before Bealnablath, at which Neeson claimed that the decision to assassinate Collins was taken, though it appears that O'Hegarty himself was not at the meeting.[32] This suggests that he was more than a mere peace negotiator – and, like O'Donoghue, certainly not a neutral. His looking for funds from Ernie O'Malley in the months after Collins's death would appear to confirm this.

Apart from O'Donoghue getting eye trouble in later life, these are the only mentions of ill health that I am aware of in his correspondence. Interestingly, later in life O'Hegarty was to become a virtual recluse, living in his home in Cork and barely opening the door to anyone. O'Hegarty's withdrawal from activities in the immediate aftermath of Collins's death, 'now that all responsibility is off his shoulders', according to Liam Lynch, is confirmed by a memo from Tom Crofts to Lynch on 9 September: 'I do not believe that Sean H. is interfering at all at present.'[33]

On the subject of the peace negotiations, O'Donoghue and O'Hegarty were involved over the summer of 1922 and were to resume in February 1923. During the intervening months peace efforts in Cork were being made by Canon Tom Duggan and the future president of University College Cork, Alfred O'Rahilly, who were trying to intervene between the Republican leadership and Generals Tom Ennis and Emmet Dalton on the Free State side. Indeed, Ennis met with the Republicans in October in Crookstown in what looks like a rerun of the attempted meeting Collins may have been going to attend on the evening of the day he died. O'Donoghue was not in the picture at this time. Aware perhaps that the wrong kind of information might leak out, however, he warned Ernie O'Malley many years later regarding what he might hear about these peace moves: 'He [Duggan] is not reliable unless he centres himself.'[34] Considering that Canon Duggan – a genuinely heroic figure – did more than anyone else to try to bring about an end to the Civil War,[35] and failed through no fault of his own, this seems to be a particularly unfair statement. Duggan laid the blame for the failure to end the Civil War firmly on the shoulders of Liam Lynch: '"I'm back to the bedrock of a Republic," Duggan quoted Lynch as saying, "and there I'll stay." Liam Lynch was the most unfortunate of the lot.'[36] Considering that Lynch, a man of integrity but rigid to the point of absurdity, had no interest in peace, there is no doubt that the negotiations in the summer of 1922 came largely from the so-called Neutral IRA of O'Donoghue and O'Hegarty, rather than from Lynch himself. Most of those involved in the peace negotiations both during the summer of 1922 and in the spring of 1923 were acting out of the highest of motives, were tired of the slaughter and simply wanted peace. The argument here is that they were being used.

What all this tells us is that O'Donoghue and O'Hegarty were in no fit state to deal with political matters in the autumn of 1922 for health reasons. They could of course have been simply ill, but if they were, they were ill for a long time. This is all pointing in one direction: that O'Donoghue and O'Hegarty may well have been at Bealnablath and may have been involved either directly or indirectly in the death of Collins; that anti-Treaty elements in the IRB did indeed plan to kill Collins after finding him guilty of 'treason' for implementing the Treaty; that O'Donoghue pulled Collins into the trap as part of that plan; that the trap was either to have been in Crookstown or as part of the Bealnablath ambush; that some persons, perhaps even O'Donoghue, may have been wounded when the National Army convoy fired on them around the time Collins was shot.

This interpretation of the shooting of Michael Collins, as we have seen, merely reflects the simple logic commonly held by Republicans at the time, as distinct from what they claimed to believe many years later. From their point of view Collins was the greatest of traitors. As Count Plunkett, author of the scathing 'People's Rights' manifesto that pointed out Collins's 'treason', put it in a letter to the Archbishop of Tuam in early October, in what which is clearly a reference to the death of Collins: 'Your Grace reminds us of the fate of those who "live by the sword"; and the records of the past few weeks should give pause to those who think they can make war with impunity against the rights of a determined people.'[37] It should be noted that Plunkett had been demoted from the Dáil cabinet by de Valera in August 1921 for his implacable opposition to any kind of negotiation with the British. (In fact, he ignored the wishes of the electorate, who voted in a large majority for Collins in June 1922 – although there were clearly enough 'determined people' to have Collins killed.)

This does not necessarily mean that O'Donoghue or O'Hegarty fired the fatal bullet. The shooter was more likely to have been a marksman, armed probably with a Mauser sporting rifle, if we are to go by the view of General Costello and the forensics of the ghastly wound on the back of Collins's head. Did one or two of the assassination party make themselves visible after the ambush appeared to be over – and effectively was over, since it was minimal in the first place and the ambush party had left the scene by then – in order to draw Collins out of his cover and present him as a clear target? The evidence is suggestive of this, even if it can probably never be proved.

And these were not the last people likely to have died as a result of Bealnablath. On 7 December 1922 Seán Hales, who had been Collins's go-between in trying to set up the meeting that led Collins to Bealnablath in the first place, was himself assassinated in Dublin. This is usually put down to a simple reprisal on the part of the Republicans for the execution of Erskine Childers a fortnight earlier and for the general policy of executions brought about by the Public Safety Bill that had come into operation in mid-October, but which was not implemented until 17 November when five IRA prisoners were officially taken out and shot for having been caught with arms. This boneheaded and excessive policy was to damage the reputation of the new state greatly, even in the eyes of its own supporters, and was to be divisive over several generations.

Liam Lynch, at least on paper, ordered that prominent supporters of the Provisional Government, including TDs who had supported the Public Safety Bill, were to be assassinated. But IRA men on the ground were reluctant to go around shooting their former comrades; Frank Henderson, for instance, claimed that he could have shot several pro-Treaty TDs if he had wanted to but he decided against it.[38]

Hales was the most prominent pro-Treaty figure assassinated during this period. He was leaving the Ormond Hotel on the Liffey quays in the company of Pádraig Ó Máille, the Leas Ceann Comhairle of the Dáil, when he was shot dead by an IRA Active Service Unit. Ó Máille was wounded in the incident. The immediate result, as we have seen, was an appalling intensification of the Provisional Government's reprisals policy when Rory O'Connor, Joe

McKelvey, Liam Mellows and Dick Barrett, all prominent Republican leaders, were taken from their cells at Mountjoy Gaol and summarily executed on foot of an emergency cabinet meeting. As Michael Hopkinson put it: 'No argument could detract from the fact that these were killings of untried and unconvicted men.'[39]

The anti-Treatyites claimed subsequently that the intention had been to shoot Ó Máille for voting for the Public Safety Bill and that Hales, who had not voted for the bill, had been killed accidentally. However, the Military Pensions application of Joseph Kelly, one of the men involved in the shooting, makes it clear that the intention was to assassinate Hales and that the Dublin Active Service Unit carried out the killing after getting a tip-off from a member of staff at the hotel that Hales was staying there.[40] Quite a number of commentators on Bealnablath have made the point that Hales was in the process of investigating the death of Collins when he was killed, and indeed may have been on his way to discuss that very matter with William T. Cosgrave. Whatever the circumstances of Hales' death, the only man in a position to point the finger firmly at those who led Collins into the trap that was Bealnablath was now dead.

None of this of course is conclusive proof of O'Donoghue's involvement in Collins's death. Historical evidence is always fragmentary, and finding out what happened is doubly difficult when evidence has either been covered up or ignored or when false trails have been laid. So perhaps now is a good time to lay out the evidence we have so far encountered.

- Florrie O'Donoghue met with Collins on the morning of Bealnablath. What he did after that we don't know. What we do know is that he was attached to the anti-Treaty IRA command in the area, since he was receiving his correspondence at anti-Treaty HQ up until the week of Collins's death (see chapter 15).

- O'Donoghue and Seán O'Hegarty were among the most vociferous opponents of the Treaty with Great Britain, making their objections known before negotiations even started.
- Using their influence within the IRB, primarily in Munster, they made considerable efforts to turn their fellow IRA/IRB officers and the rank and file of the IRA in the south against the Treaty.
- Despite these efforts they were then, along with Tom Hales, involved in trying to establish 'army unity' between Collins and the anti-Treaty IRA. These efforts used IRB connections and went on behind the backs of the Republicans. Collins ignored their 'Pact' Army Council.
- Strident calls from the more extreme wing of Republicanism for Collins to be tried for treason for the crime of signing the Treaty and for being a 'perjured traitor to the Republic of Ireland' are reflected in O'Donoghue's records of IRB meetings over the summer of 1922, which state that a decision had been taken for Collins to be 'done away with'.
- Over the summer of 1922 O'Donoghue, having technically resigned from the IRA, was instrumental in the setting-up of a 'People's Rights Association' – named on the back of Count Plunkett's manifesto – in Cork with a view to ending hostilities between the two sides.
- When the People's Rights Association efforts failed to bring both sides to the negotiation table, the 'Neutrals' brought their own proposals, which were almost certainly too generous to the Free State side to be acceptable to Republicans. Nonetheless, this was one of the reasons why Collins came to Cork and a major factor in why he chose to travel via Macroom on both stages of his journey to west Cork.
- There is evidence of a sniper creeping up on Collins and of 'an Irregular with a revolver' being near Collins at the time he was killed, and evidence that the revolver man was shot by one of Collins's drivers.

- Isherwood's evidence suggests that some wounded man (or men) was brought to Youghal in the aftermath of Bealnablath for medical treatment and that a significant cover-up operation, including the shooting of witnesses, may have been put in place to keep this from becoming public knowledge.
- While there is no evidence that O'Donoghue was one of the wounded individuals moved to Youghal, both he and O'Hegarty claimed they were too ill to work for several months afterwards.

14

Doing Away with Michael – the Aftermath

As we have seen in Chapter 7, the original piece of evidence suggesting that Collins's assassination was planned and executed by anti-Treaty elements in the IRB was an extracted intelligence report in Collins's own British Intelligence file.

Since it is quite clear from accounts of the death of Tomás MacCurtain and the arrest of Terence MacSwiney that death threats supposedly made by 'the IRB' were used during the War of Independence to cover activities of British Intelligence, the presence in Collins's file of a supposed IRB plot to kill him has to be approached with caution. In other words, we have to be wary when the desires of British Intelligence and what they liked to term 'the IRB' appear to coincide.

However, the original intelligence report of 29 July 1922 in the Collins file does appear to be genuine. It can be cross-referenced against similar threats made against other prominent pro-Treaty men. The report stated that Collins was found guilty of treason and sentenced to death 'by a court of the Inner Circle of the Irish Republican Brotherhood'. However, when one looks at the equivalent file for Seán MacEoin, one finds that he was also tried, found guilty and sentenced – though of course he was not killed.[1] The original report came from the United States, but independent intelligence reports 'from different sources in Dublin point to the assassination of prominent pro-Treaty leaders – MacEoin has been mentioned as having received notice to this end', as was Richard Mulcahy a month later.[2]

It is Mulcahy's file that gives the most detailed version of this alleged plan. Again it is probable that the 'Inner Circle' of the IRB refers to the O'Donoghue/O'Hegarty wing of the IRB and its parallel command in the Munster IRA:

> It has been reliably reported that the Inner Circle of the Irish Republican Brotherhood have tried Michael Collins and Seán MacEoin for treason to the IRB and sentenced them to death. Arthur Griffith was tried and acquitted. Twelve trusted men were given orders to carry out the sentence on Collins and MacEoin and have joined the Free State Army, *three of these are natives of Cork city* [emphasis added]. Richard Mulcahy is also expected to be convicted and sentenced to death and five other Free State officers have already been convicted, two of them being ex-members of the RIC now serving with commissions in the Free State army. Collins, I am informed, is aware of the sentence passed on him. According to my information, seventeen prominent Free State men have been tried, two acquitted, including Griffith, three killed in action and the remainder to be killed as opportunity arises.[3]

While this is the usual somewhat speculative material associated with 'I' reports, it does contain three potentially useful pieces of information: first, that Collins was aware that he was on a death list – which, as we saw, might partly account for his depression in the week or two before his death – and, second, that the net of assassination was spread wider than to catch just Collins. As he himself put it to Cosgrave on 4 August: 'The Government is aware of plots to murder the members of the Government who are carrying out the people's mandate to restore law and order in the country. They are further aware that certain Officers in the Army whose military services are well known are marked down similarly.'[4] This suggests that British military intelligence in this instance had passed its information to Collins. Clearly, the policy of 'doing away' with Collins had by now been extended to his most prominent lieutenants.

But the most useful piece of information from our point of view is the statement that three of the would-be assassins – remember, this report was compiled before Collins was killed – were believed to be natives of Cork city, which, given their prominence in the IRB, might point in the direction of O'Donoghue, O'Hegarty and one other. And while they did not join the Free State army as such – though O'Donoghue almost did – they did publicly declare their neutrality while secretly still being part of anti-Treaty operations. Besides, someone planning to join the National Army in July might not actually have gone on to do so. Indeed, O'Donoghue sat so adroitly on the fence that he was considered to have been on both sides at the same time. Garda Hickey, in his investigation on Bealnablath, established that 'one officer of the [ambush] column was delighted. He had been active during the War of Independence and had been promised a commission in the Army. This did not come through ... and that was the reason for his bitterness.'[5] Who was this individual? While O'Donoghue was not a native of Cork, he had lived for so long in the city that you would have to wonder how many outside his own circle knew that he had been born in County Kerry. Furthermore, he had been nominated as Adjutant General of the army back in June but resigned after the failure of negotiations with Richard Mulcahy on army reunification as a result of a disagreement over who would be chief of staff.

Quite clearly what this means is that there must have been a third Cork city man in the picture, who by definition must have had close IRB connections, and most likely was intimate with O'Donoghue and O'Hegarty. While this could have been any anti-Treaty Cork city IRB man, one candidate immediately springs to mind, although there is no evidence that he was at Bealnablath. This is Joseph O'Connor, O'Donoghue's best friend and best man at his wedding, one of the few leaders in the city who, along with O'Donoghue and O'Hegarty, managed to evade arrest by the British all through the War of Independence.

Joe O'Connor had been the Quartermaster of 1st Cork Brigade for much of the War of Independence and became the Quartermaster General for the 1st Southern Division in the months leading to the Truce. At the outbreak of the Civil War, he took the anti-Treaty side and remained Quartermaster General of the 1st Southern Division during the early phase of the war. It was he who took charge of the consignment of Mauser sporting rifles when they were landed at Helvick Head in April.[6] He was then promoted to Acting Quartermaster General of the entire anti-Treaty IRA from October 1922 until he resigned in early April 1923. During the latter period he was based in Dublin. However, from June to October 1922 he was based in Munster.[7] According to a letter sent by Liam Lynch on the very day of Bealnablath, 'the QMG can be got in touch with through Cork No. 1'. In other words, he had not strayed too far from his own patch at that point.[8] According to Ernie O'Malley, O'Connor was the most senior officer in the south in the early stages of the Civil War when Liam Lynch and Liam Deasy were in Dublin.[9] As Quartermaster of the 1st Southern Division, he states in his IRA pension application form that he was engaged in 'General Operations of the QMG department', that is to say 'procurement of arms, ammunition, explosives etc.'[10]

This means that, as the man in charge of IRA arms stores, he had responsibility for keeping the stock of Mauser sporting rifles and its ammunition for the 1st Southern Division. (Some of these weapons had gone the Northern Division of the IRA in May 1922 for attacks in Northern Ireland.) This was a topic Ernie O'Malley tried to bring up with O'Connor when he interviewed him in the late 1940s. O'Malley's brief notes on this encounter are worth quoting: 'Joe O'Connor ... QMG in the Civil War, not inclined to talk years later. I realized he was a brother of Fr. Dominick [*sic*] ... The first day he would not talk to me. The following day when I saw him in Cash's Stores [where O'Connor worked] I stood at the end of a counter. He was thin, had aged even, and had lost weight.' O'Malley went on to question him about the Mauser rifles: 'Cork received some of the first shipment of arms from Germany in the Truce, the sporting rifle which was armour-piercing. J. O'Connor did not even know that the sights were soldered on. He had no list of arms and equipment in the Div[ision] nor has he any HQ papers.'[11]

O'Connor would give no further information to O'Malley and clearly did not want to be reminded of the events of 1922. He had no wish to talk about the Mauser rifles and, perhaps understandably, wanted to put the whole topic of the Civil War behind him. There is no doubt that Joe O'Connor was a pleasant, shy and retiring man who was very well liked in Cash's Department Store in Cork, where he worked for most of his life. In the early 1960s he turned down an invitation to give the annual oration at the grave of Liam Lynch at Kilcrumper, outside Fermoy – a singular honour for any Republican – stating that he would not be able to do justice to Lynch's memory. 'I have given the matter very serious consideration, so there will be no use in asking me to reconsider.'[12] He was also wary when the subject came up of the return of the remains of his brother, Father Dominic O'Connor, Chaplain of the Cork No. 1 Brigade, who died in the United States in 1935 and whose remains Republicans both in the United States and in Ireland wanted repatriated in view of the priest's own wishes. 'In June 1949 I was asked for my consent to the removal of Fr. Dominic's remains to Ireland and I refused as I felt the time was not opportune.'[13] At some point between 1954 and 1957, however, Joe O'Connor changed his mind, though his advice to O'Donoghue was to focus on Dominic's pre-Truce activities so that 'it would cut out any idea of the 1922 period'.[14] O'Donoghue eventually organised for the return of the remains of Father Dominic, thus earning a letter of congratulation from the Taoiseach, Eamon de Valera, 'on the perfection of all the arrangements for the transfer'.[15]

Was Joe O'Connor part of the plot to kill Collins, and was he reluctant to talk about it as a result? He is named as having been present at the shadowy IRB meeting at which the decision to 'do away' with Collins was noted. Given that some of Collins's men had vowed to avenge his death and had sworn to shoot his killer, and were still talking about doing so in the 1940s, such caution has a certain logic. A photograph in the O'Donoghue Papers suggests that O'Donoghue, even thirty-six years after Collins's death, was prepared for such an eventuality. It shows O'Donoghue, by now an elderly though still a fit-looking man, shouldering Father Dominic's coffin with something that looks suspiciously like a revolver spoiling the line of his right trouser pocket and another in the lining of his jacket.[16] O'Donoghue was not a man who would leave anything to chance.

The most curious thing about Joe O'Connor's service history is what happened to him at the end of the Civil War. In his Military Service Pension application, he states that he resigned from the IRA at the beginning of April 1923 – before the death of Liam Lynch and the effective end of the Civil War.[17] He then went to England, where he was to remain until 1925. The reason he gave for going to England was that he needed an operation for an injury he had received over a year earlier. He states that he had been involved in an accident when travelling between Mallow and Fermoy to supervise the handover of Fermoy Barracks to the IRA in early February 1922. He states that he was in hospital for four weeks, from 9 February to 11 March, and implies – though does not state directly – that this was the reason he had to go to England in April 1923. But surely if he needed urgent medical attention as a result of the accident – an accident, by the way, for which there is no independent evidence – he would have had it in the five months between the beginning of February and the outbreak of Civil War at the end of June. Instead, he waited for over a year to have the operation.

Furthermore, when the Pensions Board queried the medical certification for O'Connor's stay at Cork's South Infirmary, where he said he was treated, they contacted Seán O'Hegarty, who worked at the nearby workhouse – later St Finbarr's Hospital – rather than at the South Infirmary. Surely the Board could have got some doctor to vouch for O'Connor, especially since many of the medical staff of the South Infirmary in 1934 would still have been in a position to vouch for O'Connor's injuries? Then O'Connor suddenly withdrew his application for a disability pension.[18] However, if he was injured, he was not too seriously injured since he was acting in lieu of O'Donoghue in 'Peace Proposal' activities in October 1922.[19] This, if nothing else, confirms O'Donoghue's indisposition at this time and his inability to carry out duties he would otherwise have undertook.

Garda Hickey refers to the group who killed Collins as a 'rearguard', covering the retreat of the others, which appears to be literally correct since the forensics suggest they were to the rear of the ambush position. 'In the rearguard there was a Kerryman, a man from the borders of Cork and Limerick and three Corkmen.' This may suggest that the British Intelligence information that three Corkmen were among the group planning to assassinate Collins was correct. It would also substantiate Eoin Neeson's claim that it was officers of the 1st Southern Division, rather than members of the 3rd Brigade, who were primarily involved in planning and carrying out the killing. Since Hickey's account was compiled close to the event, it has to be given credence over accounts written much later and, taken with the British Intelligence report, what it says is that the assassination was organised by officers of the 1st Southern Division – almost certainly former IRB men –

rather than the members of the 3rd Brigade who set up the peripheral ambush as we understand it.[20]

Hannah Desmond (neé Corcoran), a local member of Cumann na mBan, kept a detailed diary of her activities during those months. In it she records looking after the IRA party who organised the Bealnablath ambush. She stated that on the night before the ambush, she 'prepared beds and served meals for 15 officers and men for ambush at Bealnablath'. The following night, however, she prepared meals for only ten of these men. Clearly the other five dined elsewhere.[21]

In an interesting sideline to this, Hickey claimed that: 'The army also held an investigation into this. One of the results of this was that an Army Officer was suspected of leaking information to the Irregulars. He was stationed in the Cork garrison and confirmed the movements of Collins to the Irregulars. The Army investigation failed to unearth the mysterious officer although I heard some years later that he had been dismissed.'[22] This confirms the suggestions of collusion that were coming out of the Cork Command in the autumn of 1922 and which were picked up by the inquest into the army mutiny of 1924.[23] One suspects that the guilty party may have been among those dismissed as a result of the army mutiny.

In two recent papers, Denis Linehan suggested a further cover-up. He believed that Dr Leo Ahern, who was attached to the National Army in Cork and was one of the doctors present when Collins's body was brought to Shanakiel Hospital, travelled to Dublin immediately afterwards in order to influence Gogarty, who was to carry out the embalming of Collins's body, into believing that Collins had been killed by a ricochet – in order to 'divert blame from any one person on the anti-Treaty side'.[24] 'Dr Leo Ahern remembered "distinctly" Dr Gogarty asking him if there was any other head wound and I told him there wasn't. He checked the forehead for marks while I held the bandages.'[25] In one of the volumes of his autobiography Gogarty wrote that Collins's wound was 'a ricochet, evidently' but it seems he was not entirely taken in since he told Connie Neenan in New York many years later that there was another wound 'the size of a fingernail', something that was confirmed by Bill McKenna.[26] Ahern, who rose to the rank of colonel in the army, was dismissed in the wake of the 1924 mutiny as part of Liam Tobin's attempted *coup d'état*.[27] All this points to a cover-up among officers stationed in Cork at the time — which might include Liam Tobin himself, who in his National Army pension application is notably reticent about his service in Cork.[28] (He was the leading intelligence officer who landed with the National Army force at Passage West on 8 August 1922 and was still serving in Cork at the time of Collins's death a fortnight later.)

What all this adds up to is that the assassination of Michael Collins was, in all likelihood, planned by a group of IRB men who were now attached to the 1st Southern Division rather than the 3rd Brigade, that they received help from 'sleepers' within the Provisional Government forces, and that O'Donoghue and O'Hegarty were principals among them.

But this still leaves open the question of the identity of the men who comprised the rearguard action — five men, three of them possible casualties, either wounded or dead. And it sheds no further light on the identity of 'the man who shot Michael Collins' — which probably will always remain a mystery. Indeed, the identity of the actual shooter is of relatively minor significance compared to the nature of the plot and the identity of the men who planned and organised it. Nonetheless, it is worth speculating because the circumstantial evidence — and it has to be emphasised that it is circumstantial, and not by any means definitive — points in one direction and it is a direction that has been suggested by others, though not quite in the way it will be done here.

15

Blinding the Fool's Eye

If we are to believe Florrie O'Donoghue's account, he was on his way to visit his sick mother when he was arrested in Macroom the day before Bealnablath and thrown in the 'clink' by 'some fool' of a soldier. Purely fortuitously, he claimed he was released on Michael Collins's orders when he noticed the latter passing outside the following morning. He had received passes to travel through both Free State and Republican territories and, he presumably would have us believe, he went on his way to see his mother after his accidental encounter with Collins. O'Donoghue even told Eoin Neeson that he had been arrested *twice* in Macroom.

O'Donoghue would also have us believe that his chief concern during 1922 and well into 1923 was the 'reunification of the Army' and that he spent his time trying to heal the wounds between the warring factions and contriving to bridge the split over the Treaty. He was, almost every historian now believes, a 'neutral' – a man 'out for peace', as a Free State memo at the time put it; a man of integrity whose only concern was the common good. That he failed to prevent the slip to Civil War and failed to bring it to an earlier and more honourable conclusion could surely not be his fault.

Yet most if not all of this is little more than a carefully constructed fabrication. O'Donoghue was the first to foment trouble for Collins within the ranks of the IRB. Even before Treaty negotiations started, he organised his fellow Centres in Munster to oppose the Treaty, and was almost certainly party to the decision to have Collins killed. Yet at the same time, as early as April 1922, he was trying to curry favour with Collins, suggesting to him that war might still be avoided if he were to meet the anti-Treaty faction. Over the summer O'Donoghue was regularly going back and forth, trying to get the two sides to come together. This might be construed as meaning that he wanted peace were it not for the fact that the pro-Treaty Seán Ó Muirthile blamed O'Donoghue and O'Hegarty fairly and squarely for swaying their fellow IRA officers towards the drift to war in the first place – to the extent, as we have seen, that he could barely bring himself to write their names.

O'Donoghue was on the IRA GHQ Staff as Adjutant General after the Executive convention and election of 9 April 1922. Yet he was also named in government proposals to serve as Adjutant General to the Army Council on 9 June, in a council consisting of equal numbers of pro- and anti-Treaty officers. So he came within a whisker of becoming a very senior officer in the National Army.

When the Civil War broke out, O'Donoghue claimed that he could not bring himself to serve in the Republican forces. In his letter of resignation to Liam Lynch, written on 3 July, he stated that he had fundamental objections to a Civil War from which no good could derive: 'I have thought over the matter carefully and at length, and to my mind there is nothing in the circumstances of the origin of the present conflict which would justify my taking part in it.' This is a spectacular about-turn, given his machinations against the Treaty in late 1921 and early 1922. 'It is only in the event of the return of the English that I could take up arms again. Should that happen, and I think it will, I'll be in the ranks somewhere.' In a splendid piece of constructive ambiguity, O'Donoghue concludes his letter to Lynch: 'If at any time I can be of any use, I hope you will call on me. As I cannot wish for your success, I will hope that your work will in its result help to bring us nearer to the ideal we have at heart.'[1]

And yet, according to Eoin Neeson, far from being neutral, the 'indiscreet Neutrals' were present at the meeting at Ballyvourney on the Saturday night before Bealnablath, at which the decision was taken to attempt to kill Collins, and were back at 1st Southern Division meetings as late as the spring of 1923. Edward O'Mahony names O'Donoghue as having been at the Ballyvourney meeting, though stating that he was following 'a neutral policy'.[2] O'Mahony suggests that O'Hegarty was not at the meeting because he was supposedly 'involved in peace negotiations and pursuing an uncommitted role'. O'Mahony lists those present as 'Dan "Sandow" O'Donovan, Dick Langford of Milltown, Co. Kerry, Pat O'Sullivan, Commandant, 1st Southern Division, Mick Murphy, Commandant, 1st Southern Division, Tom Hales, Dan Corkery and F. O'Donoghue'. Neeson also stated that the group who shot Collins were present at Bealnablath well before the 3rd Brigade met to set up its ambush.

In an attempt to get Neeson to remove this claim from his book, Jim Hurley, one of the survivors of Bealnablath, in a statement in 1964 claimed that the 3rd Brigade got information that Collins was in the area only that morning. However, he contradicted this when he also said that

> when the four [3rd] Brigade officers reached the Beal na Blath district a substantial number of men were in place and preparing the position. Several Divisional officers and some of the Battalion commandants were there. The decision was taken, most probably, on Divisional initiative and, of course, we took our places. The full party consisted principally of those from Cork 3 with a fair proportion of Cork 1 Volunteers as the districts adjoin about that area. The party that remained to protect the main party when it was decided to give up was a Cork 3 section.[3]

Neeson stated the obvious when he replied to Hurley that 'there were sufficient senior officers of Battalion, Brigade and Division seniority present at Beal na Blath *on the night of August 21* and in the early morning of August 22 to lay the ambush on the forenoon of the latter day [emphasis added].'[4]

And yet the Republicans did not entirely trust O'Donoghue either. An IRA memo of early 1923 went: 'This association call themselves the Neutral IRA. They should not be allowed to do so. F.O.D. [Florrie O'Donoghue] Cork is the principal organizer in the city and probably in the county. They are running the organization in Cork along the same lines as it is being run throughout the country. I am keeping an eye on them.'[5]

So when is a neutral not a neutral? And where did O'Donoghue go after his meeting with Collins on the morning of 22 August 1922? Garda Hickey makes an interesting claim in his report. He states that the men who killed Collins were in position from 9.00am at Bealnablath on the morning he passed through, something that O'Donoghue in his various denials implies could not possibly be true. In this Hickey agrees with Neeson. However, he was adamant that Collins did not pass through Bealnablath on the morning of the ambush. He claimed rather that Collins's party, after they had left Macroom, did not travel as far as Bealnablath but turned south earlier from Doonisky Cross on the Cork–Macroom road and drove straight through Kilmurry village, 'nearly as far as Coppeen crossroads' before getting directions that brought them close to Enniskeane on their way to Bandon. This must have been the case since Dinny Long, the scout who is credited with having spotted Collins passing on the road, was, according to his own Military Pensions application, on armed guard for Divisional and Brigade officers, including de Valera, on the night before the ambush.[6] Since de Valera and those with him stayed that night at Muinegave, some 5 miles to the south-west, this must have been where Collins was seen to pass through, not through the Bealnablath ambush site.[7]

(It is unlikely he could have passed both Muinegave and the ambush site since they are on different roads. Most published accounts have him coming into Kilmurry and then turning left to take in Bealnablath. The local view, however, is that he passed straight through Kilmurry and bypassed Bealnablath.) De Valera *did* call to the pub in Bealnablath later that morning, but by that time Collins had long gone.

O'Donoghue, however, stated that 'the sentry at Long's where some of them stayed on the Monday night saw the convoy in which Collins travelled pass in the direction of Bandon on Tuesday morning. He recognized Collins and reported it.'[8] This is a subtle piece of distortion because it implies that Collins drove past Long's pub at Bealnablath that morning. Dinny Long was a farmer's son but was not a member of the family who owned Long's public house at Bealnablath.[9] It was perhaps convenient for people like O'Donoghue, who wanted to muddy the water that Dinny Long shared a surname with Mrs Long who ran the Bealnablath pub, so it was easy to transfer his alleged sighting a few miles to the north-east and claim that he was actually at Bealnablath itself while the convoy supposedly passed through. Of course, it also adds to the mythology surrounding the day.

If this was the case and Collins did not pass through the valley of Bealnablath that morning, and the ambushers were in place from 9.00am, were they initially planning to shoot Collins on his way south only to be thwarted because he took an unexpected route? Was O'Donoghue holding Collins up in Macroom in order to allow his men to get in position at Bealnablath? Hickey's investigations suggest that this may well have been the case, since he states that de Valera left the house at Muinegave at 9.30am, 'by which time most of the column had gone to Beal na mBlath ... because they had instructions from the previous night to be in position'.[10]

O'Donoghue, of course, is adamant that nobody had any idea Collins was in the area until he passed though that morning. This is almost certainly a lie. Lily Holland was an eight-year-old girl living in one of the farmhouses closest to the ambush site. She remembered that on the night before the ambush the family had to leave and spend the night with neighbours further away because of the dangers the ambush might pose. The IRA commandeered a cart from the farm to create the roadblock. If the entire episode was a spur-of-the moment decision made on the morning of the 22nd, this would not have been the case. Lily Holland's memory suggests that planning went into the ambush and that such preparations were going on the night before Collins passed through.[11]

The other side of the coin, of course, is that Collins would have had to return via the Bealnablath route if he was to meet with Canon Tracy that evening in Crookstown, which, according to Hickey, the IRA officers were also more than aware of.[12] They had planned for that, so it was worth their while staying put in case he did.

Whatever about that morning, from IRA documentation of the following weeks we can make an educated, informed and probably accurate guess that O'Donoghue was part of the anti-Treaty forces on the day that Collins was killed. For on 1 September, just over a week after Bealnablath, in reply to a letter from Tom Crofts, the Adjutant of the 1st Southern Division, the Adjutant of the Cork No. 1 Brigade wrote that they would try to forward his correspondence – which clearly had been sent on by the 1st Division to 'Flor Donoghue and D. Cronin'.[13] We can infer from this that until that week O'Donoghue was receiving his correspondence care of the 1st Southern Division. This would hardly have been the case had he been a neutral or if he had been in a 'clink' in Macroom. It also suggests that the Cork No. 1 Brigade had trouble tracking down O'Donoghue in the weeks after Bealnablath. If O'Donoghue was lying low in Youghal in those weeks, as can be clearly inferred from the previous chapters, this would make sense. He claimed in his IRA pension application that he began working at his job as a rate collector in Cork city on 28 September 1922 – a few weeks later – implying that he was busy at his new job from that point.[14] This is almost certainly another fabrication, since the rate collectors' jobs – of which there were several arising in the county at that time – were not advertised until the beginning of October. In fact, the job O'Donoghue finally got was not advertised until early December.[15] I think it is fair to assume that he was hardly working as a rate collector before the job was advertised.

16

The Evidence of Garda Hickey

The simplest scenario, and one that may account for much of the evidence that emerges from the day of the ambush, is that Pete Kearney and two others – possibly including Liam Deasy – had departed for the south (rather than, as they said, for the north) before the ambush, that they returned upon hearing the firing, that they hugged the roadside and shot Collins as he meandered south in their direction, and that they were wounded as they did so. This would account for both the 'sniper' and the 'Irregular with the revolver' who was shot around the time Collins was shot, especially since both Kearney and Deasy may have been wounded during that week. The problem with this is that nobody else has ever placed them there. For this to be true, a large number of people would have to have sold Meda Ryan a bundle of lies. Furthermore, this scenario, while straightforward and plausible and not to be dismissed, overlooks a raft of other information.

We have seen how Hannah Desmond, a local Cumann na mBan girl living in the Bealnablath area during the Civil War, kept a diary in which she recorded her daily activities – down to the number of pairs of socks and sets of underwear she washed – on behalf of the anti-Treaty IRA. The night before the ambush, she recorded that she prepared beds and served meals 'for 15 officers and men for Ambush at Bealnablath, August 22nd 1922'. After the ambush, however, she prepared meals for only ten men/officers.[1] This is a minor detail but an important one, because it suggests that five of the original ambush organisers were not in a position to partake of a meal and did not need a place to sleep in the area after the ambush. It also confirms that the ambush was planned well before Collins's arrival in the area. The earlier chapters also suggested that at least some of the party had been wounded round the time Collins was killed – probably more seriously than Kearney and Deasy were wounded – and may have been trying to make their way to Youghal where their injuries were to be attended to (with lethal consequences for doctors and drivers, as we have seen).

The number five is important here, because this is also the number of men who Garda Hickey claimed made up the 'rearguard' who shot Collins: 'An officer and four Irregulars were left to cover the retreat of the other men.'[2] According to Hickey, these were a Kerryman, a man from the borders of Cork and Limerick, and three Corkmen. Of course one has to approach this with caution, since it is entirely possible that whoever from the Republican side gave this information to Hickey may have wanted to send him on a wild goose chase, and it does not correspond with any of the accounts left by the members of the 3rd Brigade who are known to have been there on the day.

But if it is correct, it more likely refers to a group of 1st Southern Division officers since the 3rd Brigade consisted almost entirely of men from west Cork. The Kerryman might have been O'Donoghue, but then again he might not. The point is, though, that the 3rd Brigade men had no such people in their recollections. According to Hickey, the man who fired the fatal shot was a Corkman who was still alive in the early 1970s. This is usually interpreted as meaning Tom Kelleher, who may have thought he did so, but it is unclear what this conclusion is based on. (It may also have been Pete Kearney, who died in 1969 but lived most of his life in Dublin. Hickey states that the man who shot Collins later spared his life at a roadblock he had set up in the wake of the shooting-up of a navy launch at Cobh by Republicans in March 1924. If that was the case, then the likely candidate is Dan 'Sandow' O'Donovan, who along with Frank Busteed and the Gray brothers carried out that shooting. Sandow was still alive in the early 1970s and it was he, as O/C of the 1st Cork Brigade, who had chaired the meeting in Ballyvourney at which it was decided to shoot Collins. However, he has never been mentioned as a possible candidate and since he was Neeson's principal source in pointing the finger of blame at the 'Neutrals', he is unlikely to have been the shooter.)

In Hickey's account, the organisation of the ambush was a lot more complex than is widely believed. He claimed that three separate 'columns' were involved, comprising forty men. Yet we have accounts from only one of these columns, namely the men of the 3rd Brigade. As we have seen, the second column – the cavalry column commanded by Seán Hyde – was also in the area and counted Sonny O'Neill among its members. Its existence has become apparent only with the release of the IRA pensions files. I believe it was the third 'column' that killed Michael Collins, that it probably consisted of five men and was organised by a shadowy anti-Treaty IRB group, including Florrie O'Donoghue and some close associates, and was in position on the curve of the road on the southern side of the ambush site. This, I believe, was the core unit that was there all day with the clear intention of assassinating Collins and who fired the first shots of the ambush that shattered the windscreen of Collins's car but missed him. After the ambush, the three 'columns' went off in three different directions: one went to Crookstown, another went to Kilmurry and the third, comprising the assassins, retreated to 'Killeymey' (almost certainly Killumney). Later that night, Hickey claimed, they moved to east Cork and Waterford, bypassing the city.[3] This

I believe was the assassination group, heading to Youghal – against the flow of Republican traffic, so to speak – and carrying whatever casualties they may have had.[4]

Hickey, as we have seen, claimed that while most of those he made contact with deeply regretted Collins's death, there was one notable exception: 'one officer of the column was delighted. He had been active during the War of Independence and had been promised a commission in the Army. This did not come through ... and that was the reason for his bitterness.'[5] According to Hickey:

> I still continued my investigations and took a personal interest in the ambush. In fact, almost two years later I found some spent shells in the ditch and amongst the high grass on the spot where the column had ambushed the convoy. I kept them for years until my children used them as playthings when I was a Garda stationed at Newmarket-on-Fergus.[6]

But the most surprising detail Hickey reported is his claim that three Republicans had been shot dead at Bealnablath.[7] 'During the ambush the Irregulars lost some men ... this has never been known.'[8] Hickey claimed 'they left the public house to rejoin the column and in doing so three were shot'.[9] This is an astonishing claim because nobody on the Republican side seems to recollect a group of three men being shot dead – and there is no evidence of bodies being found around the site of the ambush or of anyone being buried as a result. And if they were shot, who shot them as they 'left the public house'? Yet Hickey stuck to his claim, repeating it in 1976 in an article in the *Evening Herald*.

Hickey claims that the killings took place after the men left the pub on first hearing the shooting. If this was Deasy's group in the pub, then they heard the shooting and made their way back to the ambush by the high road half a mile to the east. If they were that far away from danger, it is hard to believe that any of them could have been shot while doing so. However, if three men were shot and were to survive their wounds, then Hickey's claim would make sense in the context of the previous chapters. So we need to look at other claims that there may have been casualties on the Republican side.

Commandant O'Connell, in his account published in the *Cork Examiner* on 25 August 1922, stated that after ten minutes of the first phase of the fight, 'the Irregulars had been dislodged from their position in the hills and had sustained at least two casualties'.[10] Lieutenant Smith also claimed to have witnessed casualties on the Republican side – and stated that there was some firing and therefore enemy personnel on both sides of the road: 'One party then immediately opened fire on the attackers at both sides of the road with a Lewis gun and rifles.'[11]

> At the lower end of the road we kept on firing and after some time drove back the ambushers on the right-hand side of the road. They seemed to retreat over the top of the hill and the firing from this direction practically ceased. I went up around the brow of the hill [up the lane to Murray's farmhouse] after a little in order to reconnoitre and as far as I could see this section of the Irregulars had gone back over the hill. This gave us the opportunity to open a more intensified fire on the attackers on the other side who were concealed around the farmhouse and amongst the shrubbery and bushes across the stream. We picked off a couple of them and we could see them fall. Another was seen crossing a gap and was hit when fired upon.[12]

Both these statements, made in the days after the ambush, agree that there were Republicans on both sides of the road and that there appear to have been Republican casualties. They have been regularly dismissed as exaggeration but they might actually be true. If so, the group on the right who retreated over top of the hill were in all likelihood Liam

Deasy's party, for this is roughly the position that Deasy and Pete Kearney claimed they were in during the action. The men whom Lieutenant Smith saw being hit and falling were on the left-hand side. It is likely in this case that Smith was referring to John O'Callaghan and Jeremiah O'Mahony, who were both shot in the backside but not seriously wounded, particularly since the IRA column found O'Callaghan difficult to locate after the ambush and feared that he had been hit. But neither Smith's nor O'Connell's account finds three men being shot dead.

If such men had been shot dead on the Republican side at Bealnablath, then why would Tom Crofts, writing the following day, in internal documentation to his own commanding officer, state that they had suffered no casualties? If there had been casualties, there appears to be no reason why he would not inform his own chief. Instead, Crofts is categorical: 'our casualties were nil'.[13] The only hint from the Republican side that there may have been casualties comes from Margaret Lordan, sister of John Lordan, Vice O/C of the 3rd Brigade, who took part in the ambush and was, according to Meda Ryan, in the position described by Seán O'Connell above where a couple of men were hit. Margaret Lordan, who was from nearby Newcestown, was a committed Republican activist all through the War of Independence and Civil War period and stated in her Military Pension application that during this period she 'brought wounded men to safety' from a 'local ambush', as well as informing the IRA of enemy movements.[14] She does not state specifically that this refers to Bealnablath, but given that this was the most significant ambush in the Newcestown/Crookstown area in that summer, it is more than possible that she is referring to it. In fact, it is quite possible that John Lordan himself may have been wounded in the affray since he died at a comparatively young age only eight years later.[15]

Perhaps there is a clue to this in Crofts' statement, because in it he writes that while 'I have learned since that Ml. Collins was shot dead during the engagement' and 'our casualties were nil', he also wrote that his men claimed to have wounded 'at least three more of the enemy'. Given that they claimed they did not know that Collins had been killed until afterwards and that it was not possible to get off an aimed shot, it is hard to see how they could have known there were three further casualties on the Free State side – though there was one, Lieutenant Smith. Is it possible that, as in the case of the exploding Mauser bullet, Crofts was turning round the three casualties from one side to the other? It is possible, but we will almost certainly never find out.

17

Kerry Connections

We saw in Chapter 1 how Bobs Doherty, a Kerry IRA man returning with a fellow Republican across the fields to Kerry after the fall of Cork, chanced upon the Bealnablath ambush and left an account in which he claimed that he saw Collins being shot. This is the only Republican account that fits with what the basic forensics suggest must have happened. After stumbling upon a group of men in position on the eastern side of the road – 'I was above the road. I was covering the road' – Doherty claimed that he watched as one of them shot 'the big man' as he walked away from the convoy on the road below: 'I heard a man say: "I put two into him." That's all I know.'[1]

There is no doubt that Doherty was at Bealnablath. His commander in the Glenflesk Company of the IRA, James 'Tod' Healy, stated to the Military Pensions Board that, at the outbreak of the Civil War, Doherty 'went to Killarney Barracks and from that to Ballincollig where he was operating with a column and was at the ambush at Beal-na-Blath before returning home'.[2] This is likely again to refer to the cavalry column operating under Seán Hyde, since Doherty stated to Father Twohig that he went to Ballincollig to join a cavalry unit.[3]

But, astonishingly, Twohig found another Kerryman who also claimed that he had witnessed Collins fall. Mike

Donoghue, the Intelligence Officer of the Glenflesk Company and a neighbour of Doherty's, was also returning from Cork to Kerry. He too maintained that he saw the convoy in the valley below him and claimed that the man beside him fired off a shot that he believed might have killed Collins. This looks suspiciously like what Doherty reported, though there are differences in detail: 'We saw an army column stopped on the road below. Of course we threw ourselves down. The shooting had stopped now. There was a Whippet armoured car at the end of the line and there was a big man like he was standing on top of it looking around. The fellow next to me put up his gun and fired a shot and we saw the big man fall. I hit the gun down like that and said to him: "What did you do that for? Do you want to draw them on us?" and we skedaddled. We didn't know anything until the next day we got the *Cork Examiner* and we saw that Collins was kilt at this place, Bealnablath.'

Father Twohig believed that this was most likely the shot that killed Collins. Yet it seems rather odd that two Kerry Volunteers who were neighbours, colleagues and members of the same company could each have observed the exchange of gunfire without one acknowledging that the other was there. They surely exchanged their versions of events at some point. Twohig implies that Doherty was the man with Donoghue who fired the shot and that subsequently he may have diluted his role. Twohig further relates how the following evening a group of 'armed and weary' Kerry Volunteers visited a house at Ballyvourney where a distressed younger member of the group said: 'Yesterday one of us shot Michael Collins', to which his commander replied 'Shut up! You're talking too much.'

Twohig then further complicates matters when he relates the story of one Jimmy Ormonde, a County Waterford Volunteer who was travelling from Bandon to Cork and was approaching the ambush site from the south when he claimed his group also fired a few shots and saw 'the big man fall'.

Like Doherty, Ormonde was in the right place, south of the ambush site, to have witnessed Collins being killed. Given that these stories all emanated from emigrant Republicans in the United States, it is possible that they are all versions of the same thing. They may all be correct, but the only one for whom we have independent evidence that he was there is Bobs Doherty.[4] Indeed, Mike Donoghue's alleged colleague/shooter may, like Sonny O'Neill and Emmet Dalton, be another fall guy to distract attention from the real killer, since Mike Donoghue was well known to Florrie O'Donoghue and may even have been related to him.[5] Was this a piece of bluff to counter rumours emanating from Kerry and from emigrants in the United States that Kerry Volunteers may have had some hand in Collins's death? Mike Donoghue gave no hint as to the identity of his colleague who allegedly fired the fatal shot.

All this led Twohig to the conviction that it was a group of Kerry Volunteers who killed Collins. They certainly may have thought – like others – that they had done so. Talking to veterans in the Glenflesk area years later led Twohig to the belief that the man who shot Michael Collins was likely to be a Kerryman. 'If only Tod Healy was alive, he could tell you all,' one veteran told Twohig. This was James Healy, the captain of the company who vouched for Doherty in his pension application. However, Twohig claimed that Healy's wife had told him that Healy himself was not at Bealnablath, although the fact that he knew that Doherty was there might suggest otherwise.

Twohig also quotes a letter from Mike Donoghue's niece in which she recalled her uncle claiming in Ballyvourney in 1964 that 'he saw the man who shot Michael Collins'. This appears to suggest that what Doherty and Donoghue saw – or claimed they saw – may have been the same thing. Given that we have independent verification that Doherty was present, Doherty's version – that there were men in position on the southern end of the site when he came over the hill and that it was one of them who fired the fatal shot – has to be given preference over Donoghue's.

Given all this, is there any further evidence that Kerry Volunteers might have been there on the day and that Kerrymen were involved? Apart from reminiscences, there are some contemporary indications of the involvement of Kerry Volunteers in the affair, particularly in relation to Florrie O'Donoghue. Kerry was the main centre of IRB activity in Munster, going back to 1916 and beyond. Most of the Kerry leaders of the IRA had also been members of the IRB and were strongly anti-Treaty. As we have seen, the Free State pursued the Kerry IRB men with particular ferocity during the Civil War, especially after Collins's death. It would make sense that if O'Donoghue, himself a Kerryman and a leading IRB man, wanted to target Collins, he might use Kerry Volunteers to help him. There are grounds for believing that this may have been the case. Dick Langford of Milltown, County Kerry, described as 'the best organizer in the Division',[6] was on Liam Deasy's staff and was present at the Ballyvourney meeting at which it was decided to ambush Collins at Bealnablath. Langford was a very capable officer and had on occasion crossed the Cork/Kerry border to co-operate with Seán O'Hegarty during the War of Independence.[7] Dan Mulvihill of Kerry was acting O/C of the Division on 17 June – with O'Donoghue as his adjutant.[8]

And there may have been another Kerryman even closer to the centre of affairs. Because the man to whom, along with O'Donoghue, Tom Crofts was trying to direct correspondence during the week after Bealnablath, 'D. Cronin', may also have been a Kerryman. The Brigade had trouble tracking him down in the weeks after Bealnablath. In mid-October, in reply to another inquiry by Tom Crofts, the 1st Brigade stated that they believed Cronin might have been hiding out in the 6th Battalion area – that is to say, in the mid-Cork area – but they seemed vague about it.[9] After that, he seems to have vanished off Brigade correspondence.[10] The only 'D. Cronin' on the staff of the 1st Division was Denis Cronin of Killarney.[11] However, Denis Cronin's Military Pension application has recently been released and, while the information in it is ambiguous, it appears that he may have been serving with the IRA in west Limerick rather than mid-Cork at the time, so he is probably not the 'D. Cronin' in question.[12]

None of this is proof that any of these individuals were at Bealnablath; it merely shows that they were in the area that week. But it cannot be divorced from the many suggestions, pursued with no small amount of diligence over many years by Father Twohig, that Kerrymen were involved in some way in the death of Michael Collins. This, of course, is speculative, but it needs to be explored to the extent that it can be explored.

What can reasonably be deduced is that the man who shot Michael Collins must have been an accurate marksman, probably an army sniper. Highly trained and experienced snipers were a rarity in the IRA. The IRA's way of death was usually rough and ready: revolvers, shotguns, close-up killing. There are not too many instances of accurate sniper assassinations in the War of Independence. There was one, however; it was widely celebrated for many years – perhaps it still is – and it was carried out by a Kerryman.

This was the assassination of Major John Mackinnon, the notorious commander of the Auxiliaries, in Tralee in April 1921. Mackinnon was shot twice in the head while lining up a shot on the third green of Tralee Golf Course, having been at the top of a wanted list by the IRA for shooting dead two Volunteers around Christmas 1920. His assassin was Con Healy, a Tralee native and a former British army marksman then serving with the Kerry No. 1 Brigade of the IRA. The way the assassination was carried out has many similarities with the killing of Michael Collins, with a covering party protecting the sniper opening fire with all the weapons they had after the target went down.[13]

Healy might have been a candidate for the shooting of Collins were it not for the fact that he had died of TB some six months earlier.[14] However, there is one, albeit tenuous, link between Healy and Collins's death.

On 27 August 1922, some five days after Bealnablath, James Healy, the younger brother of Con Healy and also a well-known marksman and ex-British soldier, was dragged out of bed in Tralee by armed and masked men, along with a neighbour, John Moriarty, another ex-soldier and IRA man. Their captors claimed the men had bombed the local post office, something they denied. They were taken to a field at Balloonagh on the edge of the town and, in an eerie parallel with the attempted killing of Edgar Isherwood, shot, execution-style. Moriarty was killed; James Healy was merely wounded in the stomach and managed somehow to survive and make his way to safety. Moriarty's death was the first of the many unauthorised murders perpetrated by Provisional Government forces in County Kerry that were to blacken that theatre of the Civil War.[15]

There is little doubt that the murder of Moriarty and attempted murder of Healy were carried out by National Army men. While they went to considerable lengths to pretend that they were Republicans – and perpetuated that myth at the subsequent inquiry by giving the impression that the two men had been abducted for visiting the barracks and attempting to join the National Army – they were clearly lying. They informed Healy before he was shot that they were members of the Dublin Guard, effectively Collins's men stationed in Kerry, presumably because they expected that Healy would not live to tell the tale. Healy himself was in little doubt that they were Free State men, and said this in a sworn statement. They asked him if he was glad Collins was dead, and he said he wasn't. They said to him: 'Say your prayers. Have you any souvenir?' Healy gave them his brother Con's mortuary card. Healy's would-be assassin, though he was a few yards away and fired six shots, managed to hit him only once. Healy claimed that after being unconscious for a few minutes, he heard the shooting of Moriarty some distance away.[16]

Twohig wrote that two cars were commandeered from the Muckross estate outside Killarney and were brought to the Robbers' Glen near Glenflesk in east Kerry. He seems to imply that these cars were used to bring the assassins to Bealnablath and even names the driver of one of them as Mick Dan Paddy O'Donoghue of Coolies, Muckross (not to be confused with Mike Donoghue).[17]

There was no shortage of ex-British army marksmen fighting with the IRA in Kerry during the Civil War and who might conceivably have been at Bealnablath. Two others whom Twohig mentions were the brothers Fred and Pats Healy from near Rathmore, Florrie O'Donoghue's home town. The Healys were part of a column led by Dick Langford, who had attended the Ballyvourney meeting of 20 August, so they too are likely to have been in the area.[18]

Another possible candidate is John 'Gilpin' Griffin, an ex-gunner and well-known IRA figure from south Kerry. Griffin had been part of the IRA group that had attempted to defend the route to Cork city when Provisional Government troops landed at Passage West in early August and moved on the city.[19] Griffin, like the others, would have been moving west along with the retreating Republican forces to the area surrounding Bealnablath during the week of the ambush.

Twohig mentions one Dan O'Connor from Cloghane, Glenflesk, as the most likely candidate for the dubious honour of being 'the man who shot Michael Collins'. According to Twohig, O'Connor went on the run after Bealnablath, jumped on a train outside Killarney when he was surrounded by Free State forces, left the train at Mallow and made his way to Limerick where he was, apparently, tried in a Republican court for shooting Michael Collins and dismissed from the IRA as a result! While this may seem far-fetched, Twohig produces a strand of evidence to support it. This was the visit of a family called McNamara to Bealnablath in the 1970s.[20]

According to Twohig, they claimed that their great-uncle, one Maurice McNamara, was the judge at the Republican court at Cappamore, County Limerick, who presided over the case, before joining the Cistercian monastery at Mount Melleray. It turns out that a Maurice McNamara of Araglin, Cappamore, was indeed the judge over that court and presided at hearings in the Cappamore/Bilboa area.[21] Unfortunately, however, the period between late August and October 1922 fell into the inter-judicial period between the last of the official Republican courts and the decree for the abolition of the courts outside of Dublin, issued on 26 October.[22] The last recorded court case from Cappamore for which records survive was held on 8 June.

Local sources in Killarney, however, suggest a very different reason for O'Connor's sudden departure from the area. It appears he was involved, along with another young Volunteer, Michael Sullivan, in sniping at Free State troops on the Cork road some miles outside Killarney in early November. They came under fire from a Free State party and Sullivan was wounded. The following morning the house where the injured man had taken refuge was surrounded, and Sullivan was dragged out into the yard and shot dead by Free State troops. O'Connor, who had fled the night before, left for the United States with a question mark over the reasons for his sudden departure. This suggests that the man allegedly tried in Cappamore for shooting Michael Collins was not Dan O'Connor.[23]

None of this, of course, is proof that any of the above or indeed any Kerry IRA men were involved in Bealnablath. However, the balance of evidence, even if it is speculative, points in that direction. It will probably never be possible to identify precisely who these men were and, by extension, to identify the sniper who in all likelihood killed Michael Collins, but it seems clear that assassination was the likely manner of his death. We can say the following with a reasonable amount of certainty.

- Michael Collins was assassinated by a group put in place for that very purpose.
- Collins was not killed by a ricochet, an accidental shot by an IRA man or by a member of his own party.
- He was most likely killed by a sniper shooting from the roadside to the south of the ambush position or from behind the ditch on either side of the road as it was then.
- The most likely scenario is that the party on the bend of the road fired the first shots of the ambush which smashed the windscreen of the touring car and hit the clock on the dashboard, and that this was the original assassination attempt, which missed its target.
- Members of this group remained in place in the ensuing fight and, during a lull in the firing, began to inch their way in the direction of the convoy, which at that point would have been out of their line of vision.
- One of these men shot Michael Collins as he walked around the bend in their direction.
- One or more of these men were injured in the affray – shot by one of Collins's drivers – and required subsequent medical treatment.
- Collins was killed by a shot from a Mauser sporting rifle using a soft-nosed .416 inch bullet.[24]
- Collins was drawn specifically into the trap at Bealnablath by the promise of peace talks with his opponents on the anti-Treaty side from the time it became apparent that he was coming to visit County Cork – something nobody but the officers of the 1st Southern Division seemed to know about in advance.
- Most, but not all, of Collins's opponents were ultimately to regret his death, though that was not what they thought at the time.
- There may have been some help from within the Provisional Government forces, members of which leaked Collins's itinerary to the anti-Treatyites.

- Florrie O'Donoghue was a primary figure in all of this: meeting Collins on the morning of Bealnablath and also on the previous day, thereby pulling Collins into the trap with the promise of further meetings that evening. Furthermore, O'Donoghue, after causing much dissension in the IRB and Munster IRA over the winter of 1921/22, played both sides in the summer of 1922 and probably deliberately brought Collins to Bealnablath to enable the sentence handed down by a shadowy Republican court to have Collins executed for treason to be carried out.

- One or more Republicans were wounded at Bealnablath, which necessitated medical attention being brought to Youghal in the days after the ambush. Furthermore, one or more Republicans may have been killed there.

- A large-scale cover-up was implemented, which extended from minor matters, such as disguising the fact that Collins visited O'Donoghue's sister at the IRA headquarters in Cork city, all the way to killing anyone who knew about what actually happened at Bealnablath, including Seán Hales, the man who was liaising on Collins's behalf with the anti-Treaty forces before the ambush.

- It is unclear how much of this was known in advance to people like Liam Deasy and Liam Lynch and whether or not it was planned with their knowledge. However, if 'Flor Donoghue' and 'D. Cronin' were central to the plot, then Liam Deasy and Tom Crofts must have been aware of it, since it is to questions from Crofts as Adjutant of the 1st Southern Division that the 1st Brigade was replying in its efforts to track down O'Donoghue and Cronin after Bealnablath. Deasy's extreme reticence in his interviews with Father John Chisholm on the subject of Bealnablath suggests that he knew more than he let on in his other interviews and in his published work.

- The evidence is that there was a plan put in place by anti-Treaty elements within the IRB to have Collins executed:

more specifically by the Munster Centres of the IRB, through the offices of the 1st Southern Division, though how far this extended beyond O'Donoghue and those who attended the meeting at Ballyvourney is open to debate.

- It has not been possible to identify 'the man who shot Michael Collins'; my view is that this is a relatively minor matter compared with identifying the circumstances that brought about his death.

In summary, there is an awful lot more to the death of Michael Collins than meets the eye, especially when the eye has been deliberately blinkered for almost a century. All the evidence presented here suggests that Collins was assassinated rather than being killed by a random bullet. And yet this still leaves many unanswered questions: were others killed at Bealnablath? Who were those carried to Youghal after the ambush who were in need of medical treatment, and why were they driven by a Free State driver? Is this further evidence of collusion on the Free State side? Even if we do know who was calling for Collins's head for the crime of treason to the Republic, who exactly constituted the 'Court' that court-martialled him *in absentia*? Why was most State documentation on Collins's death destroyed? Why was it that people like Brennan-Whitmore with Free State sympathies smeared Emmet Dalton with the crime of shooting Collins while Republicans attributed the shooting to Sonny O'Neill? Was it because they were both former British army men and thus convenient scapegoats? Meanwhile, while Republicans were being hunted down and shot mercilessly all over the country, O'Hegarty was back at his job in the Cork Workhouse and Florrie O'Donoghue landed himself a nice cushy job as a rate collector in Cork.

Clearly, while I have uncovered significant new evidence, this is nothing near the full picture. However, one thing is certain: for almost a century a major cover-up has been going on over the death of Michael Collins. Trails of misleading information were put in place to cover almost every aspect of Bealnablath, from the route Collins took on the day to the timing and planning of the ambush, to the forensics of the wound in Collins's head, the positioning of the IRA men involved and the fact that, far from being a 'virtual accident', this was one of the most carefully planned and executed operations carried out by the anti-Treaty forces during the Civil War. It was, of course, the most pyrrhic of victories, since all it led to was the destruction of Republicanism until de Valera raised it from the grave a decade later, using the very philosophy that Collins had used. It was the victory that led to total defeat.

Acknowledgements

I wish to thank the following, without whom this book would not have been completed: Dick Kenny for being my sounding board during the research and for reading the manuscript; Eddie Bourke for first suggesting to me that all was not as it seemed when it came to the death of Michael Collins; Paul Maguire of Carlow Military Museum for his ballistics expertise; Donald Wood, Colum Cronin and Evelyn Nolan for their knowledge of the mid-Cork area; Jim Herlihy for his help in trying to track down the gardaí who investigated Collins's death; Rea Jordan and Michael Keating for helping me access the Emmet Dalton material; my brother Mike for drawing the maps and for making several important suggestions with regards to the ambush site; Barbara Kinsella and Orla Foley of the library at Institute of Technology Carlow, who organised a great number of inter-library loans on my behalf.

I also wish to thank the following for passing on various useful pieces of information: Philip McCarthy, Eve Morrison, T. Ryle Dwyer, Jimmie Parkes and Eunan O'Halpin. Also my colleague Brian O'Rourke for reading the manuscript and for listening to me for what seems like years going on about Bealnablath.

As ever, none of this work would be possible without the courtesy, patience and help given by archivists and librarians in the various institutions where the research was carried out. In particular I'd like to mention Gregory O'Connor of the

National Archives in Dublin who, as ever, always went the extra mile to help out. Also Brian McGee and his staff of the Cork City and County Archives, Seamus Helferty and his staff at UCD Archives, Lisa Dolan and Noelle Grothier and the rest of the staff at Military Archives, the staff of the Local Studies departments of Cork City Library and Cork County Library, and also Carlow County Library and the National Library of Ireland.

Others who helped in various ways over the past few years were Ann-Marie Byrne, Mary O'Leary, Denis Sullivan, Richie Lally, Rachel Richardson and my brother James, who first suggested the real significance of the photos taken at Bealnablath and who also suggested some useful amendments.

Access to Agnes Hurley's photographs was vital to this book. I wish to express my gratitude to her niece Mim O'Donovan and the Cork City and County Archives for making these photographs publicly available.

I also owe an enormous debt of gratitude to all those who previously wrote on Collins's death, particularly in times when it was not possible, owing to various sensitivities, even to come close to anything like the truth. Most credit in this regard must go to Father Patrick Twohig, Eoin Neeson and Tim Pat Coogan, who were not afraid to publish what they found, even when it was bound to frighten at least some of the horses, and also Meda Ryan for interviewing many of the participants and producing an accessible and fair-minded synthesis of her research.

None of this, of course, would have been possible without the support of my wife Mary and our children Áine, Grace and James, who will no doubt be greatly relieved that the uninvited guest to our house, Michael Collins, for all his good qualities, has finally moved out.

Appendix I
IRA Report on Ambush at Bealnablath

A/G, 1st Southern Div. To C/S, 24 Aug. 1922[1]

1. On Tuesday 2nd [*sic*] inst at 8.35 a party of Free Staters about 30 strong passed Beal na Blath on the road to Bandon. They were preceded by a motor cyclist and travelled in a Touring Car, Lorry and armoured car. Ml. Collins was one of the party.

2. A picked column 32 in number was mobilized and took up a position about ¼ of a mile from Beal na Blath to await their return.

3. At 6 pm we got definite information from Bandon that the party had gone to Clonakilty. At 7.45 pm we gave up hope of anything and decided to withdraw for the night.

4. Some of us had got as far as the Cross at Beal na Blath when a messenger came in great haste with information that the party had returned & were held up on the road by our Barricade.

5. Fortunately 6 of our men had not left their positions and three more managed to get back. Fire was immediately opened on the enemy by this section. The rest tried to get back to assist their comrades but were never in a position during the engagement to render any real assistance.

6. The firing was terrific; the enemy relied chiefly on his machine guns. Now and then you could hear the crack

of a rifle from our little party, who never budged an inch from their position.

7. The engagement lasted one hour. The enemy managed to remove the barricade; our men were to[o] far away to cover this part with their fire. They beat a retreat, leaving the motor cycle behind, towards Cork, our men continuing to fire on them.

8. I have since learned that Ml. Collins was shot dead during the engagement. Our casualties were nil.

9. The greatest praise is due to the 9 men who stuck to their positions under such heavy fire. They claimed to have wounded at least three more of the enemy.

10. The enemy used explosive bullets in whatever little firing they indulged in.

11. During the journey Ml. Collins travelled in the touring car and made himself very prominent.

Appendix II
Florence O'Donoghue's corrections to Eoin Neeson for his forthcoming book, *The Civil War in Ireland* (written in 1964)[2]

It took something over a week after the fall of Cork City on August 11 before anti-Treaty reorganisation at Brigade & Div[isional] level could be adjusted to a new situation. One of the many versions of the circumstances in which M.C. was killed is that it was an accident of war due to the prevailing lack of anti-Treaty military cohesion. Another is that if it was known that Collins was in the convoy it would not have been attacked. Neither version contains the entire truth.

After the evacuation of the occupied posts the anti-Treaty forces were forced to revert to the tactics which had been employed against the British, viz: attacks on convoys, on communications and on military posts. These were the only possible[?] means of furthering[?] and sustaining the struggle. In fact, that type of activity had commenced in a partly fortuitous way, before August 22. General O'Duffy's convoy had been ambushed three times during a tour of County Kerry, in an ambush at Liscarroll, Comdt. Cregan had been killed, and in a similar action at Ninemilehouse near Clonmel, Col.

F[rank] T[hornton] had been severely wounded and was the only member of his party to survive.

The immediate circumstances which resulted in the ambush at Bealnablath were that a meeting of the Brigade and Battalion officers of Cork No. 3 Brigade with officers of the 1st S[outhern] Div[ision] was called for Tuesday 22 August. The purpose of the meeting was to consider whether some honourable means could be found to end the conflict. The meeting had been called without any reference to the possibility of an ambush and without any knowledge that Collins was in the area. A few anti-Treaty officers arrived at B[ealnablath] on Monday night, 21st, the majority on Tuesday morning.

The first intimations any of these officers had that Collins was in the South was received on the morning of Tuesday, the day of the ambush. Allegations which have been made of the issue of a general order to the anti-Treaty forces to ambush the Collins convoy are completely unfounded. The only officers who could have issued ambush orders were present at B[ealnablath] and they had no knowledge before Tuesday morning of his intention to undertake a tour of the Cork posts. The sentry at Long's where some of them stayed on Monday night saw the convoy in which Collins travelled pass in the direction of Bandon on Tuesday morning. He recognized Collins and reported it. On the possibility that the party would return by the same route, it was decided to attack if it did so. The 20 to 25 officers and men available locally took up a position 400 yds from the crossroads. They were armed with rifles and revolvers only.

Appendix III
Army Report on Peace Negotiations Prior to Bealnablath[3]

On the 18th August 1922, General E. Dalton was handed terms by prominent Cork citizens, and, after consultation with his staff, agreed to communicate them to General Michael Collins:

1. A week's truce to be immediately arranged on the basis of the existing military position.
2. During this interval facilities are to be afforded to the Republican Military and Political leaders to hold a meeting to discuss the making of peace on the following lines:

    (1) Republican opposition to the Government and Parliament to be on constitutional lines.
    (2) Members of the Republican Forces who desire to return to civil life will be allowed return to their occupations without molestation or penalization.
    (3) Members of the Republican Forces who wish to join the National Army will be received therein with due recognition of rank and service.
    (4) Arms and Munitions in possession of Republican Forces will be handed over to a committee to be mutually agreed upon.
    (5) There will be a general amnesty for all political prisoners.

The above was wirelessed to General Collins, C.I.C., at Portobello Barracks, Dublin, who replied early morning of the 19th August to General Dalton requesting names of prominent citizens making the offer, and if Republican Leaders, Military and Political, agreed to the offer and if it was on their behalf.

General Dalton replied in the affirmative and gave the following names: M. Alward [sic], Frank Barrett, Frank Aiken.

Gen. Collins agreed to a meeting, and the Republican Forces supplied ([as] far as possible) General Dalton with details of land mines, mined bridges, etc., generally assuring a safe 'conduct' for the C.I.C. As the time would not allow the contacting of every outlying post, and for this reason only, an armoured car escort was included, to serve as it were both deterrent to possible attack, and, or, identification.

Appendix IV
Count Plunkett's Manifesto to the People of Ireland
Adopted at a Conference of the available Deputies of the Republican Party[4]

FELLOW COUNTRYMEN AND WOMEN:

A brazen usurpation masquerades as Constitutional Government in Ireland today with the approval of a corrupt press and the benediction of all the traditional enemies of our national liberty. Trusted men of our race, sent to London a year ago to explore possible avenues to a lasting peace, have prostituted the authority conferred upon them and arrogated to themselves an authority never conferred upon them.

A year ago, Dail Eireann, the elected Parliament of the Irish Republic, chose these Deputies [*sic*] to London in the full conviction that the English Government was not then prepared to complete an agreement which the Irish people would regard as acceptable. Each of the Delegates moreover had twice over sworn an oath of allegiance to the Republic. Their terms of reference further required them to sign no agreement in London without first submitting its final draft to Dublin. While they were in London, the President of the Republic took the occasion of a letter to His Holiness the Pope to proclaim to the world that the Irish people acknowledged no allegiance to the King of England. Finally, when the foreseen crisis was reached, the Delegates were summoned back to Dublin and instructed to be adamant on the questions of Partition and alien allegiance.

On their return to Dublin, however, the Delegates violated their oaths of allegiance, their terms of reference, their President's public declaration of the national will and his Cabinet's final instructions by voting – under threat of 'immediate and terrible war' – for a 'Treaty' which provides an alien Governor-General and an oath of allegiance to an alien king 'by virtue of common citizenship with Great Britain', invests England with permanent control of our leading strategic and commercial ports together with the right to erect military air bases in association with them and in time of war or of strained relations with other Powers to violate our neutrality by using our railways and other means of communication. The 'Treaty' also gives England complete control of all wireless and cable stations in Ireland and empowers her to establish others at her will, while denying us any similar right. Further, it involves Ireland in undefined financial obligations calculated, unless drastically handled, to lead to national insolvency, engender industrial discontent and perpetuate economic unrest and turmoil.

Finally, the signed 'Treaty' was given to the world without even being reported back to Dublin and naturally was publicly repudiated, as soon as read, by the President of the Republic, his Minister of Defence and his Minister of Home Affairs.

After an unconstitutional, unwarranted and abortive motion for the ratification of the Treaty, it was subsequently approved in Dail Eireann by a slender majority, misled by the clamour of a corrupt press, deceived by false promises of a satisfactory constitution, or weaned from their allegiance by offers of preferment and patronage. When later submitted, as requested by its own terms, for approval by the elected Representatives of Southern Ireland – a body never authorized or recognized by the Irish people – only half the entire representatives could be induced to attend, even though the 'Treaty's' advocates were now augmented, for the first time, by the Representatives of Trinity College.

At this stage English duplicity again manifested itself. The New Provisional Government, just set up by England's Lord Lieutenant to supplant the so-called 'Parliament of Southern Ireland' was denied the essential powers previously promised save through the issue of a General Election. To provide for this Election, on a hopelessly inadequate Register, a Free State Bill never referred to in the 'Treaty' or during its discussion was hurried through the British Parliament, where it was incautiously admitted that the expected effect of the Election would be disestablishment of the Army of the Republic, as the Volunteers were permanently disbanded in Grattan's day to leave the Nation utterly defenceless.

A special National Convention of the Sinn Fein Organization, mindful of the defective state of the parliamentary Register, which left at least one fourth of the qualified electorate without votes, directed in reply, that no election be held for three months. In the interval, persistent efforts of the 'Provisional Government' to seduce the Army of the Republic brought the country to the verge of Civil War. To avert this menace, a Pact was arranged between Messrs Collins and De Valera which provided amongst other things:

> That a National Coalition Panel for this Third Dail representing both parties in the Dail and in the Sinn Fein Organization be sent forward on the grounds that the national position requires the entrusting of the Government of the country into the joint hands of those who had been the strength of the national situation during the last few years without prejudice to their present respective positions ... That after the Elections the Executive shall consist of the President elected as formerly, the Minister of Defence, representing the Army,

and nine other ministers – five from each party to choose its own nominees. The allocation will be in the hands of the President ... That in the event of a Coalition Government finding it necessary to dissolve, a general Election will be held as soon as possible on adult suffrage.

This Pact was endorsed by Dail Eireann [on] May 20th, by the re-assembled Sinn Fein Convention a few days later. The Convention, which proved the Nation's shield during an anxious crisis, had no sooner dispersed in Dublin than Mr Michael Collins, Minister of Finance under Dail Eireann and Chairman of the 'Provisional Government', true to his public record, took the earliest opportunity, in the great city of Cork, to violate the Pact bearing his signature, a deed of treachery in which he had associated with him his Postmaster General, his Minister of Education and other instruments of his 'Provisional Government'. Through these and similar acts of betrayal, coupled with the unsatisfactory state of the Register and the poisonous clamour of the lying Press, the muzzled Republican Party, as anticipated, suffered a temporary reverse and Ireland after the most glorious struggle in her chequered story has suffered disastrously in prestige. The long intrigue with Under-Secretary Cope of Dublin Castle had produced an inevitable fruit: it has divested trusted men of the sense of principle and left them reckless, just as the treacherous exertions of the well-rewarded William Cope, reinforced by the exhortations of the organ of the Sham Squire, induced Reynolds to become informer against the United Irishmen in 1790.

The closing Session of the Second Dail had been announced for June 30th, the opening session of the Third Dail for July 1st. Meanwhile, the corrupt press and the selfish and unthinking section of the community claimed that the 'Agreed Election' – at which avowedly the Treaty was not an issue and the unpublished though long promised Constitution less so – gave a national mandate for a Provisional Parliament on the basis of Partition, which the whole people had indignantly repudiated. Unquestionably it gave a mandate for the declared objects of the Election, the Unification of the National Army under Coalition Government with the fairest prospects of averting Civil War. A self-seeking clique, however, has sought to circumvent the mandate by the most outrageous acts of political usurpation known to history. Two days before the final date fixed for the final session of the Second Dail and three days before that fixed for the inauguration of the Third, with its special mandate, the Minister of Defence under the Dail wantonly provoked Civil War, which the Parliament hoped to avert, by using the English Artillery of the 'Provisional Government' to bombard the Four Courts, Headquarters of the citizen soldiers who remained absolutely loyal to the Republic. The alleged reason for this bombardment was the arrest of a Free State Military Officer as a counter-blow to the previous arrest of the Republican Director of Belfast Boycott, the great Constitutional weapon against Partition which the Chairman of the 'Provisional Government' vainly tried in London to have discarded, without the previous authority of Dail Eireann or the subsequent approval of the country. The real reason for the bombardment Mr. Winston Churchill disclosed in the British Parliament the previous day when he said of the operations of Ireland's citizen soldiers in the Four Courts:

> The time has come when it is not unfair, premature, or impatient of us to make to the strengthened Irish Government and new Irish Parliament a request in express terms that this sort of thing must come to an end. If it does not come to an end, if through weakness, want of courage, or some other less creditable reason it is not brought to an end and a speedy end, then it is my duty to say, on behalf of His Majesty's Government, that we shall regard the Treaty as having been formally violated, that we shall take no steps to carry out or legalize its further

stages and that we shall resume full liberty of action in any direction that may seem proper, to any extent that may be necessary to safeguard the interests and the rights that are entrusted to us.

In meek response to this threat, uttered on the evening of June 26th, Dublin was awakened in the small hours of June 28th by the bombardment of the Four Courts, the deliberate continuance of which prevented the convening that week of Dail Eireann – old or new. The reckless bombardment was pursued after the fall of the building until the hands of its authors was stained with the blood of Cathal Brugha, bravest soldier, truest patriot of our race, the lion-hearted hero who emerged from the struggle in 1916 with more than a score of wounds, soon rallied the soldiers of the Republic and was deservedly honoured three years later as its first constitutionally elected President. Eventually he was chosen Minister of Defence and to his unostentatious courage and personal determination more than to all the efforts of our people, Ireland owes her immunity from the conscription sought to be imposed upon her by England. One of his last acts in Dail Eireannn was to invite the Chairman of the Provisional Government to abandon politics and accompany him in a crusade for the defence of our oppressed countrymen in 'Ulster'. The invitation was declined and Cathal Brugha has met his death at the hands of the champions of the 'Treaty'.

Haunted by the infamy of their guilt, the Provisional Government and the Dail Ministry – none of them now armed with National authority – issue contradictory Proclamations, try to suppress the Parliament of the Republic while continuing to employ its authority and financial resources in their lawless campaign; declare the Republican Courts irregular and unlawful, swell their mercenary army with recruits of questionable antecedents dressed in a uniform designed for the flower of Ireland's young manhood; 'prorogue' parliaments again and again, indulge in frenzied shuffles and redistribution

– in the interests of their inexperienced cliques of posts instituted for tyrants, and eventually, after the manner of all tyrannies, set up a military dictatorship while each successive day's happenings reveal more and more clearly how baseless are their pretensions to popular approval or sanction, just as the publication of the enslaving Constitution reveals to their duped soldiers the worthlessness of the promise that it would be such a document as all Republicans could subscribe to. Of their claims to the authority they thus try to usurp we may verily say in the words of a recent ecclesiastical pronouncement:

> Such a claim is a claim to military despotism and subversive of all civil liberty. It is an immoral usurpation and confiscation of the people's rights.

The Irish People, young and old, private citizens and public representatives will sustain the soldiers of the Republic – the heroic men and women who prefer death before dishonour – in their struggle against these new instruments of England in Irish garb as they sustained them against England's Black and Tans through the dark night of the recent Terror.

GEORGE NOBLE COUNT PLUNKETT, Chairman
SEAN T. O CEALLAIGH, Secretary.
July 15th 1922

Appendix V
Laurence Ginnell's 'Legal' Case against the Signatories of the Treaty, July 1922[5]

MR GINNELL: In order to substitute impartial justice for vituperation and its natural consequences, I propose that the Supreme Court of the Republic, recently rendered inactive, be revived in full power to compel the production of witnesses and evidence, to try Arthur Griffith, Michael Collins and Eamonn Duggan, members of Dail Eireann, on the charge of HIGH TREASON to be substantiated under the following headings:

1. Having on the sixth day of December 1921 and subsequently wilfully acted as mortal traitors to the Republic of Ireland which they had on the sixteenth day of August 1921 solemnly sworn to support and defend against all enemies, foreign and domestic.
2. Having for this purpose by trickery got themselves appointed as delegates to ascertain what final terms British ministers offered for settlement with Ireland, and to report to Dail Eireann the terms so ascertained.
3. Having, when so appointed, disregarded the limitations and without reporting to Dail Eireann, and without authority to sign, signed British terms, thereby violating their trust and jeopardising the Republic and the Nation.
4. Having so signed worse terms than those which they knew

that Dail Eireann had already unanimously rejected, and would therefore in the absence of some new complication again reject.

5. Having wilfully by their signature and by prematurely publishing their personal satisfaction and without waiting for the judgment of Dail Eireann or its cabinet, so complicated the situation that humanly speaking it was no longer possible to get the judgment of either Dail Eireann or the nation, on the merits of either the document they had signed or their conduct in signing it.

6. Having traitorously usurped authority to accept, and traitorously accepted, in the name of the nation terms involving the extinction of Irish nationality, the partition of Ireland, the submergence of its parts in the British Empire, subject to that empire's naval, military, economic and financial control and to the cost of its universal aggression to an indefinite amount to be fixed by the British, with an Irish army under British command to hold Ireland within the British Empire.

7. Having signed the document voluntarily and then applied the British threat of 'immediate and terrible war' as the only alternative to force their unwilling colleagues to sign.

8. Having afterwards admitted that the said threat was bogus and that its sole use was to obtain the signatures of their colleagues and the consent of the Irish people to their treachery.

9. Having by their conduct broken that solidarity of the Irish nation which had commanded the respect of the world, forced Britain to call a truce and, but for the treachery, made Ireland's sovereign independence an immediate moral certainty.

10. Having undermined the fidelity and broken the solidarity of the IRA, which while solid had been the efficient and esteemed instrument of our glorious progress and made us masters in our own country.

11. Having, after their status as ministers had lapsed through the general election, prevented Dail Eireann from assembling to elect ministry.

12. Having, without any legal authority whatever, in obedience to British ministers, without the consent of Dail Eireann, wantonly armed, paid and incited one section of the IRA, with English help, to wage in reality 'immediate and terrible war' on the other section, to the delight of all the enemies of Ireland, foreign and domestic, the destruction of our prestige throughout the world, the loss of many precious lives and limbs, the sufferings of numerous dependents and the diminution of our much-needed resources by the destruction of immense property which innocent civilians will be called upon to make good.

13. Considering, as Irish ministers after they had lost that status, with British ministers in all this, and in other ways to be proved on the trial, to perpetuate British domination in Ireland and to weaken Ireland's power of resisting British aggression.

14. Doing all this in direct violation of the Republican policy which the accused persons had been parties to formulating and had sworn to pursue, thereby becoming perjured traitors to the Republic of Ireland.

15. Having, as Irish ministers after they had lost that status, on the thirteenth day of July 1922, in obedience to British ministers illegally purported to dissolve the Supreme Court of the Irish Republic without the consent of Dail Eireann which had created that Court and which alone had power to dissolve it and illegally purported to revive the jurisdiction of the British Courts in Ireland.

16. Having in the seven months since they thus usurped power gone from bad to worse, brought the nation which they found united and triumphant into domestic antagonism and chaos, illegally censored truth out of the Press and allowed only malicious falsehood to reach the public, illegally broken into dwelling houses at

dead of night to the terror of their occupants, marked Republicans specially to be shot or maltreated while themselves pretending to be Republicans and given such licence to criminality as has brought our country to its present disgraceful condition:

WHEREFORE, I propose that the said Arthur Griffith, Michael Collins and Eamonn Duggan be now arrested and kept in safe custody pending adjudication on these charges.

Appendix VI
The Real Story of the Beal na mBlath Ambush by John Hickey[6]

Part 1[7]

Michael Collins, Commander-in-Chief, arrived in Mallow, Co. Cork on 19th August 1922 on a tour of inspection. On that night he reached Cork city. He had a two-fold purpose: inspection of military posts and a search for peace. It was arranged that he should meet Mr. de Valera and Mr. Childers. By a strange coincidence both these men were in West Cork at that time.

The intermediary was Canon Tracy of Crookstown[8] who had arranged a tentative meeting, although a place had not been decided. On the evening of 20th when Michael Collins arrived in Cork he made arrangements to meet Canon Tracy between three and four the following day on the way back from the inspection of Macroom Barracks.

The Irregulars received this information and planned an ambush in Farran because that was the route Collins was taking on the morning. They mined the road, and trees were already cut but held with wire. The column waited to about four [o'clock] in Farran but Collins did not return to visit Canon Tracy on that evening. While in Macroom, Michael Collins received a phone message; it asked him to return to the Imperial Hotel in Cork as an important dispatch had arrived which could not be disclosed over the telephone.

I spoke to the officer who received that phone message and it was that Fionan Lynch, a Government Minister, was on his way from Dublin with certain peace proposals. These were to be placed before de Valera and Childers at the peace meeting which had yet to be arranged.

Much speculation still surrounds the circumstances in which the Irregulars received their information. How they achieved this is very important and crucial to the whole tragedy and my investigation unearthed the following facts: Canon Tracy's housekeeper was told on August 20th by the Canon that visitors could be expected on the following day. A curious woman, she wanted to find out who were the important guests, so the Canon told her. In preparation for the guests, the housekeeper had to buy extra food and refreshments. To do so, she went into the village of Crookstown. She entered a certain shop to purchase the groceries and started to talk about the great Michael Collins coming on a visit to Canon Tracy. It was a licenced premises and three Irregulars drinking at the bar overheard the conversation. From this information, the ambush for Farran was arranged for the 21 August.

From investigations, I have learned that the ambush planned for Farran was to be a spectacular kidnap attempt with Michael Collins as the victim. The trees were cut two-thirds of the way through and held with wire staples, the purpose of this being to cut off the car carrying Collins so as to facilitate an easy kidnap bid. But as we now know, Collins did not visit Canon Tracy that day.

When the Collins convoy failed to pass through Farran, the Irregulars dispatched a scout to Cork to find out the reason. He contacted a girl who was a waitress in Hoskins Hotel, Prince's Street; she was sympathetic to the Republican cause and in turn went to another waitress in the Imperial Hotel, to try to discover the movements of the convoy on the following day, 22 August.

The waitress found out the information from some troops who were drinking at the hotel bar and also discovered their destination and the time of departure from Cork. This information was then conveyed to the Commander of the column in Crookstown where the Irregulars were billeted. The Irregulars were now in possession of the vital moves Michael Collins would make on that tragic day. The visit to Canon Tracy, which Collins failed to make on 21 August, was now definitely arranged for 22 August. This was relayed to Canon Tracy by a message sent to Crookstown Post Office from an officer of the Cork garrison. The Irregulars also knew of the visit for on that morning Canon Tracy's housekeeper again entered the village of Crookstown and had a conversation with the owner of the public house. She revealed that Michael Collins was definitely coming and that the Canon had planned a four o'clock lunch.

As the Collins convoy slowly departed from Cork city on 21 August a member of the Cork Civic Patrol who was on Washington St corner, told the Army motorcycle scout, Lt. Smith, that the road to Crookstown was blocked. This was the road that the convoy intended to take but now they had to re-plan the route. But now on 22 August Michael Collins continued the Macroom inspection and then went to Clonakilty, Rosscarbery and Skibbereen. At two o'clock the convoy reached Rosscarbery, the area where Collins was born. He took time out from his crowded journey to visit a number of childhood friends in the village.

Michael Collins then left for Skibbereen, completed his inspection, and at 5.15 set off again for Rosscarbery where he met more friends and allowed the troops to enter a public house. At this time he was in the final stage of his journey. An old friend of his, Freddie Callinan, owned the pub. Here Michael Collins had one pint of Guinness with the time now around half-past five.

Being in the countryside where he was born, Michael Collins left the pub and talked with several people while on a short walk with some of his officers. While the troops were still in the pub a disagreement arose; some soldiers were the Dublin Guards and others were local troops on escort duty. The row arose over McPeake [sic], known as 'Jock the Scotsman', who took a bottle of whiskey off the pub shelf. McPeake was the gunner on the convoy, and he was involved in a heated argument, until one of the officers separated the factions.

Michael Collins was not aware of this incident as he was visiting an ex-RIC man who was a friend of the family since their house had been burned down by the Black and Tans. During the discussion Michael Collins revealed that he was on his way to Canon Tracy and that he had high hopes of peace talks within a few days as he was to meet with Mr. de Valera and Childers before returning to Dublin. 'I wish to God it was all over,' said Collins. That ex-RIC man later told me during my investigations that although Collins appeared to be in a good mood, something overshadowed his mind and by the way he acted, the man felt that Collins was worried.

Back at the pub the drinking continued and at 7.30 when the troops left, some of them had a good deal of drink taken. The convoy set out on the road for Crookstown where Michael Collins was due to call on the Canon. On the way there ... the convoy would have to pass through Beal na mBlath ...

Part 2[9]

It was a clear Tuesday evening when Michael Collins set out to call on Canon Tracy, who was arranging a meeting to discuss peace. As the convoy lurched along that narrow Co. Cork road the thoughts of Michael Collins must surely have examined all that had happened during the previous few hours. He had departed from the Imperial Hotel in Cork city shortly after 6 o'clock that morning to continue his inspection of the Macroom Military Post.

He travelled the Cork road as far as Donniskey. Before arriving there the convoy passed through Ballytrasna where they had removed an obstruction off the road. When the

Michael Collins convoy reached Donniskey, it stopped and enquired from some farmers standing outside the co-operative store the way to Bandon. There was a blacksmith's forge beside the stores. A driver of one truck asked the blacksmith if he know anything about engines as it was overheating. So the blacksmith looked at the engine and filled the radiator with water.

One of the soldiers bought a bottle of lemonade in the co-operative store and asked the best route to Bandon. He was directed to go into Kilmurry, turn left and go right because the other road was blocked. When the convoy reached Kilmurry, it went straight ahead, and nearly as far as Coppeen crossroads, and there they were directed how to reach Bandon. So therefore the convoy by-passed Beal na mBlath on the morning of the 22nd and came nearer to Enniskeane. It was around 12 noon when the convoy arrived in Bandon. From there Michael Collins set out for Clonakilty, Rosscarbery and Skibbereen. However, all the movements of Collins had been noticed by Irregular scouts. These had been watching the convoy all the time. The Irregulars had scouts in Kilmurry village and these reported back to the main column at Beal na mBlath that Collins had passed on his way to Bandon.

The main flying column was in position since nine o'clock on that morning at Beal na mBlath waiting for Collins. We know that the Irregulars had received this information the previous night from the waitress in the Cork hotel but the Collins convoy by-passed Beal na mBlath on that tragic morning. The Irregulars also knew that Michael Collins was due to call on Canon Tracy between three and four o'clock that day, so they waited to ambush the convoy on the return journey. The scene was now set for one of the greatest tragedies of the Civil War. The Irregulars lay in wait, knowing that Michael Collins would have to pass by Beal na mBlath. Michael Collins journeyed through his native Cork and talked with old friends. Canon Tracy waited hopefully …

At this point the tall and aloof figure of Eamon de Valera enters the story. The facts are that there was a split in the IRA which arose following a July meeting in Tipperary. De Valera wanted peace – to make terms. He was supported by Dan Breen. [Liam] Lynch and the others who could be described as 'hardliners' wanted to fight. De Valera explained that it was useless to continue as the Government was getting stronger and had more troops, with the result that the IRA would be beaten into pockets. Therefore de Valera contended it would be wise to come to terms.

De Valera was brought to Beal na mBlath for the purpose of boosting the morale of the Irregulars because there was a certain amount of friction between the three flying columns. This arose because some men wanted to leave the columns and in order to unify the local commanders de Valera was brought in to speak to them. I have this from the men who were in the column at the time.

De Valera had no knowledge of the ambush taking place. Another thing I can disclose now is bound to cause some controversy. Certain elements in the IRA were trying to discredit de Valera because they were trying to break his leadership – and it almost worked. This is fact and people never realised or knew what happened. This is from the men who were there and is borne out by documents later recovered during my investigation.

Childers was in the Bantry area at the time and he met de Valera, who had already arranged peace talks with Collins. These talks were on the way – he knew about the peace talks and an arrangement was made to meet Collins on 23 August. Canon Tracy was involved in this meeting. The Canon had been in contact with Michael Collins, Mr Cosgrave and Fionan Lynch. Canon Tracy often talked to me and reading between the lines I came to the conclusion that he was acting more or less for the Bishop. The Canon was also in contact; all was arranged through certain channels. Both sides were confident of having a meeting on 23 August and this is borne out by what Collins said to Fred Callinan in Rosscarbery before he set out for Beal na mBlath and death.

We have established that the officers of the flying column knew about the Beal na mBlath ambush, although some of the men had heard nothing of the plan. There were around 50 men lying in wait. De Valera came into the area about 7 o'clock on the evening of 21 August with the intention of inspecting these men. De Valera did not know the area as he had never travelled there before but on this evening before the ambush he was driven on a side car accompanied by four men. One of these was the commander of the flying column. He was conveyed to the house of a farmer called Sullivan who later gave me an amount of information. The Sullivan farmhouse was about two and a half miles from Beal na mBlath. De Valera and his party had tea in Sullivan's and were joined later by three other men and they had discussions. At 8.39 de Valera left with the commander of the flying column and he was then introduced to all of the officers. He did not inspect the entire column as the men were billeted in different houses; some were in Kilmurry village drinking; more were in Beal na mBlath and others in Crookstown.

De Valera, accompanied by three officers, went to another farmhouse in Poulanargid which was nearer to Beal na mBlath and stayed there for the night. And to prove that, the woman of the house showed me the bed in which de Valera slept on the night before the ambush. He was given breakfast in the morning and left about 9.30 by which time most of the column had gone to Beal na mBlath to wait in ambush for Collins, because they had instructions from the previous night to be in position. The men who had stayed in Sullivan's house met de Valera that morning and went to Long's Public house in Beal na mBlath. They were taken into what was called the 'tap room' with the time now being around 10.30am. They were inside in that room and the door was closed. During my investigations, I spoke to Mrs Long and the following, in her own words, is what she told me:

She took in several drinks and then one man came out and asked her if she could provide a meal. She did. Some of the men of the column came in, she did not know who they were, and had drinks in the bar. Mrs Long also told me during my investigations that at one point she heard knocking coming from the tap room. She thought the men were calling for drinks and opened the door. Mr de Valera was standing up with some papers in his hand. She sensed there had been an argument and heard de Valera say: 'I do not agree.'

As I have already said: the Irregular scouts were out and had noticed the movements of the Collins convoy. The scouts now came to Beal na mBlath with this information. At this time, one of the scouts came into the pub and knocked on the tap room door, inside which de Valera and other officers were having discussions. One of the officers came out ... the scout said: 'Collins is in Rosscarbery'. The officer immediately put his finger to his lips cutting off the scout's words. This action of the officer's was noticed by Mrs Long behind the pub bar. I was thinking afterwards when I discussed this incident with Mrs Long that it could have been possible that the officer did not want to let de Valera know of the Collins ambush. Mrs Long agreed with this and that it seemed that some officers were shielding information that Collins was in the area from de Valera.

The ambush was expected to take place anytime between three and four o'clock because the Irregulars already knew of Michael Collins' appointment to meet Canon Tracy. De Valera and his party then left the pub between two o'clock and half past and went on to Watergrasshill, bypassing Cork city. The commander of the column stayed behind in Beal na mBlath, waiting for Michael Collins. The Irregulars decided to barricade the road at a spot about half a mile from the pub.

While this preparation was in progress the man who was to be the victim of the ambush was meeting friends in the area where he had been born. Michael Collins was in Clonakilty and Sam's Cross, where he invited his troops into his cousin's pub for a drink. On the way to Rosscarbery the Commander-in-Chief passed his old home which had been burned down by the Black and Tans. After his lunchtime visit to Rosscarbery, Michael Collins left for Skibbereen. He left there after inspecting the post and journeyed back to Rosscarbery arriving at 6.30 in the evening where he stood the troops another drink in Fred Callinan's pub. Here Michael Collins was warned of the Beal na mBlath ambush.

This dramatic but unheeded warning came about because two farmers who were drawing lime from a quarry near Beal na mBlath had been prevented from passing on the road by the obstruction placed there by the waiting Irregulars. The two farmers were coming from Castlemore Lime Quarries. They were both from the Newcestown area and would have been able to pass through Beal na mBlath to reach home. When they arrived at the Pass of the Flowers [Bealnablath], there had been an obstruction on the road. The time would have been around noon. They removed the old cart from the road and in doing so became involved in a heated argument with members of the Irregulars who were near the obstruction. Armed men replaced the obstruction on the road.

One of the men was a distant relative of Collins and when he reached home sent his son to Fred Callinan's pub with word of the ambush. Fred Callinan received the message from the boy and when the convoy arrived told Collins of the ambush. But the Commander-in-Chief was not worried and shrugged off the warning. 'There's no fear ... they won't do anything ...' It would have been around six o'clock when Collins was told of the ambush.

At that time in Beal na mBlath, the Irregulars, after a wait which began at 9 o'clock that morning, were now tired and hungry. Slowly they began to move away, convinced that Collins would not arrive.

Now as the Collins convoy lurched along towards Beal na mBlath a mist began to descend on the valley. Up ahead, the motorcycle scout, Lt. Jack Smith, kept his eyes on the narrow road. He was 100 yards or so in front of the construction truck which was followed by Collins's touring car. Behind the car came another truck and taking up the rear was the armoured car, the Slievenamon.

The Irregulars had by half-past six received no information from their scouts. Most of the column then moved on; they were tired; they were there all day. Some went to Crookstown, some went to Kilmurry and another section moved on to Killeymey [Killumney?]. They were moving to East Cork and Waterford. Late at night they would by-pass Cork city because there was an arrangement with another column to ambush Collins on the Fermoy/Cork road near Watergrasshill on 23 August.

About 15 men remained in position at Beal na mBlath. As they were about to move at around 8 o'clock or half eight, two of them went down to the main road and pushed the cart into the side. Fate intervened in the form of a donkey and cart and it is quite possible that but for the action of this donkey the ambush would not have happened. There was a carter, who had a donkey and cart and he was delivering stout to Long's pub. After doing so he went inside for a drink. While he was inside the donkey wandered along the road, feeding on the grass margin. The cart was out on the road as the donkey walked. Lt. Smith's motorcycle roared along the mist wet road; the Irregulars were leaving their positions; the donkey was feeding on the grass margin.

In the dull summer's evening a farmer walked his dog; a few soldiers dozed in the convoy winding its way along narrow roads; Michael Collins raised a rifle to his knee; Lt. Smith rounded a bend and screeched to a halt. In the nearby field the farmer walking his dog heard the throb of engines fill the evening. He watched the motorcycle and convoy come round the bend and then he heard the shots. The beautiful sounding but insignificant Beal na mBlath was about to stamp itself on Irish history ...

Part 3[10]

The farmer in the field overlooking the valley saw the convoy trucks reverse back and soldiers, rifles at the ready, leap out to commence return fire. He was the only independent witness we had but after a few minutes he became frightened and left the scene.

It was now becoming dark and the shooting continued. Michael Collins and some officers worked their way back toward the armoured car. According to one of the Irregulars to whom I spoke the exchange went on for about twenty minutes and then the Irregulars decided to retreat. An officer and four Irregulars were left to cover the retreat of the other men. There was a lull in the fighting and I will give the words of the man who shot Michael Collins exactly as he told me.

'It was becoming dark and from my position I could see the turret of the armoured car looking up out of the mist. I aimed at it and emptied my magazine.' It was one of these bullets which glanced off the armoured car and killed Michael Collins.

In the rearguard there was a Kerryman, a man from the borders of Cork and Limerick and three Corkmen. The man who fired the fatal shot never told the others. It was only at a later stage that he confided in other people who were not at the ambush. He was a Corkman and he remained active in the Irregulars. I was the first man to find out who shot Collins because nobody knew exactly – there were so many mentioned and so many boasted that they had shot Collins that the truth became clouded. But from investigations, they were all eliminated. I believe this man is still alive. During the ambush the Irregulars lost some men. This has never been known.

The Irregulars retreated, the shooting died down and Michael Collins lay dying on the narrow road. Peace returned to the valley as shocked officers lifted their dead Commander-in-Chief into the touring car and prepared to take the nightmare road back to Cork.

The five men of the rearguard party departed from Beal na mBlath and re-joined the column in Crookstown, still unaware that they had shot Michael Collins.

The convoy slowly moved away from the ambush site leaving behind the motorcycle of Lt. Smith, who had been wounded. After half a mile it reached Long's pub. Here an officer went inside and asked for a cloth to wipe the blood from the face of Collins. Another soldier requested water for one of the engines. They revealed that Michael Collins had been shot dead.

Sitting in the pub were some Irregulars and, though members of the column, they had not taken part in the ambush. They set out with the startling information to tell the column commander. The convoy was stopped outside Long's pub at about 9.30 when it left and drove to Crookstown. Before reaching the village the convoy came across three or four men standing at the entrance of Bellmont Mills and from them an officer in the convoy asked the way to Cork and where to find a priest. One of the men said that the nearest priest was Canon Tracy. Another told them the best way to Cork was to call to Cloghdubh and that a curate was there also. Another officer asked how would they know the house, to which a man told them to stop at the chapel. The convoy drove through the village of Crookstown and did not call on Canon Tracy. The reason for this is that no one knew of the secret meeting arranged by the Canon. They did not call on his house because it would bring them out of their way.

As the convoy passed through the village, some Irregulars came out of a public house, the Irregulars did not know it was Collins's convoy; they watched it pass, unaware that Collins had been shot. The convoy reached the outskirts of Crookstown and came to a junction: one road led to Farnanes and the other to Cloghdubh. They met a man at the cross. He lived at Castlemore and they asked him where they could find a priest. He directed them to go on the straight way.

The convoy arrived at Cloghdubh and pulled up outside the church. There was a shop on the right hand side and two men stood outside the church gate. They asked the men where the priest could be located. One of the men accompanied a soldier to the door of the curate's house and knocked. It was opened by the housekeeper. I will give you what she said in her own words:

'A soldier in uniform asked if the priest was inside, as if he wanted him to attend a soldier who was dying. He did not mention his name. I told him to wait and I called the priest – Fr. Tim Murphy. The priest came out to the convoy with the soldier and civilian. I will tell it now as the priest told me: "I went out with the soldier, the night was dark, it was around 10.45 and the soldier stood around. I was shown where the soldier lay. He was on the back seat of an open car. His head was lying on an officer's lap. One of the soldiers brought a carbide lamp and shone it into the dead soldier's face. The young officer cradled the head of the soldier. He was a very young officer and in the light I saw tears stream down his face." The priest gave absolution and it was only then that he was told the dead soldier was Collins. The priest told them to wait until he went to the house for the oils to anoint Collins. But when he returned the convoy was gone.'

One of the men who had stood at the church gate later told me that he heard an officer say: 'That so-and-so priest is not returning. You better drive away.' While the soldiers were waiting for the priest and while he gave absolution, some soldiers entered the shop and were given a bucket of water for the engine which was causing trouble. The convoy would have been stopped for around twenty minutes. Rumour still surrounds this episode and it is possible that the driver or officer misunderstood the request of the priest.

The convoy moved on, travelling through the village of Aherla and to Kilmurry where other members of the flying column were in a pub. They still did not know of the death of Collins. The convoy went to the Macroom railway bridge which was blocked so the convoy took to a narrow laneway and reached the Carrigrohane road, leaving the truck which was causing trouble behind.

The convoy arrived at the corner of Washington St/Grand Parade, Cork around 1.30 am on 23 August. They met two members of the Cork Civic Patrol and they accompanied the convoy to Shanakiel Hospital. This now would have been about two o'clock in the morning. In the hospital, Collins was examined and anointed. It has been said that Collins did not receive the rites of the Church. This is not so and Fr. Murphy was wronged.

The position now is that the convoy has reached Cork, Collins is dead in hospital, de Valera has gone to Watergrasshill and the rest of the column members are in the countryside. The way the Irregulars found out about the death of Collins is interesting and I doubt if it ever before has been revealed.

One of the column commanders was in Crookstown. He was the man with complete control of the columns. He was in a public house with other members when three or four men arrived from Long's pub at Beal na mBlath. These men had been in the pub when the convoy called asking for a cloth to wipe the blood from the face of Collins. They told the commander that Collins had been shot. At first the commander doubted the news. Three of the officers held a top level discussion in view of the information and decided the best thing to do would be to send a message to Mr. de Valera who had moved to Watergrasshill. They appointed a man to go with the message, which was both written and verbal. This man received instructions to make sure that when he arrived in Cork that Collins was dead. The messenger was accompanied by another man, who later returned to Crookstown and informed the commander of the column that Collins was indeed dead.[11]

In the middle of the night, unarmed and on bicycles, they journeyed through the sleeping countryside. They arrived in Cork and went to the hospital and found out from a nurse that Collins was dead. There were a large number of people in the hospital and the two Irregulars were unnoticed. The original messenger then set out for Watergrasshill – Collins was dead and he had to tell de Valera. A few hours before dawn on 23 August the messenger approached the house where de Valera was staying; he was stopped and checked by a guard. The messenger from Crookstown was accompanied by a local Irregular [and] they were stopped. The messenger told the news but the guards did not believe him. Eventually he convinced them to let him see de Valera to personally deliver the message and the following I will give in his own words as told to me during my investigations:

'I was not allowed to go beyond the door. The guard went inside. There was another man in the kitchen. This man when he heard the message went and woke up de Valera. One of the men lit a candle. It was now around four o'clock in the morning.'

De Valera was told that a messenger was waiting for him. The messenger entered the kitchen as de Valera came downstairs. He was told verbally by the messenger.

'It's not true. Where and when did it happen?' asked a shocked de Valera.

The messenger gave the details and then the other man handed the written note from the column commander in Crookstown. De Valera took the note and slowly walked to the table on which stood a lone candle. The candle threw out light in eerie rings about the kitchen; the tall and aloof figure of Eamon de Valera looked nearer. He read the note, then shook his head and said: 'What a tragedy.'

Part 4[12]

In the light of a flickering candle set on the kitchen table of a Co. Cork farmhouse Eamon de Valera learned of the Michael Collins ambush. After a long night journey through the sleeping countryside a messenger reached Watergrasshill and gave the tragic news to de Valera. The messenger returned the way he had come and on the evening of 23 August reported back to his column commander in Crookstown that the mission was completed.

National reaction was swift and only in death did a divided people come together and mourn a dead soldier. The Capital prepared to receive Michael Collins who only ten days previously had walked behind the hearse of Arthur Griffith, resplendent in his uniform of Commander-in-Chief.

The man who killed Michael Collins was strangely silent. No boast came from his lips. Instead a deep sorrow overwhelmed him and for months he kept his secret. At the time many rumours were circulating and I agree with the late admission of Mr Con Crowley that he himself did not shoot Michael Collins. The fatal shot came when most of the column had [been] dismissed. Mr Crowley was at that moment in Long's pub enjoying a quiet pint of stout. The painstaking investigation led to the man who did shoot Michael Collins. Later he admitted all to me: 'The mist was coming down and I saw the turret of the armoured car and a figure. I aimed and emptied my magazine. I was the last to fire.'

De Valera left Watergrasshill on the morning of 23 August and moved on, I think, to a place called Donoughmore. But once I had accounted for his movements up to and after the ambush this satisfied the terms of reference of the investigation.

The column was now in disbandment – some men had left for the West Cork/Kerry border and others went to Limerick and Tipperary. The whole country knew Collins was dead and looking back on that tragic Tuesday I noticed that Collins and de Valera had a strange thing in common. Both of them had very little money on them. Collins had stood his men a drink at Sam's Cross but de Valera never bought a round in Long's pub, but maybe that was because he did not drink himself.

The Irregulars did drink but contrary to rumour at the time a certain gathering was not by way of celebrating the death of Michael Collins. This took place on 23 August at a pub in the village of Aherla where members of the local flying column stopped after leaving Beal na mBlath. It has been said that the man who shot Collins was in the pub. This is not so. He was not there. In fact, this man regretted the shooting of Collins but it was not a question of being filled with remorse. It was an ambush and when a man fires a gun it is to kill but of course he regretted the death of Collins whom he admired as a man.

At the end of the investigation I wrote out the name of the man who shot Michael Collins and placed it separately in a sealed envelope and sent it with the report to the Government. I have promised that man who is still alive and living in Cork city that I will not reveal his name. If, however, he contacts me and now decides with the passage of time that his name can be revealed I will do so.

After the ambush the rumours were rife. Four main theories were advanced as to how Collins was shot. The first, it was alleged that de Valera had shot him; second, [that] the armoured car gunner McPeake [*sic*] had shot Collins; third that Collins had been shot by one of his own officers; and fourth, that he had been accidentally shot. Our six months' investigation eliminated all these rumours and discounted the theories put forward. The Government of the day took no action against the man who shot Michael Collins but I feel myself that the main purpose of the investigation was to discover the whereabouts of de Valera during the ambush.

I believe Eamon de Valera knew nothing of the ambush, having traced his footsteps on those days. I spoke to all the people who played a part in the last hours of Michael Collins and even Mrs Long at Beal na mBlath offered me the cup, saucer, plate, knife and spoon which de Valera used when he had a meal in her pub a few hours before the ambush. I also became a friend of Canon Tracy, who after the death of Collins spoke out against 'the violent men'. Shortly after the ambush a military post was established in Crookstown. In retrospect, if only it had been there before Collins was to visit Canon Tracy, the Commander-in-Chief might still be alive.

During the investigation I received information about the missing motorcycle which had been left behind by the Collins convoy after the ambush. We found it in a hayshed about three miles from Beal na mBlath. The 'S' Branch from Bandon also conducted a general search and some rifles were also found. A letter from Liam Lynch to the commander of the ambush flying column was discovered among other documents. It referred to the ambush and said it was a pity that Collins was not taken alive, presumably to bargain for favourable peace terms. It also criticized the column commander with the words: 'you should not have allowed the column to attack at that hour without your being present'.

As I have already outlined, the commander and the major section of the column waiting in ambush at Beal na mBlath had left, thinking that Collins would not return on the Crookstown road. The letter from Lynch also said: 'It's unfortunate he was shot and Dan Breen is very upset.' Dan Breen was on the Irregular side but I think he was not taking an active part. Ending the letter Lynch said: 'You will be notified of a conference at a later date and this matter will be fully discussed.'

The Army also held an investigation into the ambush. One of the reasons for this was that an Army officer was suspected of leaking information to the Irregulars. He was stationed in the Cork garrison and confirmed the movements of Collins to the Irregulars. The Army investigation failed to unearth the mysterious officer, although I heard some years later that he had been dismissed.

Suspicion of being involved in the Irregulars was also cast on the convoy gunner McPeake [*sic*], known as 'Jock the Scotsman', especially when he deserted. He was brought back from Scotland to Cork in 1923 to face charges of alleged larceny of the armoured car Slievenamon. He was interviewed about the ambush and I believe he is still alive. Later during private investigations I spoke to Army experts and they finally discounted the possibility that Collins could have been shot by the machine gun. The range was so close that it would have blown his head off. It has also been established that Collins was alive until the last shots were fired. Michael Collins was also near the armoured car and 'the man' fired the last shots, covering the retreat of the other members of the column.

One officer of the column was delighted. He had been active during the War of Independence and had been promised a commission in the Army. This did not come through, and that was the reason for his bitterness.

I still continued my investigations and took a personal interest in the ambush. In fact, almost two years later I found some spent shells in the ditch and amongst the high grass on the spot where the column had ambushed the convoy. I kept them for years, until my children used them as playthings when I was a Garda, stationed at Newmarket-on-Fergus. My own life had a strange parallel with the life of Michael Collins. I was stationed where I first met him, at William St. Barracks, Limerick and I was stationed where he was born. I was the first Garda into Crookstown near where he died and I was also posted to Mountjoy, near his grave in Glasnevin. In 1925 I left Crookstown and was posted to Garda H.Q. I spent two years in Rosscarbery and still continued to speak to people who were involved in the ambush and discovered further information.

I came to Limerick in 1956 and five years later retired from the Gardaí and stayed in the city. I was born in Irremore, Lixnaw, Co. Kerry. At the time of my investigations there was nothing to mark the place where Collins died. There was only a little wooden cross – someone put the cross there. In 1924 a limestone cross was erected. When the base was put down it was knocked. After this incident I and other members of Crookstown station party had to do night duty, from 10.00pm to 7.00am, for a period of eight months before and after it was erected.

Last month, for the first time since I investigated the ambush, I went back to visit the scene. The place had changed completely. It brought back many memories. Many was the cold night I spent there and nobody with me. We never knew who moved the base of the first limestone cross, but we had suspicions but could not prove it.

I would say if Collins had not been shot peace would have come within a fortnight. I do know this. Part of the message that Collins received was unconditional surrender. This message came from the Government. They wanted unconditional surrender. An Army officer told me that Collins wanted no conditions, only peace, something similar to the 1921 Truce. That was the day when the people were united; there was no bitterness; it was 11 July 1921. Now fifty years after the death of Michael Collins, when for the first time he had been honoured by the Army, I would like to see one day of mourning for all those who died. I would suggest a National Day of Mourning for the 11 July as on that day in 1921 all the people were united. That was the day when the people came together and surely that is not too much to hope for after 50 years of divided bitterness.

'The Real Story of the Beal na mBlath Ambush' will be told by Mr. Hickey in book form. The book will also contain some of his experiences and will be called: 'Forty-Five Years a Garda'.

Four years later John Hickey was interviewed by Martin Brennan of the Evening Herald. *In this interview Hickey reiterated many of the points he made in the* Limerick Weekly Echo *articles, including the claim that three of the attacking party at Bealnablath were shot dead. As one might expect, it tends to focus on 'The Man Who Shot Michael Collins' and also on the question of whether Collins received the Last Rites from the curate at Cloughdubh. The following is the text of that interview.*

I Spoke to the Man who Shot Michael Collins
Absolutely incorrect to say priest refused to give Last Rights[13]

Today, 48 years after the shooting of General Michael Collins, one of the two-man team who spent six months investigating one of the greatest tragedies in Irish political history speaks out to contradict what he calls many 'gross inaccuracies' which surround reports on the death of the founder of the National Army.

John Hickey (65) of Lixnaw, Co. Kerry, has retired from the Gardaí after 45 years' service and now lives in Limerick. An IRA volunteer, he joined the Army after the Treaty and a year later was one of the first men to join the Garda Síochána. His first posting was to Crookstown, Co. Cork, only a short distance from where Collins died at Beal na mBlath. One startling disclosure he makes is: 'I spoke to the man who shot Michael Collins – he later saved my life.' Another piece of information revealed in an exclusive interview with the *Evening Herald* is the heretofore undisclosed fact that three of the attacking party on the Michael Collins party were shot dead. Also, Mr Hickey says that 'very important leaders of the Irregulars, who were later members of the Government, were in Beal na mBlath on the day of the shooting'.

John Hickey, father of four children, got his information first hand from the people directly involved when, with another policeman, he was ordered by the Government of the day to investigate rumours that one of Collins's own party had shot their leader. He spent months writing reports which, he says, were never acted upon and which he now feels have been lost or destroyed. He now speaks out in defence of a priest of whom it was said that a soldier attempted to shoot him when it was thought he would not give the Last Rites to Collins after he had been shot.

Mr Hickey throws more light on a confused corner of history. Of the man who shot Michael Collins he will only say: 'He was a fellow countyman of Collins. He was a West

Cork man. He told me he shot at a shadow in the late dusk of an August night. Like many of the attacking party he did not know Collins was in the convoy. He was very remorseful afterwards – maybe he still is.'[14] Mr. Hickey adds: 'This is not the time to disclose his name. Anyway, I am not sure if the man is still alive. There are many things I could say but this is not the time just yet.'

'The man who fired the fatal shot at Collins later saved my life. It happened in 1924 when a number of IRA shot and killed British troops at Spike Island. The evening after the shooting they were travelling by car and when I stopped them they were going to shoot me. The man was in the car and spoke up: "Let him go. I know him." I met him several times afterwards before I was transferred from Cork and I thanked him for what he had done. He did not know that I had reported what I knew to Dublin.'

In his own words, John Hickey states: 'I want to tell the true facts about what happened. I have decided to break my long silence because of the grossly inaccurate articles which have appeared from time to time. These articles are giving a completely wrong impression, possibly not intentionally, but they certainly do not give the facts. I feel it is time the people of Ireland and indeed the world should be given some of the facts of what happened on the fateful day in August 1922 and on the days before and afterwards.' Mr Hickey pointed out the accuracy of what he had to say could be checked against the records of the investigation which was carried out with the late Sergeant L.P. Clear, who was a Tipperary man.

'When I joined the police force in 1923 instructions were issued thorough the usual channels that both Sergeant Clear and I were to investigate the shooting of Collins. At first people were very hostile. We were unpopular because many people did not trust the new police force. Eventually, we gained their confidence and gained much valuable assistance from the late Canon Tracy of Crookstown. We were strangers and he put us in touch with the people who were able to help us. At this stage I would like to refer to a newspaper article in which

Emmet Dalton gave disclosures about the shooting of Collins. He is wrong on a number of points. His reference to the priest, who he says refused to give the Last Rites. This is absolutely incorrect. He says he does not know the name of the priest. I know it. I spoke to the man during my investigations and later he became a personal friend.

'His [the priest's] exact words as to what happened on that night are as follows. I remember them clearly as he often told me about it when we talked about the incident. He told me "between 11.00 and 11.15 pm there was a knock on the door of my house. My housekeeper answered the door. She called me and said I was wanted outside. A soldier and a civilian (who lived locally) were standing at the doorway. The soldier asked me to come outside as there was a soldier shot. It was a dark night and the soldier carried in his hand an old carbide lamp which was giving very bad light. I walked out to the roadway where the convoy had stopped. There was a soldier lying flat with his head resting on the lap of a young officer. The young officer was sobbing and crying and did not speak. There was blood on the side of the dead man's face. I said an Act of Contrition and other prayers and made the Sign of the Cross. I told an officer to wait until I got the Holy Oils. I went to the house but when I returned the convoy had gone."'

Mr. Hickey said the priest also told him that just before the convoy pulled away the civilian heard an Army officer say: 'that priest is not coming back' and he ordered the convoy to drive away. Some of the soldiers were hysterical.' Mr. Hickey adds: 'I want to clear up this point once and for all in view of what has been written. This is as I was told it by the priest concerned.'[15]

Another point which Mr. Hickey makes in the interview refers to the consumption of alcohol by members of Collins's force. They had been to Skibbereen and Rosscarbery. 'My investigations revealed that some of the convoy were "merry" on leaving Rosscarbery at 7.30 pm that evening. They had been drinking at a public house there, where Collins himself had one pint of Guinness.'

There are many points about the ambush which people do not know of, according to Mr Hickey. 'During the month of August there were five ambush attempts to get Collins in Cork, Limerick and Kerry. The day before he was shot there was an ambush attempt arranged for Farran on the road to Macroom but for other reasons he did not travel that road. There was also an ambush arranged for Watergrasshill for August 23 if the ambush at Beal na mBlath failed.'

In a reference to the actual ambush Mr. Hickey confirms a view already expressed by researchers of the Civil War period that Collins gave the order that led to his death. 'The convoy had got beyond the point of the ambush but Collins ordered them to stop and go back and fight,' he said. 'There were about 49 men in three columns and they had planned to ambush the convoy at 3.30 pm. They had been waiting since 9 am. Because of the delay in Skibbereen and Rosscarbery – Collins was with relatives – many of the men in the ambush party left to go away at 7 pm to Crookstown about two and a half miles away. Another six or seven of the men went into a local public house for a drink and were still there when they heard the shooting. They left the public house to re-join the column and in so doing three were shot.

'The purpose of the investigation was to clarify who actually shot Collins as there were strong rumours at the time that some of his own escort were responsible for the shooting. This, I am convinced, was believed in Government circles at the time. The investigation established without any doubt who shot Collins but apparently the Government decided not to take any action. The investigation cleared up without any doubt that it was not anyone of Michael Collins's party who fired the shot that killed their commander.'

Mr Hickey met Michael Collins only once, in Limerick on 12 August. He was a member of an escort which was to bring him to an inspection tour through Limerick and Kerry. The tour did not take place as Collins had to return to Dublin because of the death of Arthur Griffith.

Notes

ABBREVIATIONS USED

AG   Adjutant General
BMH   Bureau of Military History
CCCA   Cork City and County Archives
CD   Contemporary Documents
CiC   Commander in Chief
CO   Colonial Office
C/S   Chief of Staff
CW   Civil War
IRA   Irish Republican Army
IRB   Irish Republican Brotherhood
NA   National Archives (Dublin)
NCO   Non-Commissioned Officer
NLI   National Library of Ireland
MA   Military Archives (Dublin)
MSP   Military Service Pension
MSPC   Military Service Pension Collection
PRA   People's Rights Association
TNA   The National Archives (UK)
UCD   University College Dublin
WO   War Office
WS   Witness Statement

Prologue

1   In my own book *The Year of Disappearances* (Dublin, 2010) on the matter of the killing of 'spies and informers', but more generally from a military point of view by William Sheehan in his book *A Hard Local War* (Stroud, 2011) in which O'Donoghue's version of events is often flatly contradicted by reality.

Introduction

1 Liam Deasy, *Brother Against Brother* (Cork, 1998), p. 81.
2 Florence O'Donoghue, *No Other Law* (Dublin, 1954), p. 274.
3 See Appendix II for one such missive.
4 Eoin Neeson, *The Civil War in Ireland 1922–1923* (Cork, 1966). See Chapter 3.
5 Neeson, *The Life and Death of Michael Collins* (Cork, 1968).
6 Denis Linehan, 'The Death of Michael Collins: Who Pulled the Trigger?', *The Irish Story* (online), February 2014. Linehan has carried out detailed and valuable analysis of the contradictions between the various accounts before coming to the conclusion that extracting the truth from the morass of conflicting information left by the various parties is next to impossible.
7 S.M. Sigerson, *The Assassination of Michael Collins*, 2014 edition, available at Amazon.com.

1. In the Wrong Place at the Wrong Time

1 A/G 1st Southern Div. to C/S, 24 August 1922, Moss Twomey Papers, UCD, P69/93 (177). Reproduced in Peter Hart, *Mick: The Real Michael Collins* (London, 2005), pp. 410–11.
2 Dalton would never forget it or be allowed to forget it. O'Connell called the house he lived in subsequently in Dublin 'Beal na mBlath'.
3 See photo on page 15. CCCA, SM865.
4 Patrick J. Twohig, *The Dark Secret of Bealnablath* (Cork, 1991), pp. 180–2. A bastable cake was a loaf of soda bread baked in a bastable or pot oven over an open fire.
5 *Ibid.*
6 Ellen Allen, quoted in the TV documentary *The Shadow of Béal na mBláth*, RTÉ 1989.
7 I am grateful to my brother James for first pointing out the more obvious relevance of the bloodstain when I was initially interested in the collar, and also to my brother Mike for establishing the fact that the spot in question is where the monument now stands – on the other side of the road.
8 See photo on page 16.
9 I am grateful to Paul Maguire of Carlow Military Museum for his help in this analysis.
10 In the TV documentary *The Shadow of Béal na mBláth* (RTÉ, 1989), State Pathologist John Harbison was dubious about the claim that Collins may have been killed by either. He was also dubious about the likelihood that a dum-dum bullet killed him, on the basis that an exit wound in that case would have been no more than about two or three inches in diameter. The entire back

of Collins's head was blown off, indicating that the bullet that struck him was of a much higher power than most of those used at that time in infantry rifles.

11 The cap, which is in the National Museum of Ireland, has inevitably been the subject of debate over the years, with some claiming that it is Dalton's. However, the rip in the back suggests that it is not. Meda Ryan has pretty much established the provenance of the cap. All the evidence suggests that it is in fact the cap that Collins wore at Bealnablath. Meda Ryan, *The Day Michael Collins was Shot* (Cork, 1989), pp. 140–5.

12 Carlton Younger, *Ireland's Civil War* (London, 1985), p. 435, quoted in Linehan, *op. cit.*, p. 12.

13 Cagney told Seán McGarry of the IRB that the bullet entered behind the left ear, making a small entry wound and that Collins's long hair hid it. Tim Pat Coogan, *Michael Collins* (London, 1990), p. 421.

14 Bill McKenna account. Seán O'Mahony Papers, NLI, MS 44,102/5. Commandant Frank Friel and Nurse Eleanor Gordon, who washed Collins's face and bandaged his head at Shanakiel Hospital, both confirm that there were two wounds, an entrance and an exit wound, in his head and that the entry wound was on the hairline. However, for many commentators this has mysteriously migrated from the hairline behind his left ear to the hairline of his forehead, which neither the cap, the greatcoat, the death mask nor the photos of Collins lying in state supports. Ms Gordon also claimed there was a singed hole in the back of his tunic that might indicate a second bullet wound, though she does not claim an equivalent wound in his back. The greatcoat, however, appears to have no such hole. Sigerson, *op. cit.*, pp. 390–2.

15 Connie Neenan in *Survivors*, ed. Uinseann MacEoin (Dublin, 1980), p. 246.

16 Twohig, *op. cit.*, p. 209.

17 Edward O'Mahony checked the weather records for that day and states that a trough of low pressure crossed the area late in the day, which would account for the dark conditions. However, it must have brought little or no rain with it. He also states that sunset was around 20.45 to 20.50 'modern' time. Chapter 12, Edward O'Mahony, *Michael Collins: His Life and Times* (1996). Available at http://generalmichaelcollins.com

18 *Irish Times*, weather forecast 22 August 1922.

19 Twohig, *op. cit.*, pp. 180–2.

20 *Ibid.*, pp. 245–6.

21 *Ibid.*, p. 36.

22 Interestingly, while investigating this point, I found a very old rusted sheet of corrugated iron hidden deep under the grass on

the ditch at the left (eastern) side of the road. Might this have been thrown across the dense thicket of watercress behind the ditch to keep someone's feet dry? It may seem far-fetched that it might still exist. Nonetheless, it was there, hidden under thick grass at the end of June 2016.

23 Twohig, *op. cit.*, p. 36. Twohig has two other witnesses at the southern or south-eastern side of the ambush site, Mike Donoghue from Glenflesk, Co. Kerry, and Jimmy Ormonde, a Volunteer from Co. Waterford, who claimed to have witnessed something similar. All three use the phrase that they 'saw the big man fall'. Denis Linehan shrewdly suggests that these may all have been versions of the same story, seeing as they appear to have emanated from Republican emigrants in the United States. Either that or three different men witnessed Collins fall. Whatever the source of this, either Doherty or all three were the only person or persons known to be in the right place to see Collins being killed. Linehan, *op. cit.*, pp. 20–1.

24 Edward O'Mahony, *Michael Collins: His Life and Times*, www. generalmichaelcollins.com/on-line-books/foreword-life-times/

2. Bealnablath: Some Essential Facts

1 Bill McKenna report on the death of Collins. Seán O'Mahony Papers, NLI MS 44.102/5. O'Mahony's papers are a useful source of material on Bealnablath. The papers contain letters from one Simon Dalton, who states that he was Emmet's nephew and that Emmet claimed before he died that he had shot Collins. While a Simon Dalton did exist, there is no evidence that he was even related to Emmet. The conspiracy appears to have emanated from Simon Dalton's solicitor, who claimed to have a letter to that effect and, amazingly, to have destroyed it! There is also a supposedly first-hand account from one Robert Flynn, who claimed he was one of the Free State soldiers at Bealnablath and stated that he saw Dalton shooting Collins. However, the account contains so many other outlandish statements – such as the claim that Michael Brennan and Liam Tobin were also at Bealnablath and orchestrated a major cover-up – that it is clearly the work of a fantasist. It appears that Flynn was borrowing other stories to bolster his account, such as his claim that an attempt was made to kill him in a Dublin theatre – probably a garbled reference to a shooting carried out by Frank Teeling in 1923. Flynn claimed he was from County Meath and that he was born in 1896 – something for which there is no evidence in the births records. Nor is there any record of a Robert Flynn

(or O'Flynn) in the 1922 National Army census. Robert Flynn: Statement under oath, O'Mahony Papers NLI MS 44,103/1.

2   Bill McKenna report on the death of Collins. O'Mahony Papers, NLI MS 44.102/5.

3   *Ibid.*

4   Neeson, *The Life and Death of Michael Collins*, pp. 128–9.

5   *Limerick Weekly Echo*, 9 September 1972 (Appendix VI). Greg Ashe in Ernie O'Malley, *The Men Will Talk to Me, Kerry Interviews*, ed. Cormac K.H. O'Malley and Tim Horgan (Cork, 2012), p. 126.

6   Twohig, *op. cit.*, pp. 16–37.

7   *Ibid.*, p. 240.

8   *Limerick Weekly Echo*, 26 August–9 September 1972. (Appendix VI.)

3. Evasive Actions

1   Daniel Murray, 'Evasive Manoeuvres: An Examination of Florence O'Donoghue's Account of the Death of Michael Collins, 10 June 2013, The Irish Civil War 5', *The Irish Story*. www.theirish story.com/2013/06/10/evasive-manoeuvres-an-examination-of-florence-odonoghues-account-of-the-death-of-michael-collins/

2   Neeson, *The Civil War in Ireland*.

3   Account of Bealnablath, O'Donoghue Papers, NLI, MS 31,305.

4   *Ibid.*

5   Murray, *op. cit.*

6   O'Donoghue's loose notes on the attempted negotiations, 9 July 1922, O'Donoghue Papers, NLI, MS 31,187.

7   AG to CiC, 25 July 1922, Mulcahy Papers, UCD, Pa/50.

8   Dáil Éireann Debates (Treaty), 3 May 1922, p. 259. Quoted by Kevin Edward Girvin, *The Life and Times of Seán O'Hegarty*, MA thesis (UCC, 2003), pp. 100–1.

9   Collins Notebook, O'Donoghue Papers, NLI, MS 31,256.

10 A.J.S. Brady, 'The Briar of Life', accessed at castlehotelmacroom. blogspot.ie.

11 John M. Feehan, *The Shooting of Michael Collins* (Cork, 1981) p. 57.

12 Interestingly, O'Donoghue had a pass for Mallow – issued by himself in March 1922 as Divisional Adjutant of the IRA – in his papers, but none for Macroom. O'Donoghue Papers, NLI MS 31,243.

13 Florrie O'Donoghue in O'Malley Notebooks, UCD, P17b/95.

14 Interview with Dalton by Cormac MacCarthaigh, in Feehan, *op. cit.*, p. 105.

15 Florrie O'Donoghue, O'Malley Notebooks, UCD, P17b/95.

16 The ambush was finally carried out there on another convoy on the day that Collins was killed. *Cork Examiner*, 23 August 1922.

17 Richard Mulcahy, 'Talk on Michael Collins', 19 October 1963. Mulcahy Papers, UCD, P7/D/66.

4. Some Orchestrated Manoeuvres in the Dark

1 See correspondence between Cork and Dublin via Cope, July/August 1922 in Mulcahy Papers, UCD, Pa/50.
2 Neeson, *The Life and Death of Michael Collins*.
3 Neeson, *The Civil War in Ireland*.
4 Neeson, *The Life and Death of Michael Collins*, p. 103. Hurley was a member of the 3rd Brigade, not the 1st Brigade.
5 *Ibid.*, p. 105.
6 *Ibid.*, p. 136.
7 *Ibid.*, p. 101.
8 *Ibid.*, p. 112.
9 *Ibid.*, p. 105.
10 Twohig, *op. cit.*, pp. 44–6.
11 *Ibid.*, p. 134.
12 Coogan, *op. cit.*, pp. 399–400. See also *Limerick Weekly Echo*, 26 August 1972–19 September 1972.
13 O'Donoghue Papers, NLI, MS 31,334.
14 Letter from Breda Lucci, dated 28 January 1990, quoted in Twohig, *op. cit*, p. 46.
15 Harry Boland and Lady Lavery were other recipients. Chrissie Osborne, *Michael Collins Himself* (Cork, 2003), p. 99.
16 Agnes McCarthy, MSP34REF60655.

5. The Lead-Up to Bealnablath

1 Memo from Lynch to O'Malley, 2 August 1922, P17A/60. See Cormac K.H. O'Malley and Anne Dolan: *No Surrender Here: The Civil War Papers of Ernie O'Malley 1922–24* (Dublin, 2007), pp. 82–3.
2 Con Moloney at Field Headquarters to Ernie O'Malley, 15 August 1922, Moss Twomey Papers, NLI, P69/77(83). See O'Malley and Dolan, *op. cit.*, p. 101.
3 Intercepted letter from 'Con' to Richard Mulcahy, 27 July 1922, Moss Twomey Papers, NLI, P69/77(83). See O'Malley and Dolan, *op. cit.*, p. 101. The letter Liam Lynch got with this information came from Con Moloney and the letter he quoted also came from a 'Con', who was presumably in the Free State forces.
4 John A. Pinkman, *In the Legion of the Vanguard* (Cork, 1998) pp. 168–9.
5 Peadar O'Donnell, quoted in Uinseann MacEoin, *Survivors* (Dublin, 1980) p. 28.
6 See 'Cork Harbour Board peace negotiations July 1922' documents, De Valera Papers, UCD, P150/1638.

7   Gerard Murphy, *The Year of Disappearances* (Dublin, 2010) p. 102.

8   These are quotations from O'Donoghue's loose-leaf notes taken on the days of the meetings, O'Donoghue Papers, NLI, MS 31,187.

9   Liam Lynch to Frank Daly, 14 July 1922. De Valera Papers, UCD, P150/1638.

10   Ml Ó Cuill to Michael O Coileán TD, Desmond FitzGerald Papers, UCD, P80/713.

11   Unsigned, undated note, FitzGerald Papers, UCD, P80/714.

12   Undated note, FitzGerald Papers, UCD, P80/714.

13   *Ibid.*

14   William Murphy to MD, 12/8/1922, Mulcahy Papers, UCD, P7a/50.

15   Provisional Government Minutes, 7 September 1922. NA, Taois/ 1/1/3/1 PG110.

16   F. O'Donoghue in O'Malley Notebooks, UCD, P17b/95.

6. Words, Too Many Words

1   Eunan O'Halpin, 'British Intelligence in Ireland, 1914–1921', in Christopher Andrew and David Dilks, *The Missing Dimension: Governments and Intelligence Communities in the Twentieth Century* (Oxford, 1984).

2   Liam de Roiste Diary 25.8.1922, CCCA, U271A/46.

3   Feehan, *op. cit.*

4   Seán Boyne, *Emmet Dalton: Somme Soldier, Irish General, Film Pioneer* (Dublin, 2014). Some writers claim it was MI6, others MI5. Many do not appear to know the difference.

5   Which does not mean that there are not whole files of spurious material claiming he did. Having spent many months chasing down these 'leads', it gradually became clear to me they led nowhere and that much of the material was planted by people with various political agendas. As we have seen, many of these can be found in the Seán O'Mahony Papers, NLI, MS 44, 102–7. It should be pointed out that O'Mahony's papers also contain quite a lot of very valuable material on various topics relating to the Irish revolution.

6   Boyne, *op. cit.*

7   Denis O'Neill, MSP34REF4067.

8   Ashe, *op. cit.*, p. 126.

9   Coogan, *op. cit.*, pp. 419–20.

10   Hurley was arrested on 23 November 1922, just two weeks before Hales himself was assassinated. MA, CW/CAPT/004/2/01–09.

11   Sworn statement of Charles McCarthy of Skibbereen, who interviewed Connolly on three occasions in the late 1960s/early 1970s.

12 IRA memos of 2 December 1922 and undated memo, MA, CW/CAPT/004/2/01–09.
13 Twohig, *op. cit.*, pp. 169–70.
14 See Appendix I.
15 Peter Kearney, MSP34REF54870.
16 He did repeat his claim that he and Kearney were on the hill to the north-east of the ambush position. He claimed that 'the bullet that killed Mick Collins could not possibly have come from any of the four men concerned', i.e. those on the lane opposite, since it hit him on the back of the head and they were in front of him. He suggested rather that it must have come from the machine gun of the Free State armoured car. Father John Chisholm interviews with Liam Deasy, Tape 7. I am grateful to Eve Morrison for granting me access to this information.
17 J. Anthony Gaughan, *Irish Times*, 20 August 1988.
18 I wish to thank Eunan O'Halpin for drawing my attention to O'Mahony's papers.
19 S.M. Sigerson, *The Assassination of Michael Collins* (2014) available on Kindle Direct Publishing.
20 Photocopy typescript report on the death of Collins. O'Mahony Papers, NLI, MS 44.102/5.
21 John Ranelagh to E.J.D. 9 March 1973, Emmet Dalton Papers NLI, MS 46,687 (4). A more detailed synopsis of the 'crimes' Aylward, Barrett and Aiken were guilty of is given in the undated government memo, quoted earlier, in Desmond FitzGerald's Papers, UCD, P80/714.
22 Bill McKenna statement, O'Mahony, NLI, MS 44,103/6.
23 Liam Lynch to Ernie O'Malley, 27 August 1922. O'Malley P17A/61. See also O'Malley and Dolan, *op. cit.*, p. 127.
24 Michael Hopkinson, *Green against Green: The Irish Civil War* (Dublin, 2004), p. 138.
25 Interview with Jimmy Flynn, O'Mahony Papers, NLI, MS 44,104/5. De Valera's general movements can be confirmed from many sources. His own papers contain an entire file on the subject. For example, see Ryan (*op. cit.*), Twohig (*op. cit.*) and Siobhan Lankford, *The Hope and the Sadness* (Cork, 1980).
26 However, Tim Pat Coogan mentions it.
27 Denis Long, MSP34REF7542.
28 This is in O'Malley's words in O'Donoghue, O'Malley Notebooks, UCD, P17/b/96.
29 Coogan, *op. cit.*, p. 406.

7. The IRB and the Shooting of Collins

1 British military intelligence file on Michael Collins, TNA, WO 35/206.

2   Hart, *op. cit.*, p. 378.

3   Count Plunkett, Manifesto to the People of Ireland, 15 July 1922, De Valera Papers, UCD, P150/1630.

4   Count Plunkett apparently had been inducted into the IRB by his son Joseph in the months prior to the 1916 Rising and travelled abroad in early 1916 espousing the Republican cause. O'Kelly was also an old-school IRB man.

5   People's Rights Association Resolution, 17 July 1922. De Valera Papers, UCD, P150/1638.

6   RIC Intelligence Reports 1916, TNA, CO 904/23 Part 3A pp. 46–63.

7   The Free State military apparatus was also porous to British Intelligence. It is clear, for instance, that they had a spy in Oriel House, Collins's own Secret Service HQ. In September 1922 it could list the names of every member of the staff at Oriel House, down to messenger boys and the cleaner! See British Command's Weekly Intelligence circulars for late August/early September 1922. De Valera Papers, UCD, P150/1646.

8   'Mr Ginnell – In Dáil Éireann', undated, De Valera Papers, UCD, P150/1630. Ginnell was not an IRB member but had had an association with senior 'Brothers', such as Bulmer Hobson, going back well over a decade.

9   Former loyalist and future Senator James Douglas, who played a not insignificant role as mediator in many of the conflicts surrounding the ending of the Civil War, was of the view that the decree abolishing the Supreme Court was illegal since the legislature was independent of the Dáil. See James Douglas note (undated). De Valera Papers, UCD, P150/1631.

10 Kathleen Clarke, 'Supreme Court' correspondence, De Valera Papers, UCD, P150/1630.

11 De Valera Notes on above, De Valera Papers, UCD, P150/1630.

12 Maloney arrived at Liverpool on board SS *Scythia* on 1 July 1922. It seems he then lived in Britain until 1925. Inward Passenger Lists, Ancestry.co.uk. He was to remain in Ireland at least until the week after Collins's death, when he is known to have met with Richard Mulcahy on one side and Mary MacSwiney on the other, ostensibly to explore the possibilities for peace. Maloney, whose credentials are dubious to say the least, is worthy of a book in his own right. See W.J. McCormack, *Roger Casement in Death: Or Haunting the Free State* (Dublin, 2002).

13 See O'Donoghue Papers, NLI, MS 31,240 and MS 31,421.

14 Sean O'Hegarty memo 25/5/1923. O'Donoghue Papers, NLI, MS 31,421(2).

15 O'Donoghue, *No Other Law*, Chapters 15–18.

16   Letters from O'Donoghue to Éamon de Valera. De Valera Papers, UCD, P150/3447.

17   Owen McGee, *The IRB: The Irish Republican Brotherhood from the Land League to Sinn Féin* (Dublin, 2005), pp. 327–72. McGee offers an excellent analysis of the role of the IRB during those years.

18   Leon Ó Broin, *Revolutionary Underground: The Story of the Irish Republican Brotherhood, 1858–1924* (Dublin, 1976), p. 221.

19   Eileen McGough, *Diarmuid Lynch: A Forgotten Irish Patriot* (Cork, 2013). McGough's book is a fine example of independent and specialist research. She tracked down many sources not previously used. Her portrait of Lynch is of a decent, energetic and upright man.

20   Ó Broin, *op. cit.*, p. 220.

8. The Great Divide (the IRB and the Treaty)

1   Ó Broin, *op. cit.*, p. 177.

2   British Intelligence report on Collins, TNA, WO 35/206.

3   Seán Ó Muirthile Memoir, Mulcahy Papers, UCD, P7a/209. Harry Boland, Austin Stack and Liam Lynch were also strongly anti-Treaty and Ó Muirthile reports this.

4   On the day the Supreme Council recommended acceptance of the Treaty, 12 December 1921, but before they became aware of it, the Cork City District Board of the IRB, of which O'Donoghue was Centre, called for rejection of the Treaty on the basis that it was 'treason' to the Republic established in 1916. O'Donoghue, *No Other Law*, p. 192. The IRB was organised into 'Circles'. Each Circle was overseen by a 'Centre' or commanding officer.

5   *Ibid.*, pp. 191–2.

6   Ó Muirthile Memoir, p. 177, Mulcahy Papers, UCD, P7a/209.

7   John Joe Rice, in O'Malley, *The Men Will Talk to Me*, p. 282. Rice recalled that those attending the meeting, in addition to Collins and Ó Muirthile, were Liam Lynch, Liam Deasy, Tom Crofts, Seán O'Hegarty, Florrie O'Donoghue and Paddy Cahill.

8   Meda Ryan, *Tom Barry: IRA Freedom Fighter* (Cork, 2005), p. 240.

9   Ó Muirthile Memoir, pp. 167–70, Mulcahy Papers, UCD, P7a/209.

10   See correspondence in Piaras Béaslaí Papers, MS 33,919(2). Also see O'Donoghue, *No Other Law*, Chapter 14.

11   O'Donoghue, *No Other Law*, p. 192.

12   Cork County Centre to Divisional Centre, January 1922, O'Donoghue Papers, NLI, MS 31,237(1).

13   Undated memo in O'Donoghue's hand, O'Donoghue Papers, UCD, MS 31,237(1). Cork County Centre to Divisional Centre, January 1922, O'Donoghue Papers, NLI, MS 31,237(1).

14 Florrie O'Donoghue in O'Malley Notebooks, UCD, P17b/95.

15 *Ibid.*

16 Undated memo by O'Donoghue in a debate with General Seán MacEoin (1959) over the finer points of the IRB Constitution, O'Donoghue Papers, NLI, MS 31,296(1).

17 P.S. O'Hegarty statement on IRB, 15 December 1946, O'Donoghue Papers, NLI, MS 31,333(1).

18 Ó Muirthile Memoir, p. 168.

19 Diarmuid Lynch Memoir, p. 487, O'Donoghue Papers, NLI, MS 31,598(1).

20 See McCormack, *op. cit.*

21 See Appendices IV and V.

22 McGee, *op. cit.*, p. 361.

23 Hopkinson, *op. cit.*, p. 42.

24 Cork No. 5 District to County Centre, 20 February 1922, O'Donoghue Papers, NLI, MS 31,237(1).

25 Ó Muirthile Memoir, p. 175, Mulcahy Papers, UCD, P7a/209.

26 O'Donoghue, *No Other Law*, Chapter 15.

27 'Incidents in connection with the IRA that had a bearing on outbreak of present war.' De Valera Papers, UCD, P150/1737.

28 *Ibid.*

29 Ó Muirthile Memoir, p. 190, Mulcahy Papers, UCD, P7a/209.

30 'Incidents in connection with the IRA that had a bearing on outbreak of present war.' De Valera Papers, UCD, P150/1737.

31 *Ibid.*

32 See O'Donoghue, *No Other Law*, Chapter 17.

33 Ernie O'Malley, *The Singing Flame* (Dublin, 1978), p. 53; Frank O'Connor, *The Big Fellow: Michael Collins and the Irish Revolution*, p.157, (Dublin 1937, new edition, Cork 2018).

34 O'Donoghue Papers NLI, MS 31,305(2). Rex Taylor, *Michael Collins*, p. 227. Also see the plate facing p. 208 in Taylor. It seems apparent that the comments were made on the day of the meeting and by Collins himself, and as such they are likely to be far more accurate and more significant, even if Collins was writing tongue-in-cheek. What is of equal importance is O'Donoghue's reaction to them forty years later and his attempts to denigrate Taylor in the press as a result. Taylor makes an interesting point on the these notes, commentating that they are the only place in all of Collins's notebooks and correspondence that he had access to where Collins wrote in pencil, 'for he had a particular hatred for pencilled notes and stamped signatures'. For Lynch's reluctance to talk and calls for action see: Meeting of S.C and County Centres, 19 April 1922. NLI O'Donoghue Papers, MS 31,250.

35 Langford Notes, CCCA, U156/45-50.

36 Handwritten notes on death of Michael Collins, Seán MacEoin Papers, UCD, P151/1882.

37 Piaras Béaslaí, *Michael Collins and the Making of a New Ireland* Vol II, pp. 425–6 (Dublin, 1926).

38 The journalist was one Elizabeth Lazenby. See article by Seán MacEoin in the *Cork Examiner*, 24 August 1964.

39 'Memo to R from A', 31 May 1922. Art Ó Brien Papers, NLI, MS 8424/13. IRB men routinely referred to the Brotherhood as 'The Organization' or 'The Firm'.

40 Mac Eoin, *Cork Examiner*, 24 August 1964.

41 James Creed Meredith, Report of Army Inquiry Committee, 7 June 1924. Mulcahy Papers, UCD, P7/C/42.

42 See Chapter 13.

43 Meredith Report of Army Inquiry Committee, 7 June 1924, Mulcahy Papers, UCD, P7/C/42.

44 John Joe Rice in O'Malley, *The Men Will Talk to Me*, p. 280.

45 *Ibid.*, p. 284.

46 *Ibid.*, p. 287.

47 They are among his papers in the National Library of Ireland. O'Brien had been arrested in Dublin in July but was released around the time of Collins's death. His newspaper cuttings operation went on uninterrupted right through the period of his incarceration, indicating that his office in London was well able to function in his absence. He was released two days after Collins's death. *Cork Examiner*, 25 August 1922.

48 O'Donoghue's letter of resignation to Liam Lynch, 3 July 1922, O'Donoghue Papers, NLI MS 31,187.

49 It is perhaps unfair to assume that this Commandant was O'Donoghue. However, given that he always had a foot in both camps, and in the absence of any other suitable candidate, it is reasonable to suggest that it was he, particularly in view of Collins visiting both him and his wife during his trips to Cork. Adj Cork 1 to Adj 1st S. Div, 6 September 1922. Mulcahy Papers, NLI, P7/B/93.

50 Michael Leahy, O'Malley Notebooks, P17b/1421. It appears there had been a disagreement between Collins and O'Hegarty going back to 1918 over £300 of 'Organization' funds that had gone missing. Note entitled 'Collins Diary', O'Donoghue Papers, NLI, MS 31,305(2).

9. Army Matters

1 Hopkinson, *op. cit.*, p. 61.

2 Gearoid O'Sullivan, quoted in Hopkinson, *op. cit.*, p. 62.

3   Mulcahy, quoted in Hopkinson, *op. cit.*, p. 62.
4   The Cork Harbour forts still in British hands.
5   Dalton to Mulcahy, 18 November 1922, Mulcahy Papers, UCD, P7/B/67.
6   On the night of Dalton's wedding, 18 November 1922, at the Imperial Hotel in Cork, a Sergeant Kearns was shot in the guardroom by a soldier and this was witnessed by another NCO. Boyne, *op. cit.*, p. 271.
7   Undated memo in Mulcahy Papers, UCD, P7/C/42.
8   Memo/Minutes Mutiny Meeting 19 December 1923. Mulcahy Papers, UCD, P7/B/195.
9   Jamie Moynihan, *Memoirs of an Old Warrior*, edited by Donal Ó hEalaithe (Cork, 2014), p. 234.
10 O'Sullivan to MoD, 31 August 1922. Mulcahy Papers, UCD, P7/B/195.
11 Creed Meredith Report, 7 June 1924. Mulcahy Papers, UCD, P7/C/42.

10. Not a Shred of Evidence

1   Smith account, Sigerson, *op. cit.*, p. 309.
2   Twohig, *op. cit.*, pp. 57–8.
3   *Cork Examiner, Irish Independent, Freeman's Journal*, 24–25 August 1922.
4   Garda John Hickey, quoted in *Evening Herald*, 12 September 1976. (Appendix VI.)
5   *Limerick Weekly Echo*, 16 September 1972. (Appendix VI.)
6   For instance, see Diarmuid Ó Tuama, *Cogadh na gCarad ón Chonradh go Saorstát* (Dublin, 2013); Vincent MacDowell, *Michael Collins and the Irish Republican Brotherhood* (Dublin, 1997); and of course Feehan (*op. cit.*).
7   D. Ryan to John Feehan, 9 November 1981, Seán O'Mahony Papers, NLI, MS 44,103/4.
8   *Evening Herald*, 12 July 1968.
9   W.J. Brennan-Whitmore, *With the Irish in Frongoch* (Dublin, 1917). This has recently been reissued by Mercier Press (Cork).
10 Brennan-Whitmore went on to become a senior Blueshirt with fascist leanings. Feargal McGarry, *Eoin O'Duffy: A Self-Made Man* (Oxford, 2005), p. 325.
11 Ó Tuama, *op. cit.*
12 Richard G. Lucid to O'Donoghue, 8 December 1964. O'Donoghue Papers, NLI, MS 31,303(1).
13 Draft memo and final article, *Sunday Press*, 25 January 1959, O'Donoghue Papers, NLI, MS 31,296(1).

14 C/S to O/C 1st Southern Division, 28 August 1922. Full letter quoted in Seán MacEoin article, *National Observer*, December 1958. O'Donoghue Papers, NLI, MS 31,296(1).
15 *Ibid.*
16 *Ibid.*
17 O'Donoghue to Seán Feehan, 8 January 1964. O'Donoghue Papers, NLI, MS 31, 305(1).
18 Michael MacDonagh, *The Life of William O'Brien* (London, 1928), p. 248. Quoted in Rex Taylor, *Michael Collins* (London, 1958), p. 241.
19 John Doherty to Piaras Béaslaí, 24 August 1930. Béaslaí Papers, NLI, MS 33,919(1).
20 It should also be pointed out that Eoin Neeson believed that McPeak was the most likely shooter, but the balance of evidence is against it. Also see Pádraig Ó Braoin, *Micheál Ó Coileáin* (Fermoy, 1985).

11. 'Mick turned and fell'

1 Feehan, *op. cit.*, p. 101. According to Feehan, this came from an interview with one of Collins's escort which appeared in the *Daily Express* of 25 August 1922.
2 The wearing of civilian clothing would not have been unusual for National Army men in the disorganised early stages of the Civil War. There were at least two Lewis gunners on the Crossley tender ahead of Collins.
3 Almost all accounts have Dolan, who was Collins's personal bodyguard, travelling on the armoured car and getting into a firing position near Collins. Conroy, on the other hand, is only occasionally mentioned. However, he 'was with the late Gen. Collins when [Collins was] killed' (James Patrick Conroy 24SP80). Conroy is variously referred to as having been in the armoured car or the Crossley tender or to have swapped between the two. He is also mentioned in the *Cork Examiner* of 24 August 1922 as having been present, which makes it all the stranger that he has been forgotten by almost everybody.
4 *Daily Express*, 25 August 1922.
5 Sigerson (*op. cit.*) dismisses it on the basis that she believes Collins was shot from the front 'and a sniper on his knees firing at a man standing up (as Collins would have had to be, in order to "fall") could not possibly be responsible'. She also claims the angle the sniper was at could not account for the trajectory of the bullet that hit Collins. In fact, it would precisely account for it.
6 *Daily Express*, 24 August 1922.
7 Sigerson, *op. cit.*, p. 60. Other arguments against O'Connell's account appear to be equally facile. The suggestion that he was

taken on as a guide from Mallow when the road between Mallow and Cork 'is a direct main road requiring no guidance' ignores the fact that the road was impassable and the convoy had to travel through the backroads via Whitechurch, as Siobhan Lankford (*op. cit.*) and Father Twohig (*op. cit.*) both make perfectly clear.

8 In fact, O'Connell may have been literally as well as geographically correct. There are grounds for thinking that Collins did not visit Bandon on his way to Skibbereen and that he went directly from Macroom to Clonakilty, bypassing Bandon to the west in the morning. The evidence that he actually stopped in Bandon on his way south is slim. He did of, course, call to Bandon and meet with Seán Hales on the way back.

9 'Eyewitness Recalls Death of Michael Collins', 1965. RTÉ Archive. Accessed at www.rte.ie/archives/2015/0821/722718-michael-collins/ on 14 March 2016.

12. Snipers and Drivers

1 See Appendix I.

2 *Cork Examiner*, 25 August 1922.

3 IRA Report, A/G 2st S. Div to CS 24 August 1922, Moss Twomey Papers, UCD, P69/93 (177). Republished in Hart, *op. cit.*, pp. 410–11. See Appendix I.

4 And perhaps by two others as well. See Chapter 17.

5 Twohig, *op. cit.*, pp. 169–70.

6 See Appendix VI.

7 From what I have been able to establish about Doherty in Killarney he appears to have been an upright and reliable witness.

8 And there is a significant amount of that documentation, several files in fact, in the Irish Military Archives.

9 HQ 1st S. Div to C/S GHQ, 11 September 1922. MA, CW/CAPT/004/2/01.

10 Twohig, *op. cit.*, p. 169.

11 IRA Ambush report, 24 August 1922. See Appendix I.

12 Liam Deasy, presumably. Michael J. Costello, *The Irish Times*, 3 September 1981. The Mauser sporting rifle should not be confused with the Mauser semi-automatic pistol, which had a detachable stock and was regularly used by IRA men at that time, sometimes as a pseudo-rifle, though mostly as a handgun.

13 Florrie O'Donoghue, O'Malley Notebooks, UCD, P17b/96. The Mauser sporting rifles were landed at Ballynagoul, Helvick, Co. Waterford from the schooner *Hannah* on 2 April 1922. 'The rifles were very good because, although under Peace Treaty arrangements with Germany, they were only supposed to manufacture sporting weapons, we found these Mausers could

pierce the steel shutters of barracks' (Pax Whelan in MacEoin, *op. cit.*, p. 141). A consignment of them went north to the 3rd Western Division. Michael Farry, *The Aftermath of Revolution: Sligo 1921–23* (Dublin, 2000), pp. 52–3.

14 Dalton, quoted in Neeson, *The Life and Death of Michael Collins*, p. 133.

15 Michael J. Costello, *The Irish Times*, 3 September 1981.

16 *Daily Express*, 24 August 1922.

17 *Freeman's Journal*, 28 August 1922.

18 *Cork Examiner/Freeman's Journal*, 26 August 1922. Two IRA men, John O'Callaghan and Jerh Mahony, were shot in the backside as they were making their way away from the scene. Their wounds appear to have been superficial.

19 *Evening Herald*, 12 September 1976. (Appendix VI.)

20 According to Sigerson (*op. cit.*), the drivers on the convoy on the day were Michael Corry and Michael Quinn on the touring car, Jim Wolfe and Jimmy Fortune in the armoured car and Jim Conroy and Sergeant Thomas Cooney on the Crossley tender. The drivers likely to have been near Collins were Corry and Quinn. Jim Conroy had been one of Collins's drivers during the War of Independence. And presumably Lieutenant Smith could also drive.

13. Doctors, Drivers and Wounded Plotters

1 He was incorrectly called 'Edward' in the newspaper reports of his abduction. He is listed in the National Army census of 1922 as recuperating in the Mercy Hospital in Cork in late 1922.

2 *Cork Examiner*, 30 August 1922.

3 *Ibid.*, 30 August 1922.

4 *Ibid.*, 24 August 1922.

5 Richard Kearns MSP2D80.

6 *Cork Examiner*, 31 August 1922.

7 *Ibid.*, 5 September 1922.

8 *Ibid.*, 22 September 1922.

9 *Ibid.*, 30 August 1922.

10 Cormac MacCarthaigh, *Agus*, April 1968. Many commentators claim this occurred in Clonakilty but MacCarthaigh, who seems to have been the original source, states that it occurred in Rosscarbery.

11 *Cork Examiner*, 15 September 1922.

12 O/C Cork to CiC, 18 November 1922, Mulcahy Papers, UCD, P7/B/67.

13 John Borgonovo (ed.), *Florence and Josephine O'Donoghue's War of Independence: A Destiny That Shapes Our Ends* (Dublin, 2006), pp. 147–59.

14 Walsh was close enough to Josephine that he submitted a letter supporting her claim for an IRA pension – as did Liam Tobin, who was a National Army officer in Cork at the time of Collins's death.

15 This refers to the killing by the IRA of Protestant civilians in Cork city during the War of Independence. They were often referred to as Anti-Sinn Féin League spies, even though the term 'Anti-Sinn Féin League' almost certainly refers to undercover members of the security forces rather than Protestants. See Murphy, *The Year of Disappearances: Political Killings in Cork 1921–1922*, 2nd ed. (Dublin, 2011).

16 Somebody, very likely to have been O'Donoghue himself, gave an account to Ernie O'Malley of the activities of Youghal Volunteer commandant Paddy O'Reilly, who was executed during the Civil War, in 1923. 'Information from Bde HQ notified him [O'Reilly] of a ring of spies called Anti-Sinn Fein and ordered him to shoot the Ring Leader and order two others to leave the country. This was done and the Ring Leader was shot 25/3/21.' Paddy O'Reilly, O'Malley Notebooks, UCD, P17b/107. (The supposed 'Ring Leader' was John Cathcart, a Methodist businessman in the town. Cathcart is believed to have been shot by O'Reilly himself, probably on O'Donoghue's orders. Thomas Walsh, TNA, CO762/86/9.)

17 Island View, Knockaverry, Youghal, Co. Cork. His other sister-in-law, Kathleen, was herself a nurse in Cork.

18 Richard B. Dalton death certificate.

19 *Cork Examiner*, 25 September 1922 and 26 September 1922.

20 *Ibid.*, 21 September 1922.

21 TNA, WO399/5129. She told her sister Kathleen that she was going to see Dr Dalton on the evening Cork City Hall was raided, which resulted in the capture of Terence MacSwiney. Borgonovo, *op. cit.*, p. 121.

22 Anna Cronin Compensation claim, NA, FIN/COMP/2/4/229. On the first occasion, 9 September, the houses were riddled with rifle fire from across the river. On 16 September the attack was much more determined and machine guns were used.

23 Though he was a doctor, his death does not seem to have been registered. The claim that he died of a heart attack is reported only in the *Cork Examiner*.

24 Hickey states they moved to 'Killeymey' before travelling east. This almost certainly refers to Killumney. *Limerick Weekly Echo*, 2 September 1972. (Appendix VI.)

25 Cumann na mBan HQ to C/S IRA, 5 October 1922. MA, CW/CAPT/003/1/08.

26 Ernie O'Malley to Seán O'H, 27/10/1922, O'Malley Papers, UCD, P17A/58. O'Malley and Dolan, *op. cit.*, p. 305.

27 Adj Cork 1 to Adj 1st S. Div, 6 September 1922, Mulcahy Papers, UCD, P7/B/93.

28 *Limerick Weekly Echo*, 16 September 1972. (Appendix VI.)

29 Florence O'Donoghue to Liam Deasy, 29 December 1922, O'Donoghue Papers, NLI, MS 31,240.

30 Moynihan, *op. cit.*, p361.

31 Seán O'Hegarty to O'Donoghue, undated – but it is clear from the context that it was written that autumn of 1922. O'Donoghue Papers, NLI, MS 31,240.

32 Coogan, *op. cit.*, p. 406. Also see O'Mahony, *op. cit.*, Chapter 10.

33 Div Adj to C/S, 9.9.1922, MA, CD 333/13. The memo has been subsequently annotated by hand to suggest that the Seán H. in question was Seán Hyde. However, this is not in Croft's handwriting, suggesting that it was inserted erroneously later by someone else, probably by someone in military intelligence. It is clear from the correspondence that the Seán in question was Seán O'Hegarty and that he should not continue to influence the men with regard to peace talks 'now that all responsibility is off his shoulders'. C/S to O/C 1st S. Div, 'Peace Moves of Enemy', 6 September 1922. MA, CD 333/13.

34 O'Donoghue in O'Malley Notebooks, UCD, P17b/96.

35 O'Donoghue, *No Other Law*, pp. 290–9.

36 Canon Tom Duggan, O'Malley Notebooks, UCD, P17b/111.

37 G.N. Count Plunkett to Dr Gilmartin, 5 October 1922. Trinity College Dublin, Samuel Collection, Box 1/ Ms 15/a. Accessed online.

38 Hopkinson, *op. cit.*, pp. 189–92.

39 *Ibid.*

40 Joseph Kelly, MSP34REF20910.

14. Doing Away with Michael – the Aftermath

1 Seán MacEoin, TNA, WO 35/207.

2 Seán MacEoin and Richard Mulcahy files, TNA, WO 35/207.

3 Extract from Intelligence Summary No. 319, dated 16 August 1922, File IX/1417, dated 19 August 1922. In Richard Mulcahy, TNA, WO 35/207.

4 Collins to Cosgrave, 4 August 1922, quoted in Coogan, *op. cit.*, p. 397.

5 *Limerick Weekly Echo*, 16 September 1972. (Appendix VI.)

6 'The First Southern Division was responsible for all measures concerned with the landing, and the Division Quartermaster, Joe

O'Connor, supervised the distribution and security of the arms.' O'Donoghue, *No Other Law*, p. 225.

7 The minutes of the IRA Executive meeting of 16–17 October 1922 find him still in the South. O'Malley Papers, UCD, P17A/12; O'Malley and Dolan, *op. cit.*, p. 495. By the end of November, however, he was at GHQ. Liam Lynch (GHQ Dublin) to all Divisions, 26 November 1922, Moss Twomey Papers, UCD P69/39/(134–5). O'Malley and Dolan, *op. cit.*, p. 336. See also Joseph O'Connor MSP 34REF1878, where his pension application has him moving from Cork to Limerick, Tipperary and Dublin during the Civil War.

8 C/S to O/C 1st S.Div, 22 August 1922. MA, CW/CAPT/004/2/01.

9 Florrie O'Donoghue, O'Malley Notebooks, UCD, P17b/96.

10 Joseph O'Connor, MSP34REF1878.

11 Florrie O'Donoghue, O'Malley Notebooks, UCD, P17b/96.

12 Joe O'Connor to Florrie O'Donoghue, O'Donoghue Papers, NLI, Ms 31,449(1).

13 Letter from Joseph O'Connor, *Sunday Press*, 24 October 1954.

14 Joseph O'Connor to Florence O'Donoghue, received 13 May 1957. O'Donoghue Papers, NLI, MS 31,449(1).

15 Éamon de Valera to Florence O'Donoghue, 17 June 1958. NA, Taois/S5872.

16 One of a series of photos in O'Donoghue Papers, NLI, MS 31,449(7).

17 He claims his service with the anti-Treaty forces ran from 1 July 1922 to 31 March 1923. Joseph O'Connor MSP34REF1878.

18 Joseph O'Connor MSP34REF1878.

19 Liam Lynch to Seosaimh O'Conchubhar, Sean Treacy and Micheal de Burca, 18 September1922. Mulcahy Papers, UCD, P7a/81. Just to complicate matters, there was a second Joseph O'Connor, a Dublin man, in the senior IRA command at that time.

20 *Limerick Weekly Echo*, 26 August 1972. (Appendix VI.)

21 Hannah Desmond, MSP34E8570.

22 *Limerick Weekly Echo*, 26 August1972. (Appendix VI.)

23 See Chapter 9.

24 Denis Linehan, 'The Death of Michael Collins: Was There a Doctor's Plot? Part 2 A Note of Dr Leo Ahern.' Published online at Academia.edu.

25 Ryan, *op. cit.*, p. 115.

26 Both quoted in Linehan, 'The Death of Michael Collins'.

27 Denis Linehan, 'The Death of Michael Collins: Was There a Doctor's Plot?' Published online at Academia.edu.

28 Liam Tobin, 24SP2764.

15. Blinding the Fool's Eye

1   O'Donoghue to Liam Lynch, 2 August 1922. O'Donoghue Papers, NLI, MS 31,202. In fact it is clear from a note from O'Hegarty to O'Donoghue a few days earlier that it was O'Donoghue who resigned first: 'Like yourself I am now out of a job.' O'Hegarty to O'Donoghue, 30 June 1922. O'Donoghue Papers, NLI, MS 31,187.

2   O'Mahony claims that this was a Cork No. 1 Brigade meeting. Two of these, however, Langford and Hales, were not members of Cork No.1 Brigade. Edward O'Mahony, *Michael Collins: His Life and Times*, Chapter 10, available online.

3   Jim Hurley statement, 3 January 1964. O'Donoghue Papers, NLI, MS 31,305(1).

4   Eoin Neeson to Jim Hurley, 12 January 1964. O'Donoghue Papers, NLI, MS 31,305(1).

5   Div Adj to DI GHQ, 1 February 1923. MA, CW/CAPT/004/–.

6   Denis Long, MSP34REF7542. Long claimed he subsequently took part in the actual ambush and there is no reason to disbelieve him. He does not say in his MSP application that it was he who spotted Collins that morning.

7   The IRA leadership were billeted between three houses in this area: O'Sullivans, Walsh's and Wood's. It appears that on that night de Valera stayed at the home of Richard Wood at Muinegave, sleeping on the couch in the kitchen. (Liam Deasy and Seán Culhane had already taken the only vacant bedroom, which goes to show the level of respect they had for their leader.) O'Mahony, Chapter 10. That de Valera stayed at Wood's has been confirmed for me by Richard Wood's grandson, Donald Wood. It has also been suggested that he stayed at O'Sullivans. (P. O'Neill letter. De Valera Papers, UCD, P150/1639). Practically speaking, it makes little difference. All accounts agree that he was billeted in the Muinegave rather than Bealnablath area.

8   O'Donoghue corrections to Eoin Neeson, Appendix II.

9   1911 Census. They may of course have been related. There were several families called Long living in the immediate area at the time. But the whole point here is that Dinny Long was sentry at a house that was on a different road several miles away. (This was about half a mile to the east of Coppeen cross on what was then called the Bantry Line and is now called the R585. I am indebted to Donald Wood for this information.)

10 See Appendix VI.

11 I am grateful to Evelyn Nolan, Lily Holland's daughter, for this information.

12 See Appendix VI.

13 Adjutant Cork No. 1 Brigade to Adjutant 1st S. Div 1 September 1922, MA, CW/CAPT/003/1/01. I have not been able to establish who precisely 'D Cronin' was. Interestingly, O'Donoghue wrote to Taoiseach Éamon de Valera in 1958 to request politely that these captured documents be treated in the same way as the Bureau of Military History material, i.e. be put into cold storage for fifty years so that nobody would have access to them until well into the twenty-first century. O'Donoghue to An Taoiseach, 2 July 1958. De Valera Papers, UCD, P150/3447.

14 Florence O'Donoghue, MSP34REF2091.

15 Cork Examiner, 21 October 1922, 30 October 1922, 2 December 1922, 4 December 1922, 9 December 1922, 16 December 1922. The only exception was the rate collector's job for Macroom which was advertised on 10 October 1922. In fact, the County Council had trouble filling the posts, which may account for the multiple advertisements over several weeks. The reason for this was the intimidation of rate collectors during the War of Independence and immediately afterwards. Quite a number of the vacant positions were then filled by former IRA men, who presumably would have been immune to intimidation. The multiple advertisements for the same jobs, particularly in December, are a strong indication that nobody was doing the jobs at that stage.

16. The Evidence of Garda Hickey

1 Hannah Desmond, MSP34E8570.

2 *Limerick Weekly Echo*, 9 September 1972. (Appendix VI).

3 *Ibid.*, 2 September 1972. (Appendix VI).

4 *Ibid.*, 2 September 1972. (Appendix VI).

5 *Limerick Weekly Echo*, 16 September 1972.

6 *Ibid.*

7 *Evening Herald*, 12 September 1976.

8 *Limerick Weekly Echo*, 9 September 1972.

9 *Evening Herald*, 12 September 1976.

10 *Cork Examiner*, 25 August 1922.

11 *Ibid.*, 24 August 1922.

12 *Ibid.*

13 AG 1st S. Div to C/S, 24 August 1922. Hart, *op. cit.*, pp. 410–11. There are local rumours that one IRA man crawled away after the ambush and was found dead in a barley field a few days later, but I have been unable to confirm this.

14 Margaret Lordan, MSP34REF28758.

15 Lordan's death in June 1930 was not registered, so it is not possible to establish what he died from.

17. Kerry Connections

1 Twohig, *op. cit.*, pp. 30–7.
2 Robert J. Doherty MSP34REF53155.
3 Twohig, *op. cit.*, pp. 30–1.
4 Jimmy Ormonde is named as a Waterford Volunteer prisoner in Ballykinlar Camp in 1921. Liam Ó Duibhir, *Prisoners of War, Ballykinlar Internment Camp 1920–1921* (Cork, 2013), pp. 154, 297.
5 See photo in O'Donoghue's Papers, NLI, MS 31,459(6). It shows a family resemblance between the four O'Donoghues in the picture – two Michaels and two Florries. Florrie O'Donoghue's parents came from the Killarney area and lived in Rathmore only from 1891, three years before Florrie was born, until 1922. Valuation Office Records for Rath More, Rathmore, Co. Kerry.
6 Bertie Scully in O'Malley and Horgan, *op. cit.*, p. 162.
7 Johnny O'Connor in O'Malley and Horgan, *op. cit.*, p. 217.
8 'Important' Army Notebook. De Valera Papers, UCD, P150/1737.
9 HQ Cork 1 to Adj 1st S. Div. 18 October 1922. MA, CW/CAPT/003/1/01. These notes come from documents captured by Free State forces during the Civil War which are currently in the Military Archives in Dublin.
10 If this was the Denis Cronin in question then it seems he returned to Kerry, where he found himself a member of the greatly harried Kerry No. 1 Brigade and was still at large well after the Dump Arms order by the IRA that ended the Civil War. Marguerite Synnott, MSP34REF50888.
11 IRA Membership Rolls, Kerry No. 2 Brigade, MA-MSPC-RO-102.
12 Denis Cronin was later verifying officer for the Kerry No. 2 Brigade under the 1934 [IRA] Pensions Act, an equivalent role to that played by O'Donoghue in Cork. MSP34REF23014.
13 *Cork Examiner*, 16 April 1921: John O'Riordan, BMH, WS 1117: Michael O'Leary, BMH WS 1167. *Kerry's Fighting Story* (Tralee, 2009), pp. 144–5. Tim Horgan, *Dying for the Cause* (Cork, 2015), p. 57.
14 I am grateful to T. Ryle Dwyer for this information.
15 *Cork Examiner*, 16 and 18 December 1922. *Irish Independent*, 16 and 18 December 1922. *Southern Star*, 23 December 1922.
16 Horgan, *op. cit.*, pp. 62–3.
17 Twohig, *op. cit.* p. 23.

18 Johnny O'Connor, in O'Malley and Horgan, *op. cit.*, p. 246.
19 Greg Ashe, in O'Malley, *The Men Will Talk to Me*, p. 127.
20 Twohig, *op. cit.*, pp. 280–4.
21 Correspondence between Minister of Home Affairs and East Limerick Dáil Courts, NA DECC 10/39.
22 Decree, NA DECC26/7.
23 I wish to express my gratitude to Denis Sullivan for this information.
24 The most likely model is the Mauser M98 Magnum which was adapted for use as a sporting rifle and used a .416 inch (10.6 × 7.4 mm) Rigby bullet. This was used for big game hunting and was adopted from the Mauser 98 infantry/sniper's rifle, which was noted for its range and accuracy, using more conventional ammunition – usually 7.92 × 57 mm Mauser cartridges.

Appendices

1 Moss Twomey Papers, UCD, P69/93 (177).
2 O'Donoghue Papers, NLI MS 31,503(2).
3 Seán O'Mahony Papers, NLI MS 44,102/5.
4 De Valera Papers, UCD P150/1630.
5 *Ibid.*
6 *Limerick Weekly Echo*, 26 August–16 September 1972.
7 *Ibid.*, 26 August 1972.
8 In the original, Canon Patrick Tracy's surname is spelled as Treacy. According to the 1911 Census and Guy's Cork Directory, the correct spelling is Tracy.
9 *Limerick Weekly Echo*, 2 September 1972.
10 *Ibid.*
11 The messenger was Dan Holland, MSP34REF9793.
12 *Limerick Weekly Echo*, 16 September 1972.
13 *Evening Herald*, 12 September 1976.
14 It is usually assumed that the man in question was Tom Kelleher, who fired some shots at the end of the ambush – perhaps the final shots, as he claimed. Kelleher was still alive at the time Hickey wrote his articles and it is fair to say he may have believed he had shot Collins. Three things militate against this, however. Analysis of the wound and the direction the bullet came from suggest it could not have come from Kelleher, who was at least 300 yards to the north of where Collins died – when the fatal bullet almost certainly came from the south. Also, the last fusillade that may have come from Kelleher was the fusillade that shot Lieutenant Smith as he helped get Collins onto the armoured car. So even if Kelleher fired the last shots, these were not the shots that killed Collins.

15 The controversy arose because Emmet Dalton claimed in an interview around this time that there was a perception among members of the party that the priest was refusing to anoint Collins. Dalton even suggested that one officer raised his rifle to shoot the priest but he himself prevented him from doing so. Given how hysterical the party were at this stage, this misunderstanding is just about possible.

Bibliography

Andrew, Christopher and David Dilks (eds), *The Missing Dimension: Governments and Intelligence Communities in the Twentieth Century* (Oxford 1984).

Borgonovo, John, *Florence and Josephine O'Donoghue's War of Independence: A Destiny that Shapes Our Ends* (Dublin 2006).

Boyne, Seán, *Somme Soldier, Irish General, Film Pioneer (A Biography of Emmet Dalton)* (Dublin 2014).

Brady, A.J.S., *The Briar of Life* (undated, available online).

Coogan, Tim Pat, *Michael Collins* (London 1990).

Deasy, Liam, *Brother Against Brother* (Cork 1998).

Dwyer, T. Ryle, *Michael Collins and the Civil War* (Cork 2012).

Farry, Michael, *The Aftermath of Revolution, Sligo 1921–23* (Dublin 2000).

Feehan, John M., *The Shooting of Michael Collins* (Cork 1981).

Hart, Peter, *Mick: The Real Michael Collins* (London 2005).

Hopkinson, Michael, *Green against Green: The Irish Civil War* (Dublin 2004).

Horgan, Tim, *Dying for the Cause* (Cork 2015).

Keane, Barry, *Cork's Revolutionary Dead: 1916–1923* (Cork 2017).

Kerry's Fighting Story (Tralee undated).

Lankford, Siobhan, *The Hope and the Sadness* (Cork 1980).

McCormack, W.J., *Roger Casement in Death: Or Haunting the Free State* (Dublin 2002).

MacDowall, Vincent, *Michael Collins and the Irish Republican Brotherhood* (Dublin 1997).

MacEoin, Uinseann, *Survivors* (Dublin 1980).

McGarry, Feargal, *Eoin O'Duffy, A Self-Made Man* (Oxford 2005).

McGee, Owen, *The IRB; The Irish Republican Brotherhood from the Land League to Sinn Féin* (Dublin 2005).

McGough, Eileen, *Diarmuid Lynch: A Forgotten Irish Patriot* (Cork 2013).

Moynihan, Jamie, *Memoirs of an Old Warrior* edited by Donal Ó hEalaithe, (Cork 2014).

Murphy, Gerard, *The Year of Disappearances, Political Killings in Cork 1921–1922, 2nd edition* (Dublin 2011).

Neeson, Eoin, *The Civil War in Ireland 1922–1923* (Cork 1966).

Neeson, Eoin, *The Life and Death of Michael Collins* (Cork 1968).

Ó Braoin, Pádraig, *Mícheál Ó Coileáin* (Fermoy 1985).

Ó Broin, Leon, *Revolutionary Underground: The Story of the Irish Republican Brotherhood, 1858–1924* (Dublin 1976).

O'Donoghue, Florence, *No Other Law* (Dublin 1954).

Ó Duibhir, Liam, *Prisoners of War, Ballykinlar Internment Camp 1920–1921* (Cork 2013).

O'Mahony, Edward, *Michael Collins, His Life and Times* (1996 – available online).

O'Malley, Cormac K.H. and Anne Dolan, *No Surrender Here: The Civil War Papers of Ernie O'Malley 1922–24* (Dublin 2007).

O'Malley, Ernie, *The Singing Flame* (Dublin 1978).

O'Malley, Ernie, *The Men Will Talk to Me, Kerry Interviews*, ed. Cormac K.H. O'Malley and Tim Horgan (Cork 2012).

Osborne, Chrissie, *Michael Collins Himself* (Cork 2003).

Ó Tuama, Diarmuid, *Cogadh na gCarad ón Chonradh go Saorstát* (Dublin 2013).

Pinkman, John A., *In the Legion of the Vanguard* (Cork 1998).

Ryan, Meda, *The Day Michael Collins was Shot* (Dublin 1989).

Ryan, Meda, *Tom Barry, IRA Freedom Fighter* (Cork 2005).

Sheehan, William, *A Hard Local War* (Stroud 2011).

Sigerson, S.M., *The Assassination of Michael Collins* (2014 Amazon.com).

Taylor, Rex, *Michael Collins* (London 1958).

Twohig, Patrick J., *The Dark Secret of Bealnablath* (Cork 1991).

Index